William Clark's elk skin-bound field book

THE
Lewis &
Clark
TRAIL

By Thomas Schmidt
Foreword by Stephen E. Ambrose

NATIONAL GEOGRAPHIC

WASHINGTON, D.C.

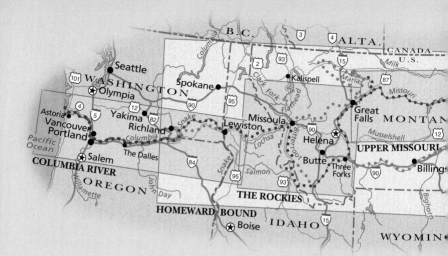

Contents

TRAVELING LIGHTLY ON THE TRAIL 6
A JOURNEY WITH LEWIS AND CLARK 8

Lower Missouri 10

Great Plains 42

Upper Missouri 74

The Rockies 94

Columbia River 138

Homeward Bound 168

NATIONAL SIGNATURE EVENTS 186
OTHER LEWIS & CLARK SITES 187
FOR MORE INFORMATION 188
ABOUT THE AUTHOR 189
A NOTE ON QUOTATIONS 189
ILLUSTRATIONS CREDITS 189
INDEX 190

COVER: "Explorers of the Marias," Fort Benton, Montana
PRECEDING PAGES: Citadel Rock on the upper Missouri River

MAP KEY and ABBREVIATIONS

• • • • • • • • • • • •   Route of Lewis and Clark
• • • • • • • • • • • •   Return Route Variations
⎯⎯15⎯⎯   Interstate Highway
⎯⎯12⎯⎯   U.S. Federal Highway
⎯⎯200⎯⎯   State Road
⎯⎯2⎯⎯   County or Local Road
⎯⎯4⎯⎯   Provincial Highway
– – – – – –   Trail
· · · · · · · · · ·   Continental Divide
⎯ · ⎯ · ⎯ ·   National Boundary
– – – – – –   State Boundary

Boundaries
N.F.   I.R.   N.W.R.

National Park .... NAT. PARK., N.P.
National Recreation Area .... N.R.A.
National Scenic Area .... N.S.A.
National Volcanic Monument .... N.V.M.
National Wild and Scenic River
National Recreational River .... NAT. REC. RIVER
Air Force Base .... A.F.B.

National Forest/-s .... NAT. FOREST, NAT. FOR., N.F.
National Grassland .... NAT. GRASSLAND

National Wildlife Refuge .... N.W.R.
National Bison Range .... NAT. BISON RANGE

State Park ....S.P.

Indian Reservation ....INDIAN RES., IND. RES., I.R.

■   Point of Interest
✪   State Capital
+   Peak/Elevation
) (Pass
| Dam
=   Falls

POPULATION

● **St. Louis**   over 200,000
● **Great Falls**   20,000 to 200,000
● Astoria   under 20,000

□   National Battlefield .... N.B.
    National Historic Landmark .. N.H.L.
    National Historical Park .... N.H.P.
    National Historic Site .... N.H.S.
    National Memorial .... NAT. MEM.
    Recreation Area .... REC. AREA

□   National Forest Ranger Station

□   National Wildlife Refuge ...... N.W.R.

□   State Historic Site .... S.H.S.
    State Historic Park .... S.H.P.
    State Park .... S.P.
    State Recreation Area .... S.R.A.

ADDITIONAL ABBREVIATIONS

Ave. .... *Avenue*
Cr. .... *Creek*
Fk. .... *Fork*
ft .... *feet*
Ft. .... *Fort*
Mt. ...... *Mount, -ain*
N. .... *North*
R. .... *River*
Ra. .... *Range*
Rd. .... *Road*
S. .... *South*
St. .... *Saint*
ST. .... *Street*
Sta. .... *Station*

Traveling Lightly on the Trail

Almost 200 years ago, Capt. Meriwether Lewis took a few last fateful footsteps up to Lemhi Pass and looked across the Continental Divide. From that spot, he could see clearly the seemingly endless ranges of mountains which forever blocked President Jefferson's vision of a Northwest Passage for trade. What must Lewis have thought as he stood there? Back in 1976, I brought my family there so we could take those last steps ourselves and wonder at all that beautiful spot had meant for our friend Meriwether and for our country.

As we approach the bicentennial of the Lewis and Clark Expedition, more and more people are taking trips to the magical places along the trail: Lewis and Clark Pass, the Missouri River Breaks, the Lolo Trail, Fort Clatsop, the intersection of the Niobrara and the Missouri, and countless others. Some of these sites are equipped to handle all who come. Many other places, like Lemhi Pass, are not. These places are quiet wilderness capable of transporting us back in time, yet they are also fragile and vulnerable.

A few years ago, visitors walking up to Lemhi Pass found their view of the grand vista obstructed by a large silver Airstream trailer. There was not a NO PARKING sign there. It must have been a bitter moment for those folks hiking up, in search of that spectacular view and for that moment of epiphany. This story served as a wake-up call for myself and the other members of the National Council of the Lewis and Clark Bicentennial, a citizen group mandated by Congress to help organize our national observance of the expedition, a watershed event in our history. Along with helping to create a series of fabulous National Commemorative Events, as well as countless arts-and-humanities projects and programs, the Council intends to see to it that visitors to the trail find what they are looking for. Of course, we need your help.

We of the Council know that most folks know how to be good visitors. Most campers know that if they "Pack it In," then they have to "Pack it Out." They know how to visit a place without spoiling it for others, to stay on trails when hiking, to be careful with fire. They "Ask First" before going on to private land. But obviously, some travelers do not. As we of the Council go about the glorious work of inviting our fellow Americans to learn about their

Clark's map of the Great Falls of the Missouri

great history and see this great country, we want to give people good information so they will travel wisely and safely. The Council encourages all enthusiasts of the Corps of Discovery to "Discover Their Trails, Explore Your Country, and Respect Our Heritage."

We are glad you have purchased this guide. The National Geographic Society has done a splendid job on it. Use it and you will make some amazing discoveries. If you want to learn more about all the great commemorative events (see page 186) occurring along the trail during the bicentennial, get in contact with tribal leaders or private landowners. Or to learn how to be a better traveler, please contact the

National Council of the
Lewis and Clark Bicentennial
c/o Lewis & Clark College
0615 SW Palatine Hill Rd.
Portland, OR 97219
www.lewisandclark200.org
888-999-1803.

Getting to know Meriwether Lewis, William Clark, and the others has been a great joy to my family. They inspired us. The time we spent traveling the trail together as a family brought my family good health, strong relationships, and great stories. We wish you and yours the same.

Happy Trails,
Stephen E. Ambrose

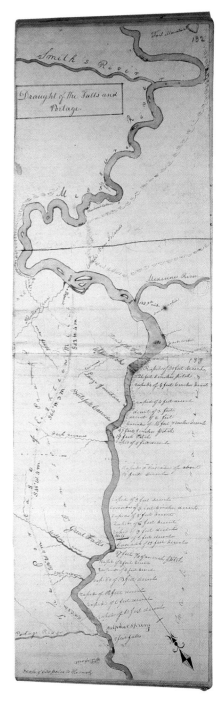

A Journey with Lewis and Clark

"The object of your mission is to explore the Missouri river, & such principal stream of it, as, by it's course and communication with the waters of the Pacific ocean, whether the Columbia, Oregon, Colorado or any other river may offer the most direct & practicable water communication across this continent for the purposes of commerce."

THOMAS
JEFFERSON,
INSTRUCTIONS
TO LEWIS,
JUNE 20, 1803

In May 1804, U.S. Army officers Meriwether Lewis and William Clark headed up the Missouri River with 45 men and a well-stocked keelboat. Their assignment was to cross the North American continent from the Mississippi to the Pacific by way of the Missouri and Columbia River systems. The trip, long a dream of President Thomas Jefferson, would spirit them into lands newly acquired under the 1803 Louisiana Purchase and far beyond.

Just getting there and back would be a major achievement, since the region was almost entirely unknown to European civilization. But Lewis and Clark were charged with more than the challenge of wilderness travel. They were to map the land, hold diplomatic councils with Indians, and study and record everything regarding plants, animals, minerals, soil, and native ways of life.

That they succeeded so well is due largely to their deep friendship—and their multiple qualifications. Like their enlisted men, Lewis and Clark were brave, resourceful, and tough. They were adept woodsmen and skilled hunters. In addition, Lewis was a competent practical doctor. Well read, he had training in botany, zoology, geology, and astronomy, and had served as Jefferson's personal secretary. Clark was the cartographer, the better boatman, the more consistent journalist, and the leveler head.

Together they logged more than 8,000 miles in the wilderness and interacted with dozens of tribes. They mapped a broad swath of the Rockies and the courses of the Missouri and Columbia. They also wrote the first scientific descriptions of a breathtaking 178 plants and 122 animals.

Sticking as close to Lewis and Clark's route as is practical today, this book guides travelers to expedition landmarks, museums, landscapes, and other sites evocative of the Voyage of Discovery. From start to finish, it weaves the expedition's story from site to site. The book uses modern landmarks and place-names to describe expedition movements, so you can easily follow along with a decent road map. Excerpts from the expedition journals, with original spellings and punctuation intact, are interspersed throughout.

Much has changed—the face of the land, the faces of the inhabitants, the flow of the great rivers. But to a surprising extent, much endures that is suggestive of the 1804-06 landscape. This book will help you find those places and tell you what happened there.

THOMAS SCHMIDT

Annual encampment of the Blood Indians, relatives of the Blackfeet

Lower Missouri

**December 1803 –
August 20, 1804**

This chapter follows the Lewis and Clark Expedition from its winter quarters near St. Louis, up the Missouri River through forest and bluff country, and onto the verge of the Great Plains, near present Sioux City, Iowa. Much of today's route leads through towns and major cities, often on busy roads that rarely provide more than a fleeting glimpse of the great river. Still, a number of sites—mostly boat landings and parks—offer a vivid sense of the land and river that Lewis and Clark experienced. You'll also find full-scale reproductions of the expedition's boats, abandoned Indian villages mentioned in the journals, and three interpretive centers devoted to the expedition. Along this leg of the journey, the Corps of Discovery honed its boating skills, held its first major council with Indians, and pressed beyond the European settlements. Sadly, it also buried one of its comrades, Sgt. Charles Floyd.

Detail of "View from Floyd's Grave," George Catlin, 1832

Lewis and Clark State Historic Site

Camp Wood, Illinois

◆ 3.5 MILES N OF I-270 ON ILL. 3, FOLLOW SIGNS

On a gloomy December afternoon in 1803, the 55-foot-long keelboat of the Lewis and Clark Expedition crept along the forested banks of the Mississippi River and landed at the mouth of the Wood River across from St. Louis. As the men set up camp beneath a dark canopy of massive cottonwoods, maples, and oaks, a violent storm charged across the Mississippi and blasted them with snow and hail. It must have felt like the right time to stop for the winter and the right place, too. For the next five months, the men could gaze west from Camp Wood across the Mississippi to the mouth of the Missouri River, their highway to the unknown.

Today, the **Lewis and Clark State Historic Site** *(618-251-5393)* encompasses a swath of land reminiscent of Camp Wood, where the Corps of Discovery passed the winter of 1803-04. The grounds include a major visitor center, a thoughtful reproduction of the expedition's fort, living history demonstrations, acres of dense riverside forest, and a fine vista across the Mississippi to the mouth of the Missouri. Here, too, a paved bike path links the site with St. Louis's famous Gateway Arch and Pere Marquette State Park.

Built in a field of over 30 species of native prairie grasses and wildflowers, the visitor center sketches the expedition's entire story and pays particular attention to events at Camp Wood. Insightful exhibits illustrate North America circa 1803, review the expedition's manifold purposes, trace its transcontinental route, summarize its impressive accomplishments, and ponder its long-range implications. The center's most striking element is a marvelous, full-scale reproduction of the expedition's keelboat, which has been cut lengthwise and partially unloaded to reveal its structure and the wide variety of tools, provisions, and trade goods Lewis and Clark packed for the journey. The boat serves as centerpiece for other exhibits that introduce the members of the expedition and describe everyday life at Camp Wood.

Outside, a short stroll leads to the fort reproduction, which is scheduled for completion in 2003. Though the exact form of the original fort is unknown, the reproduction follows one of several possible floor plans that Clark sketched in late December 1803. It is a palisaded enclosure with a barracks hut at each corner and a larger building in the center for the officers and for storage. When completed, the fort will offer visitors a chance to wander among the low-slung buildings and to get a feel for what it was like to spend a dreary winter stationed beside the Mississippi with a group of bored, impatient, and often irritable, enlisted men.

The original fort was built much closer to the river. For a vivid sense of that setting, drive a half mile through the forest beyond the interpretive center to a monument on the bank of the Mississippi River. Though the small clearing in the forest is not quite where the Corps wintered, its peaceful, evocative surroundings offer the closest match possible to what Lewis and Clark saw from their cluster of log huts 200 years ago.

Like the Wood River, the adjacent diversion channel here emerges from a towering, vine-laden forest very similar to what Lewis and Clark encountered. The grand and muddy breadth of the Mississippi still sweeps by with

Shipshape

The expedition's keelboat resembled a galley, with benches for 22 oarsmen, a deck at the bow, and an elevated stern deck above a cabin. Fifty-five feet long, it sported an 8-foot beam and drew 4 feet of water. Its 32-foot jointed mast could be lowered. Beneath the oarsmen's feet ran a 31-foot hold, while above their heads were awnings that could be stretched for shade or to repel rain. Extremely versatile, the boat could be rowed, sailed, pushed along with setting poles, or pulled by ropes.

Stashed within the hold of the keelboat was a collapsible iron-frame boat designed by Captain Lewis and Thomas Jefferson during the winter of 1802-03. The frame weighed just 44 pounds, and was to be assembled and covered with animal skins once the expedition portaged the Great Falls of the Missouri. Lewis estimated "the canoe" would carry 1,770 pounds.

Traveling with the keelboat were two smaller boats that the captains called pirogues or canoes. It's unclear exactly what these boats looked like, but they were big. Clark's diagram of a "Perogue of 8 Tuns" shows a vessel with a large central cargo area and enough room for four oarsmen at the bow, two at the stern, and a tillerman. Like the keelboat, the pirogues could be operated four different ways.

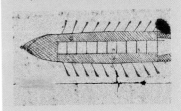

Cahokia Mounds State Historic Site

surprising force, and through the hazy tree line of its western bank you can still make out the Missouri confluence. Great egrets wade the channel. Big fish splash in the river.

The big keelboat arrived here after a three-and-a-half-month voyage from Pittsburgh. Lewis had spent the spring and summer of 1803 outfitting the expedition, and began his descent of the Ohio River on August 31 with perhaps 11 men.

It had taken a month and a half to reach Clarksville, Indiana Territory (see Falls of the Ohio State Park, p. 187), where Clark waited with a group of young Kentucky woodsmen he had recruited. As they continued down the Ohio, the captains added more men, gained valuable experience working the boat, and wrote extensively in their journals about the country and its inhabitants, plants, animals, and curiosities.

Great flocks of passenger pigeons darkened the skies. Thousands of migrating gray squirrels swam across the river. And at the mouth of the Mississippi they weighed, measured, and described a vast catfish: 128 pounds, 4 feet 3.25 inches long, with a mouth 10 inches wide.

All this was a warm-up for the impending ascent of the Missouri. But for now, they needed a place to winter. And, because the captains had decided to expand their party from 15 men to 45, they also needed more supplies, which could be obtained only in St. Louis. So Lewis remained in the city for most of the winter, buying goods, hiring French boatmen, and gathering priceless information about the Missouri. Clark, meanwhile, spent a good deal of the winter in the huts on the south bank of the Wood River.

Once the men had built their huts, shored up the boat, and transferred its cargo to the storehouse, they had little to do but hunt, haul wood, and watch sheets of ice float by on the Mississippi. Soon, they got into trouble. They sneaked away and got drunk at a nearby whiskey shop. They fought and disobeyed orders. One private even loaded his gun and threatened to shoot a sergeant.

Clark did his best to keep them busy. Some whipsawed planks and were rewarded with an extra gill (4 ounces) of whiskey for each day's labor. Others hammered away at the forge for an extra gill. A few made sugar, for half a gill, and everyone participated in a daily shooting contest to hone their marksmanship. The prize? An extra gill, of course.

Clark busied himself learning what he could about the Missouri from visiting boatmen, traders, and Indians—some of whom had been as far as the Mandan villages, near present-day Bismarck, North Dakota. He also studied an excellent map showing the river's route to that point. He could only guess what lay beyond, but by mid-January he estimated that the expedition could reach the Pacific Ocean and return to St. Louis by the fall of 1805.

He was a full year off the mark.

In early spring, as ducks and geese flew north along the river, Clark had the men refit the keelboat with a jointed mast and two rows of lockers with lids that could be raised as a breastwork. The men also parched and pounded corn into meal, dug honey out of trees, and put up 50 kegs of salt pork.

As spring wore on, other provisions, equipment, and tools stacked up in the storehouse: 3,400 pounds of flour; 560 pounds of biscuits; 750 pounds of salt, candles, coffee, peas, beans, sugar, lard, grease, axes, and saws; and 21 carefully packed bales of trade goods intended for barter and as gifts for the Indian tribes they would encounter (see sidebar p. 17).

Clark moved the men into their tents and supervised the loading of the keelboat and a pair of smaller, open boats called pirogues (see sidebar p. 13). He also divided

The Men

Lewis and Clark headed up the Missouri with roughly 45 men: backwoodsmen of the Ohio River Valley, U.S. Army enlisted men, and French settlers.

Twenty-five of the men, including three sergeants, formed what was called the permanent party, which would man the keelboat and make the entire journey to the Pacific and back. The Americans not already in the Army were sworn in as privates. At least nine French boatmen—*engagés*—were brought along to help handle the pirogues.

The captains assigned seven other men, including a corporal, to the return party, which they planned to send back partway through the voyage with the maps, notes, and specimens of plants, animals, and minerals they had prepared to that point.

Clark brought along a black man named York, his slave and companion since boyhood. Lewis brought his dog Seaman (or Scannon), a Newfoundland.

All the men were young and accustomed to arduous labor. Most were experienced backwoods travelers who could shoot, jerk and dry game, and cheerfully bear hardship. But their skills were varied in useful ways. There were two blacksmiths and one carpenter. Others knew Indian languages, and some were outstanding hunters.

the men into squads, assigned them to their boats, and issued knives, tomahawks, powder, balls, and buckshot.

By mid-May, all was ready for departure. On the afternoon of the 14th, after a full day of rain, Clark and the men bid adieu to a small crowd of well-wishers, pushed their boats into the current, and headed west into the mouth of the Missouri.

The Voyage of Discovery had finally begun.

CAHOKIA MOUNDS S.H.S.

Shortly after the men had finished building their fort on the Wood River, Clark walked out onto the broad Mississippi floodplain near present Mitchell, Illinois, and came across what he called an "Indian Fortification." It consisted of nine low earth mounds arranged in a circle, with pot sherds and stone points scattered on the ground. What he had stumbled upon were the remains of a Mississippian Indian village, abandoned for hundreds of years. Had he continued his walk several miles south, he might have come here, to Cahokia Mounds *(30 Remey St., Collinsville. 618-346-5160. Donation),* and found the remains dating back a thousand years of the largest prehistoric Indian city north of Mexico.

Today, a large, first-rate museum describes the city and the Mississippians' sophisticated culture. You can amble among the mounds and climb to the grassy apex of North America's biggest prehistoric earth structure.

ST. LOUIS

By the time Lewis began hobnobbing with the merchants of St. Louis during the winter of 1804, the city was nearly 40 years old and had a population of roughly a thousand people, mostly French. It was the hub for a lucrative fur industry that reached far into the interior of the Missouri drainage basin.

Clark spent part of February and March with Lewis in St. Louis, where they almost certainly witnessed the March 10, 1804, ceremony transferring Louisiana to the United States. During this time they attended a couple of late night balls and also traveled a short way up the Missouri to prevent a Kickapoo attack on the Osage.

Today, the St. Louis area offers several worthwhile stops pertaining to Lewis and Clark. First, a new state park, yet to be named *(S off US 67 before Alton, Ill. bridge, beyond Riverlands Visitor Center. 636-937-3697),* has been designated at the confluence of the Mississippi and Missouri. Primitive, still lacking roads, but accessible to hikers, it wraps around the northern point of land separating the rivers and offers visitors a chance to explore the same muddy banks that Clark and the boat crews passed on May 14, 1804. A narrow ribbon of willows, maples, cotton-woods, and sycamores still grow here, and you are likely to see evidence of deer, raccoons, and other animals Lewis and Clark would have seen in the same area.

Downtown and beneath the city's famous stainless steel arch, the National Park Service's **Museum of Western Expansion** *(314-655-1700. Adm. fee)* is devoted mainly to events after Lewis and Clark's era. You will find a copy of a pre-expedition map of North America reflecting how little was known before Lewis and Clark set off. Near it lie the basic tools the captains used: a reproduction of the Harpers Ferry rifle the men carried, as well as quill pens, a compass, sextant, and chronometer.

For a glimpse of St. Louis circa 1803, stroll two blocks west of the arch to the **Old Courthouse** *(11 N. 4th St. 314-655-1700)*, where paintings and dioramas depict the early town. Of particular interest are reproductions of late 18th-century flintlock muskets, a model pirogue, and a full-scale, partial repro-duction of a French colonial dwelling. Outfitted with simple furniture, wooden bowls, gourd ladles, and rustic tools, the house offers a clear portrait of the typi-cal home Lewis and Clark would have seen in St. Louis and in settlements far-ther up the Missouri.

You'll find more about early St. Louis at the **Missouri History Museum** *(Lindell Blvd. at DeBaliviere St., Forest Park. 314-746-4500)*, which tracks the city's history from its founding in 1764 to the present. One small exhibit deals with Clark's post-expeditionary life and displays artifacts from his council room, including one of his swords and some of his furniture.

After returning from the Voyage of Discovery, Lewis and Clark both lived in St. Louis. Their homes stood on what is now the expansive lawn surrounding the arch. **Clark's Grave** lies in vast Bellefontaine Cemetery *(Pick up a map at cemetery office)*, 5 miles north of downtown on Florissant Avenue.

Boatload of Cargo

In addition to tons of provisions such as corn, pork, whiskey, and tobacco, the expedition's supplies included a blacksmith forge, carpentry tools, sewing instruments, gunpowder packed in lead canisters (which could be melted into bullets), fishing tackle, cooking utensils, mosquito netting, winter clothing, blankets, medicines, and sheets of oiled linen that doubled as sails and tents. The bales of trade goods contained beads, mirrors, combs, earrings, knives, scissors, awls, fish hooks, paint, thread, and many other items.

The captains also packed folding telescopes, surveying equipment, scales, thermometers, compasses, sextants (for measuring vertical angles of latitude), and a chrono-meter (for longitude measurements). Perhaps most important, they made sure they had plenty of paper, ink powder, and pencils to prepare their invaluable journals.

St. Charles

> "A great majority of the inhabitants are miserably pour, illiterate and when at home excessively lazy, tho' they are polite hospitable and by no means deficient in point of natural genious, they live in a perfect state of harmony among each other"
>
> MERIWETHER LEWIS, ON ST. CHARLES'S CITIZENS, MAY 20, 1804

After shoving off from the Wood River site, it took Clark and the men more than two days to reach St. Charles, a distance of just 23 miles. As they struggled against the Missouri's ferocious springtime current, they watched entire riverbanks—trees and all—give way and crash into the water. The cargo in one of the pirogues was soaked, and the keelboat snagged on submerged logs three times.

As the men pulled into St. Charles, a crowd of French settlers and Indians flocked down to the bank to welcome them. Soon, Clark was walking through a town he described as being about a mile long, with roughly one hundred small frame houses and 450 people. He added that the surrounding countryside was beautiful, interspersed with alternating prairie and timber, and that Americans had settled nearby. Among them was legendary woodsman Daniel Boone, then in his late sixties and living in a four-story Georgian mansion near present Defiance.

Though white settlement at St. Charles predates Lewis and Clark by nearly 35 years, most of the buildings in its attractive historic district were built well after the expedition passed through.

The best physical reminder of how things were in 1804 remains the river itself: broad, swift, brown; smelling of muck, sand, and willow thickets; alive with sandpipers and swallows. You can walk along the river in **Frontier Park** beside the historic district, where spectacular, operating reproductions of the expedition's boats usually reside. Built, manned, and fully outfitted by the **Discovery Expedition of St. Charles** *(314 S. Main St. 636-916-5344)*, the keelboat and two pirogues will spend several months of each bicentennial year retracing the expedition's route date by date. Also in Frontier Park, you'll cross a bike path that starts in St. Charles and hugs the Missouri River for more than 150 miles. Called **Katy Trail State Park** *(800-334-6946)*, the trail follows a former rail corridor through the same forest and bluff country that Lewis and Clark saw during the first three weeks of the expedition.

On your way back from the river, you might drop by the **Lewis & Clark Center** *(701 Riverside Dr. 636-947-3199. Adm. fee)*, a grassroots museum largely occupied by buckskinned mannequins and extensive dioramas chronicling the expedition's key events.

While in St. Charles, Clark decided to shift the keelboat's cargo forward—a change that was probably suggested by the boatmen. Restowing gave the men something to do while everyone waited five days for Lewis to finish his tasks in St. Louis and rejoin the party.

As the days passed, Clark dined with the leading merchants of St. Charles, bought another 136 pounds of tobacco, and paid the men. He and some of the party also attended a dance, where Pvt. John Collins apparently enjoyed things a little too much. He was court-martialed the following day for being absent without leave and "behaveing in an unbecomeing manner at the Ball." He got 50 lashes.

On May 20, in a driving rain, Lewis arrived from St. Louis on horseback. The next day, after hours of preparation, the men finally climbed into the boats.

MAY 22, 1804

Weldon Spring Conservation Area

◆ 5 MILES W OF US 40/61 OFF MO. 94 ◆ 636-441-4554

Deeply forested, lined with high bluffs overlooking the Missouri River, and traversed by a 5.3-mile section of the Katy Trail, this peaceful spot offers a vivid impression of the country Lewis and Clark saw in 1804. They camped about 2 miles below the present boat ramp, under a dense canopy of trees that overhangs the river and casts deep shadows across the forest floor.

Missouri's Katy Trail State Park along the Missouri River

Though unidentified, the approximate site of their camp lies along an inviting stretch of the bike path, where the river coasts along within easy reach of the trail. Vines, showy wildflowers, and thickets of shrubs drape the limestone cliffs. Great blue herons stalk the riverbanks, while at dusk you might see white-tailed deer—just like the four brought into the expedition's camp by Kickapoo hunters.

While Clark and the men worked the boats upstream, Lewis walked on shore, botanizing and identifying many of the birds, mammals, and insects that still live here. It would become their pattern: Clark with the boats, Lewis out roving. Unfortunately, Lewis's activities remain sketchy until he reached the Mandan villages because either his journal was lost, or he did not keep one (see sidebar p. 50). The next day, the expedition moved slowly upriver, passing beneath the long wall of bluffs you can see across the river from the boat ramp. Late in the day, while clambering among those bluffs, Lewis slipped from a 300-foot cliff. "Saved himself by the assistance of his Knife," Clark wrote, "he caught at 20 foot."

MAY 23–JUNE 3, 1804

Defiance to Jefferson City

Roads along this segment plunge and climb through forest and bluff, cross the Missouri, and coast beside its broad floodplain to Jefferson City. Along the way, you can catch glimpses of the river corridor from boat landings at the waterfront towns, of **Washington, New Haven,** and **Hermann.**

The expedition made fairly good time (averaging about 10 to 15 miles a day) as it worked the boats up to the mouth of the Osage River, east of Jefferson City. Still, there were some tense moments. For instance, on May 24, near **Matson,** the men were onshore hauling the keelboat upriver with a tow rope when the boat struck a sandbar and broke the rope. The current swung the boat, pinned it broadside, and nearly capsized it before every man aboard jumped to the high side. There they clung until the awesome current washed the sandbar from beneath the hull and freed the boat, which swept 2 miles downriver before the crew regained control.

The next day, near **Marthasville,** they passed the last white settlement, a tiny clearing in the trees called La Charette (now gone), where they were given milk and eggs. As they pressed onward, they hailed several different trading parties returning from the interior on rafts loaded with furs obtained from the Osage, Pawnee, and Omaha tribes. These parties, and several others they would meet in western Missouri, served as floating reminders of how well-known and well-traveled this leg of the Missouri was. The captains also paused to chat with a trader who had wintered several hundred miles upriver, in present South Dakota. Such traders often lived for many years among the

Camp Routine

Every evening when the party landed, guards were posted near the boats and at the rear of the camp. The rest of the men hauled gear, pitched tents, gathered firewood, divided into seven messes, and started cooking supper.

Sgt. John Ordway issued the provisions: lyed corn and grease one night, pork and flour the next, pork and Indian meal the third. Fresh meat, when available, substituted for pork. Each mess reserved a portion of the meal for the following day because the captains wanted no delays for cooking during precious daylight hours.

Often, the men got some whiskey to wash down their meal. Sometimes Pvt. Pierre Cruzatte would pull out his fiddle and the men would dance in the firelight, cheering one another on, while Lewis and Clark worked on their field notes and journals. Each of the sergeants also kept a journal.

Though mosquitoes often plagued the men throughout the day, they could at least look forward to a relatively untormented night of sleep. Each had a mosquito bier, without which, Lewis later wrote, "it would be impossible for them to exist."

Indians, bartering guns, powder, beads, knives, cloth, and other manufactured goods for beaver pelts, buffalo robes, and other furs they sent back to the wharves of St. Louis.

The expedition halted for nearly two days at the mouth of the Osage, so the captains could measure the width of the two rivers and fix the position of the confluence by measuring the angles of the sun and the moon.

If formal monuments have an appeal, you might drive up to Jefferson City's **Missouri State Capitol** *(E. Capitol Ave. at Jefferson St. 573-751-4127)* to see the large bronze relief of men in knickers signing the Louisiana Purchase. Otherwise, the only site in town with even a loose tie to the expedition is the **Runge Conservation Nature Center** *(NW edge of town on Mo. 179. 573-526-5544),* where exhibits and short, looping trails offer a primer on the major habitats Lewis would have studied during his long, solitary walks. The nature center also features a large aquarium that allows you to get face to face with the sort of catfish Pvt. Silas Goodrich hauled from the Missouri.

JUNE 7, 1804
Rocheport

As the boats of the expedition moved slowly upriver beneath the high, sometimes overhanging bluffs beyond Jefferson City, Clark began noticing "Courious Paintings and Carveing in the projecting rock." Many of these pictographs and petroglyphs of people, animals, and spirit creatures have been destroyed, but you can still see one along the **Katy Trail State Park** *(Milepost 174.7, about 5 miles SE of Rocheport).*

On the morning of June 7th, the expedition landed just above present Rocheport at the mouth of Moniteau Creek, where the men ate breakfast in the shade of a deep forest very much like the one found there today. Lewis explored the creek, and Clark mentions landing just above it to investigate yet another set of spirit images (now gone). "We landed at this Inscription and found it a Den of rattle Snakes," he wrote. The party shot three "verry large" rattlers, and moved on.

To reach the creek, follow the Katy Trail west several hundred yards from the town's depot to a railroad tunnel. There, the sun-dappled water opens a narrow lane through the forest, passes under a footbridge, and empties into the Missouri. For a more general vista of the big river and the bluffs that tower above it, walk the Katy Trail in the opposite direction for about 15 minutes.

In the days preceding the expedition's landing at Rocheport, the boat crews dodged sandbars and large

masses of drifting trees. The carpenters mended the keel-boat's mast, which had broken against an overhanging tree. And they had met a couple of hard-luck trappers who had lost all of their furs to a prairie fire, after wintering 250 miles up the Kansas River.

Deer were so plentiful that the hunters sometimes brought in more venison than the party could eat. The surplus was jerked. Occasionally they shot a black bear, and they had seen their first tantalizing sign of bison below present Rocheport.

JUNE 9, 1804
Arrow Rock State Historic Site

◆ N OF I-70 ON MO. 41 ◆ 660-837-3330 ◆ CAMPING

Lewis and Clark had little to say about Arrow Rock, an abrupt bluff that rises directly from the current and over-looks a bottomland prairie and a swift, narrow stretch of the Missouri. The landmark, named by French boatmen 80 years before Lewis and Clark, is overgrown with forest and difficult to see. But, from the park's **Campground Overlook,** the river and surrounding country squares roughly with Clark's description: broad grassy bottomland rising gradually to gentle forested hills.

Perhaps the best reason to stop at Arrow Rock, though, is for an introduction to the Missouri and Little Osage peoples, whose abandoned villages Lewis and Clark encountered farther upriver. At the **visitor center,** por-traits, drawings, hide scrapers, pipes, trade beads, and the rusted remains of French flintlocks illustrate village life from prehistoric times to the late 18th century.

Several miles above Arrow Rock, the keelboat snagged on numerous submerged logs. "This was a disagreeable and Dangerous Situation," Clark wrote, "particularly as immense large trees were Drifting down and we lay imedi-ately in their Course,—Some of our *men* being prepared for all Situations leaped into the water Swam ashore with a roap, and fixed themselves in Such Situations, that the boat was off in a fiew minits, I can Say with Confidence that our party is not inferior to any that was ever on the waters of the Missoppie."

JUNE 15, 1804
Van Meter State Park

◆ OFF MO. 41 ON MO. 122 ◆ 660-886-7537 ◆ CAMPING

It took the expedition six days to wrestle the keelboat upriver from Arrow Rock to a camp several miles beyond this pleasant, wooded park. They struggled past sandbars

Missouri River near Washington

and disintegrating riverbanks and came close to losing the keelboat twice. The current at one point was so strong that the men could make no progress, even with a stiff following breeze, all sails set, and every oar manned. Some had to get out and haul with ropes, slogging through the mud under a collapsing bank.

They camped a few miles northeast of today's **Malta Bend,** on the river's north side. At dusk they could look across the river to a lush bottomland prairie and extensive plain where the Missouri and Little Osage tribes had built and then abandoned a pair of villages. The expedition's camp near Malta Bend is inaccessible, but the previous evening's camp lay just across the river from **Miami** (*N on Mo. 41*), where you can get a good look at the swift brown waters of the Missouri from the town's shady boat landing.

Clark wrote, "On the river in this low Prarie the *Missouries* lived after They were reduced by the *Saukees* at Their Town Some Dists. below."

That earlier Missouri village stood in what is now Van Meter State Park, at the crest of a high ridge overlooking the river. Established by 1450 and abandoned in the mid-1720s, the village had a population of about 5,000 at its height. The Missouri lived in elliptical houses made of poles covered with mats and animal skins. They grew corn, squash, pumpkins, and beans, fished the river, and hunted for deer, elk, and bear in nearby forests.

Today, you can walk the ground where the Missouri village once stood, but much of the site now lies beneath a deep forest of oak and hickory. In its heyday, when there were relatively few trees, you could have seen the river, its floodplain, and the surrounding prairie. Nearby, though, you'll find two compelling openings in the forest. One, the **Mounds Field,** contains burial mounds that predate the Missouri. The other, called the **Old Fort,** is a large space enclosed by serpentine rows of parallel ditches. The purposes of the earthworks are unknown, but they must have been very important to the Missouri, who spent many years excavating with tools made from bison scapulas.

Before driving or hiking up to the village site, stop at the **visitor center,** where a large, annotated mural depicts what the community once looked like. Here, too, you'll find examples of the catlinite pipe heads, shell beads, bone tools, and stone points the Indians used before the French arrived in 1680, with glass beads, metal tools, and cloth.

Tragically, the French also brought smallpox, which decimated the Missouri. In the 1720s, the tribe moved several miles upriver to live near the Little Osage. There, both tribes remained until the late 18th century, when pressure from the Sauk and Fox pushed them out. Lewis and Clark would meet the Missouri six weeks later in Nebraska, where the tribe's surviving members had gone to live with the Oto.

For now, though, the captains were thinking more about the Sioux—in particular the Yankton. They had the good luck to meet a French trader southeast of present **Brunswick**. Pierre Dorion, Sr., who had lived for 20 years among the Yankton, was headed for St. Louis, but he agreed to return to the Yankton as the expedition's interpreter.

JUNE 16–24, 1804

Waverly to Buckner

The expedition arrived in the Waverly area after dark on a night thick with mosquitoes. They camped across the river from the present-day **Waverly Fishing Access** in what Clark called "a bad place" crawling with ticks. The next morning they moved on about a mile and then were laid up for two rainy days. They made a new tow rope and cut oars for the keelboat and pirogues.

The fishing access, with its thick understory of shrubs and vines, is a good place to gain appreciation for the grueling labor involved in towing an awkward 55-foot barge upstream. Most of the crew of 25 would have been out on the bank or in the shallows straining against the rope, slipping in the muck, cutting their feet on rocks, and sidestepping the occasional snake. It was a monumental effort that often gained the party just 10 miles or so during a 12- to 14-hour day.

By this time, several of the men had dysentery, and two-thirds of the party had broken out in boils and ulcers. Infected mosquito bites and cuts played a role in their discomfort, but the main culprit was diet. They ate practically no fruits or vegetables, and their jerky was probably contaminated with bacteria. But with the germ theory of disease still 50 years in the future, Clark could do little but blame the muddy water.

For some distance now, Clark had observed that the land was beginning to open up near the river. The abrupt stone bluffs and deep woodlands he had seen in eastern and

A Mighty Arsenal

The Corps of Discovery headed into the Missouri River country armed with rifles, muskets, pistols, a small cannon, and two blunderbusses.

The rifles included 15 muzzle-loading flintlocks, which Lewis had picked up at the Harpers Ferry arsenal in the spring of 1803. These guns were .54 caliber, had a 33-inch barrel, could kill a deer at 100 yards, and could be fired twice in a minute.

Lewis and Clark, and some of the men it seems, carried their own civilian "Kentucky" or "Pennsylvania" long rifles. Some of the enlisted men carried Model 1795 muskets, which were .69 caliber, smooth-bore flintlocks capable of firing a single ball or a handful of shot. The captains also carried pistols.

The small cannon, or swivel gun, was mounted at the bow of the keelboat and could be turned quickly in any direction. It fired a 1-pound ball or the equivalent in smaller projectiles (16 musket balls, for instance). The blunderbusses—large, bell-mouthed weapons that fired buckshot—were mounted on swivels in the pirogues.

> *"The water we Drink, or the Common water of the missourie at this time, contains half a Comn Wine Glass of ooze or mud to every pint"*
>
> WILLIAM CLARK,
> JUNE 21, 1804

central Missouri were giving way to rolling prairies interspersed with islands of trees. This topographic transition is still apparent, especially near Waverly, but the vegetative cover has changed. When Lewis and Clark saw it, the openings were tallgrass prairies bursting with wildflowers.

JUNE 23–24, 1804

Fort Osage

◆ SIBLEY ◆ 816-650-5737 ◆ ADM. FEE
◆ APRIL–MID-NOV. WED.-SUN., MID-NOV.–MARCH SAT.-SUN.

Four years after passing this point with the Corps of Discovery, Clark returned with a detachment of soldiers from St. Louis and built Fort Osage, which operated for nearly 20 years as a government trading post for the Osage and neighboring settlers. Faithfully reconstructed on its original site overlooking the Missouri, this low, palisaded fort accurately reflects the type of rough-hewn quarters that would have been familiar to Lewis, Clark, and other Army veterans with the expedition.

The national historic landmark abounds with incidental items that help build a vivid portrait of period life and the specific tasks of some of the expedition's principal members. There are drawknives, mallets, planes, and augers such as those used by Patrick Gass, carpenter, to build the fort on Wood River. And the hand-wrought metal fittings on the fort's doors resemble those the expedition's blacksmiths might have fashioned.

Living history buffs also demonstrate more common expedition chores—tanning hides, making fire with flint and steel, or pouring hot lead into bullet molds.

Vantage points along the fort's palisade and at some of its buildings offer fine vistas of the Missouri and its broad floodplain. A short footpath leads down to the the river.

Clark stepped ashore somewhere near this point to hunt. He expected the boats to catch up with him, but headwinds pinned them down all day, stranding Clark 6 miles above the evening camp. What ensued was typical of the hardship the men routinely endured.

"I concluded to Camp, altho I had nothing but my hunting Dress, & the Musquitors Ticks & Knats verry troublesom […] in crossing from an Island, I got mired, and was obliged to Craul out, a disegreeable Situation & a Diverting one of any one who Could have Seen me after I got out, all Covered with mud, I went my Camp & [s]Craped off the Mud and washed my Clothes, and fired off my gun which was answered by George Drewyer who was in persute of me & came up at Dark we feasted of meet & water."

JUNE 25–30, 1804

Kansas City Area

As the expedition pushed upriver into what are now the outskirts of Kansas City, Clark described broad prairies approaching the Missouri on both sides. Deer, he wrote, "are feeding in great numbers on the banks of the River […] and amuse themselves running on the open beeches or points."

On June 26, they camped at the mouth of the Kansas River, where they laid up for three days and built a defensive breastwork of logs and shrubs 6 feet high from river to river. While the men repaired one of the pirogues, dressed deer skins, and dried dampened stores, Lewis and Clark fixed the position of the confluence, measured the widths of the rivers, and noted the presence of "a great number" of Carolina parakeets, a species that is now extinct.

Soon, the expedition resumed its arduous passage, and the men had another close shave with the keelboat. Near present **Riverside,** the stern mired on a sandbar and the bow swung with sickening speed toward a large snag. It missed with just 6 inches to spare.

"If the Boat had Struck," Clark wrote, "Her Bow must have been Knocked off & in Course She must hav Sunk in the Deep water below."

The French Boatmen

As the keelboat made its way up the Missouri River, the expedition had many close calls. High banks collapsed and threatened the towing crews. Wind-driven waves pummeled the boat and sometimes sent it spinning downriver, where it slammed broadside onto sandbars or crashed into overhanging branches. Masts broke. Oars snapped. The windows of the captains' cabin smashed.

Often, it was the French boatmen who quickly controlled the situation. They knew the river intimately, and navigating its manifold hazards came naturally. They knew when to swim a rope to shore, how to work the boat off a snag, or even land in a gale and winch the boat over on its side to protect it from high waves. They came from a long, proud line of boatmen and fur traders who often claimed not only French but Indian heritage.

Their collective knowledge was invaluable to Lewis and Clark, and it covered far more than the immediate Missouri River corridor. It also extended hundreds of miles up the river's tributaries. They already had names for many of the creeks, rivers, bluffs, and other landmarks the Corps encountered, and they could identify the sites of abandoned Indian villages, trading posts, and forts.

JULY 1, 1804

Fort Leavenworth

◆ GRANT AVE., LEAVENWORTH ◆ 913-684-5604

This busy Army post seems to have little to do with Lewis and Clark until you drive down to its small airfield, where the slick roiling surface of the Missouri River glides past lavish bottomland prairies and dark walls of overhanging cottonwood and willow. Quiet, hot, humming with insects, rich in birdlife, and crammed with vigorous chest-high grasses, flowers, and shrubs, this tract of land appears much the way it did in 1804—right down to the gumbo-like mud the men slipped on while hauling the keelboat's tow rope. Walks along gravel roads and unmarked trails lead through the prairies and forests.

There are no interpretive signs, but none are needed to imagine the boats struggling against the current, or to picture George Drouillard, the expedition's premier hunter, slipping through the forest with his flintlock rifle.

Cannon at Fort Leavenworth, across the river from Lewis and Clark's camp

At Fort Leavenworth's **Frontier Army Museum** *(Follow signs. 913-684-3191)* visitors will find a few modest Lewis and Clark exhibits.

The expedition camped across the Missouri from Fort Leavenworth after logging 12 miles, a respectable distance. It had been a miserably hot day—so hot, Clark wrote, that the captains had "delayed three hours to refresh the men who were verry much over powered with the heat."

JULY 2, 1804

Weston Bend State Park

◆ 1 MILE S OF WESTON ON MO. 45 ◆ 816-640-5443
◆ CAMPING

Like Fort Leavenworth, Weston Bend offers one of the lower Missouri's rare opportunities to see the land much as it was in 1804. Patches of upland prairie plants grow among the park's open hills and extend to the rim of a high bluff. There a dense tangle of tree, shrub, and vine tumbles down to the riverbank, shifting as it descends from a forest of oak, hickory, and walnut to one of willow, cottonwood, and silver maple. From an elevated platform bolted to the bluff, you can gaze over the forest to the river below. But the real prize is the river corridor itself, where willow branches arch over the eddies, swallows skim the surface, and large cottonwood branches sweep by on the fast water.

Lewis and Clark slept near this spot and heard the same suck and wash of the living river, the same plop of large fish, the same bug-loud buzz. During the day, the men replaced another broken mast and watched a huge jam of driftwood float downriver. It took a half hour to pass.

JULY 4, 1804

Atchison Area

The members of the expedition celebrated Independence Day by firing the keelboat's swivel gun at dawn and dusk, knocking back an extra gill of whiskey each, and dancing into the night. Mostly, though, the men spent the day making history in their usual laborious fashion. They pushed 15 miles upriver and camped near the present Kansas town of **Doniphan,** in what Clark described as the most beautiful plain he had ever seen.

During the day, as the expedition approached the area of present Atchison, the captains took note of an oxbow lake similar to the one that stretches along the edge of **Lewis and Clark State Park** *(5 miles S of Rushville off Mo. 45. 816-579-5564. Camping).* Clark correctly concluded that the lake, which extended for several miles, was a cutoff meander of the ever changing Missouri River. Its water was clear, Clark wrote, full of fish, and its surface crowded with geese and their young. Today's narrow lake and its immediate surroundings of farm fields, lawns, and a small town hardly resemble what the Corps would have seen. But the valley itself is beautiful, especially when a thunderstorm crosses the broad floodplain and the surrounding wooded hills recede into the mist.

Atchison's pleasant **Independence Park** *(E end of Commercial St.)* offers a lovely riverside view of the Missouri as it coasts along between its deeply wooded banks. North of the park, River Road follows the Missouri to **Benedictine Bottoms,** a wetlands area reminiscent of the riverside habitats Lewis roamed in July 1804. Many of the plant and animal species he saw continue to live on the bottoms, and an interpretive sign identifies them. For a more general vista of the river and its broad floodplain, take the loop road through the campus of **Benedictine College** *(2nd St. N, follow signs)* and walk along the bluffs behind the abbey.

JULY 7, 1804

St. Joseph

When the Corps of Discovery passed the site of this river town in 1804, Clark described the surrounding landscape as a beautiful and extensive prairie divided by narrow strips of riparian woodland. The weather was hot and humid; the labor of wrestling the boats upriver, intense. One man got sunstroke, and in the blistering days ahead several others fell victim to the heat.

In St. Joseph, you'll find a small but excellent Lewis and

"The Plains of this countrey are covered with...Cops of trees, Spreding ther lofty branchs over Pools Springs or Brooks of fine water. Groops of Shrubs covered with the most delicious froot is to be seen in every direction, and nature appears to have exerted herself to butify the Senery by...flours Delicately and highly flavered raised above the Grass, which Strikes & profumes the Sensation."

WILLIAM CLARK, NEAR DONIPHAN, KANSAS, JULY 4, 1804

Clark exhibit at the **St. Joseph Museum** *(1100 Charles St. 816-232-8471. Adm. fee)*. It focuses on expedition events in the immediate area during both the outbound and return legs of the voyage. Journal excerpts, drawings, and a modest assortment of artifacts convey a sense of the expedition's day-to-day life. Maps identify nearby campsites and compare the Missouri's course of the early 1800s to that of today. Here, too: a reproduction of Karl Bodmer's 1833 painting of the prairie St. Joseph now occupies.

A pamphlet map, available at the museum or through the chamber of commerce, identifies six local vantage points along the Missouri that have Lewis and Clark interpretive signs.

JULY 11–12 1804

Squaw Creek N.W.R.

◆ SW OF MOUND CITY, MISSOURI, ON US 159 ◆ 660-442-3187
◆ CAMPING

As Lewis and Clark approached what is now Nebraska, they noted that the forests were beginning to thin along the hills and that the land beyond the river valley had opened up and flattened. They were moving toward the edge of the Great Plains.

To get a feel for this transition, climb the short **Loess Bluff Trail** behind the visitor center. The short path leads through a succession forest of oak, hickory, and juniper to the narrow crest of a 200-foot ridge overlooking the floodplain of the Missouri. To the west, flat land extends to the horizon. A slope of knee-high grass and wildflowers before you falls away to the edge of the forest. This small clearing is one of the last remnants of Missouri's native prairie.

Across the Missouri and south of present **Rulo,** Lewis and Clark camped at the mouth of the Big Nemaha River and gave the men, who were "much fatigued" from toiling in blistering heat, a day off. The island they camped on is gone, but the confluence still offers weary travelers a pleasant spot to rest in the shade of widely spaced cottonwoods that rustle in the breeze.

While most of the men relaxed, Clark explored 5 miles of the Nemaha and rambled about on a vast floodplain prairie covered with grasses 4.5 feet high

After Clark returned, the captains court-martialed Pvt. Alexander Willard for lying down and sleeping while on guard duty—a grave lapse that could endanger the whole party. Willard pleaded guilty to lying down, not guilty to sleeping. Convicted on both counts, he was sentenced to a hundred lashes on four consecutive evenings.

"The water of this river or Some other Cause… throws out a greater preposn. of Swet than I could Suppose Could pass thro: the humane body Those men that do not work at all will wet a Shirt in a Few minits & those who work, the Swet will run off in Streams"

WILLIAM CLARK, JULY 6, 1804

JULY 14, 1804

Indian Cave State Park

◆ NE OF SHUBERT, NEBRASKA, ON NEBR. 64E ◆ 402-883-2575 ◆ ADM. FEE ◆ CAMPING

There is no indication in the journals that Lewis or Clark ever saw the petroglyphs that adorn this park's landmark cavern. But they did camp nearby, after almost losing the keelboat several miles downriver to a "black and dismal looking" storm that pinned the boat against a sand island and might have battered it to pieces if the men hadn't careened its hull to the waves. The blast continued for 40 minutes, Clark wrote, then "sudenly Seased and the river become Instancetaniously as Smoth as Glass."

Ancient petroglyph in Nebraska's Indian Cave State Park

The park is worth visiting if only to ponder the ancient carvings at Indian Cave, an overhanging brow of sandstone partway up a wooded bluff. But the site also offers a broad sample of the landscapes Lewis and Clark roamed: upland forests of oak and hickory, pockets of mixed-grass prairie stuffed with wildflowers, swamps, bottomland, and the mighty river itself. At the top of the bluffs, you'll find one of the finest scenic overlooks on the lower Missouri.

JULY 16–19, 1804

Brownville to Nebraska City

Before crossing to the east bank of the Missouri, consider a short cruise on the *Spirit of Brownville (Brownville. 402-825-6441. Mem. Day–Labor Day Sat.-Sun.; fare)*, which allows you to appreciate the surrounding landscape from Lewis and Clark's usual perspective: the middle of the river.

As the Corps of Discovery headed into what is now Iowa, Clark described a long line of grassy hills to the east that rose above a broad prairie and paralleled the river as far as he could see. He called it bald-pated prairie because

Hikers along a Loess Hills trail, overlooking the Missouri River floodplain

the range of hills was nearly devoid of trees.

He was looking at the **Loess Hills,** which still form a low wall to the east of I-29. Today, though, they are nearly covered with thick forests as the prairie fires that once inhibited tree growth have been suppressed for generations. This profound vegetative change continues along the Missouri River for 150 miles, obscuring the modern traveler's perception of entering the Great Plains until northern Nebraska.

If you had been tugging on one of the keelboat's oars back in 1804, however, you would have had the distinct impression of reaching new country along this stretch of the river. Near present **Nebraska City,** Clark followed fresh elk tracks up the western hills through a narrow strip of woodland and suddenly emerged on an open and boundless prairie. "I Say bound less," Clark wrote, "because I could not See the extent of the plain in any Derection, the timber appeared to be confined to the River Creeks & Small branches, this Prarie was Covered with grass about 18 Inches or 2 feat high and contained little of any thing else."

You can still see the eastern margin of the Great Plains from one of two vantage points at Iowa's **Waubonsie State Park** *(9 miles N of Hamburg, off I-29 on Iowa 2. 712-382-2786),* which takes in a small portion of Clark's formerly bald-pated hills. If you're in a hurry, take the **Overlook Trail.** For a more comprehensive vista, walk the mile to **Sunset Ridge Overlook.**

JULY 19, 1804

Nebraska City

Perched along high bluffs overlooking the Missouri River, this small city on the edge of the Great Plains is building one of the finest Lewis and Clark interpretive centers you'll find anywhere along the expedition's route. Scheduled to open in 2003, the **Missouri River Basin Lewis and Clark Center** *(Off Nebr. 2, follow signs)* focuses primarily on the captains' stunning success describing plants and animals new to science and celebrates Lewis and Clark's other scientific achievements.

The wooded site, and adjacent field replanted in native grasses, wildflowers, and shrubs, offers a spectacular, unobstructed view of the Missouri winding through its broad valley. Inside, the center will offer two large exhibit halls. The first includes a full-scale reproduction of the keelboat, cut crosswise to reveal its cargo area. Visitors will be able to walk the boat's deck, opening storage lockers full of reproduced Indian trade goods, provisions, tools, and specimens Lewis sent back to Jefferson. A 19th-century medicine chest will illustrate how the captains treated various ailments that arose during the voyage.

In the Great Hall of Large Animals, visitors will amble among dioramic mounts of animals large and small that the expedition either depended upon for food, shelter, and clothing or described for science. Nearby, visitors will also see a freshwater aquarium stocked with fish species mentioned in the journals.

As the expedition approached the mouth of the Platte River, the boat crews struggled past an increasing number of shifting sandbars. Lewis remarked that the Platte greatly accelerated the current of the Missouri and that its sediment "consists of very fine particles of white sand." As he crouched by the river and rubbed that sand between his fingers, Lewis would have been fascinated to learn that much of it came from the Rocky Mountains. Soon they would form the principal obstacle of the entire voyage.

JULY 22–26, 1804

Western Historic Trails Center

◆ S OF COUNCIL BLUFFS. 24TH STREET EXIT OFF I-80/I-29
◆ 712-366-4900

In 1804 trees were so scarce along this leg of the Missouri that Lewis and Clark had to travel 12 miles from the mouth of the Platte to find a shady spot to rest the weary men for a few days. They camped in the vicinity of this excellent interpretive center, which is backed up by an extensive woodland interspersed with meadows of grass and native wildflowers, including cone flower, indian blanket, black-eyed Susan, and blue flax.

The captains named the spot Camp White Catfish for a strange-looking fish caught there by Silas Goodrich, the Corps's best fisherman. White, with small eyes and a tail resembling a dolphin, it was a channel catfish, first described for science by the captains.

While Lewis and Clark estimated the camp's position and made notes, some of the men carved new oars and setting poles. Others hunted, or aired provisions, and two set off across the plains to visit the Oto and Pawnee villages on the Platte. They were sent to invite the chiefs to come speak with Lewis and Clark, but both villages were empty for the moment, the tribes out hunting bison.

The expedition's own hunters had seen bison and elk now for nearly 300 miles, but had not been close enough to shoot any. Though eager for a change in diet, the party still relied on venison as its principle staple, supplemented occasionally with beaver, geese, fish, and wild fruits.

Exhibits in today's interpretive center incorporate the Lewis and Clark Expedition as the forerunner to mass migrations along the Oregon, California, and Mormon Trails. Film loops and panels deal with some of the highlights of the expedition, but the parklands surrounding the center offer more rewards. A wide path leads through meadow and trees to the **Missouri River Overlook** (1 mile round-trip), and other trails form a 1.75-mile loop through similar terrain.

When Lewis and Clark roamed through bottomlands like this, they hiked through alternating stretches of tallgrass prairie, dense woodlands, and shallow marshes. Though you won't see an elk, a bison, or a Carolina parakeet here now, cottonwoods and sycamores still rise from an understory of dogwood and mulberry. There are grapevines, groves of willow, and marshy areas clogged with bulrush, cattail, and arrowroot. Birdsong carries on the refreshing breeze, and butterflies still waver among the wildflowers.

JULY 27–28, 1804
Omaha Area

Unable to contact the Oto, Lewis and Clark shoved off after a brief rain shower and logged 15 miles in a single afternoon—excellent progress. They camped in what is now downtown Omaha, near the Douglas Street Bridge. Nothing suggestive of the terrain remains, of course, unless you count the remarkable collection of Karl

Bodmer landscape paintings at the **Joslyn Art Museum** *(2200 Dodge St. 402-342-3300. Closed Mon.; adm. fee).* Bodmer steamboated the Missouri in the early 1830s, busily recording images of the same tribes and villages Lewis and Clark encountered farther upriver, in the Dakotas and Montana. Complementing his works are paintings by George Catlin and Alfred Jacob Miller.

For another vivid impression of how things have changed in the past 200 years, cross the river to Council Bluffs, Iowa, and visit the **Lewis and Clark Monument** *(25th St. Exit off I-29, proceed E across railroad tracks, then N on Monument Rd. to park entrance),* which overlooks Omaha, its airport, and a couple of bends of the Missouri River.

As the boats moved slowly upriver on July 28, George Drouillard, out hunting on the prairie, met a Missouri Indian who accompanied him to the party's camp just north of present Council Bluffs. The Indian told the captains that most of the Missouri and Oto were out hunting bison on the plains, but that a small band was camped nearby, hunting elk. Lewis and Clark asked him to return to his band and invite its leaders to a council farther up the river, near what would become **Fort Atkinson,** Nebraska.

The Oto

Always a small tribe, the Oto moved west from the Mississippi River during the late 17th and 18th centuries, living near or with the Iowa Indians. About 1798, the Oto were joined by the Missouri, who had been decimated by smallpox and attacks by the Sauk and Fox tribes. Thereafter, they lived as one tribe, making their way as farmers and hunters. When Lewis and Clark met them, they were living on the Platte River near present Fremont, Nebraska.

JULY 30–AUGUST 3, 1804

Fort Atkinson S.H.P.

◆ 1 MILE E OF FORT CALHOUN, ON CTY. RD. 34
◆ 402-468-5611

Originally built in 1820 on a steep bluff washed by the Missouri River, Fort Atkinson overlooked the bottomland prairie where Lewis and Clark met with the Oto and Missouri on August 3, 1804. Today, the fort's quadrangle of low log huts has been reconstructed at its original location, a broad swath of grass and wildflowers atop Council Bluff.

Two key changes in the landscape, however, keep you from building a clear image of Lewis and Clark greeting the chiefs and handing out Jefferson Peace medals. The face of the bluff, once bare, is now covered with high forest, and the river, which hugged the bluff in 1804, has shifted a few miles east. Still, the park has a lot to offer. At the **visitor center** *(Mem. Day–Labor Day daily, Sept.–Oct. Sat.-Sun.)* you'll find an authentic 1803 Harpers Ferry flintlock rifle, the very model carried by members of the expedition. Here, too, is a copy of Karl Bodmer's 1833

"From the Bluff on the 2d rise imediately above our Camp the most butifull prospect of the River up & Down and the Countrey opsd. prosented it Self which I ever beheld; The River meandering the open and butifull Plains, interspursed with Groves of timber, and each point Covered with Tall timber"

WILLIAM CLARK, AT FORT ATKINSON, JULY 30, 1804

painting of the fort site.

Outside, follow the **Grass Trail** to the fort and the edge of the bluff. From here, Lewis and Clark could gaze down onto the shimmering surface of the Missouri and see the boats tied up beside their tents. Today all you see are tree trunks, but the 1.2-mile trail beneath the bluff loops through the approximate site of their camp.

As the captains prepared for their first formal encounter with Indians, the enlisted men rested and amused themselves. Some caught and tamed a young beaver. Pvt. Joseph Fields killed a badger, which Clark described in great detail. Lewis skinned and stuffed it to send back to Jefferson. They watched swans glide by on the river and caught catfish so fat they could render a quart of oil from each fish. The hunters brought in their first elk, and Clark marked his 34th birthday with a feast of venison, elk, beaver tail, and wild fruit.

At sunset on August 2, the Missouri and Oto arrived. As a goodwill gesture, Lewis and Clark gave them tobacco, roasted meat, pork, flour, and meal. "In return," Clark wrote, "they Sent us Water millions [watermelons]."

The next morning the captains greeted the Indians in full dress uniform. Lewis delivered a long speech. He declared that the Missouri River country now belonged to the United States, appealed for intertribal peace, and asked them to send a delegation to visit Jefferson. He also urged them to trade with St. Louis merchants. If they did so, he said, a trading post would be built near the mouth of the Platte. Otherwise, access to valuable European goods could be cut off.

After the speech, the captains gave each chief a bundle of gifts (breechclouts, paint, medals). Eager for a more dependable source of manufactured goods, the Indians made no objection to Lewis's pronouncements, promised to follow his advice, and asked for gunpowder and whiskey. Clark gave them a canister of powder and 50 balls, as well as a bottle of whiskey. Lewis pumped up his air gun and fired a few rounds, which, Clark wrote, "astonished those nativs." The air gun, along with the swivel gun and various scientific instruments, would become

Sunset at
De Soto N.W.R.

standard props at all of the meetings Lewis and Clark had with Indian leaders.

Before leaving the Fort Atkinson area, consider a jaunt through the **Boyer Chute National Wildlife Refuge** *(3.5 miles E of Fort Calhoun on Cty. Rd. 34)*, where short nature trails explore a restored floodplain forest and grasslands reminiscent of the 1804 landscape. You can also follow a longer trail that hugs the Missouri's main channel.

AUGUST 4, 1804
De Soto N.W.R.

◆ E OF BLAIR ON US 30 ◆ 712-642-4121

As the expedition passed this area, the men had to maneuver through a tricky, 1-mile stretch of narrow river clogged with snags. While they dodged oncoming tree trunks, the Missouri busily ate away at the banks, caving them in and crashing more trees into the water. By now the crews took such hazards in stride, and the boats slipped by unscathed.

"at length we were surprised by the appearance of a flock of Pillican at rest on a large sand bar attatched to a small Island the number of which would if estimated appear almost incredible; they appeared to cover several acres of ground"

MERIWETHER LEWIS, AUG. 8, 1804

Today, the erosive power of the river remains evident at the refuge's **Missouri River Overlook,** which faces a densely wooded bank with exposed tree roots dangling 8 to 10 feet above the swift brown current.

The refuge, a stopover for half a million migrating snow geese each autumn, takes in a large oxbow lake that curves through restored prairie flats and floodplain forest beside the Missouri. Though Lewis and Clark missed the snow geese, they did see many of the other animals that live here—white-tailed deer, beavers, muskrat, coyotes, wood ducks, and various other birds.

The **visitor center** offers glass-enclosed overlooks of the lake and forest from spotting scopes.

AUGUST 10, 1804

Lewis and Clark State Park

◆ 5 MILES W OF ONAWA ON IOWA 175 ◆ 712-423-2829

Located on a narrow oxbow lake briefly noted in Clark's journal, this shady state park boasts full-scale operating reproductions of the expedition's hefty keelboat and the two pirogues that accompanied it up the Missouri.

Recently restored and gleaming, the keelboat is docked under a breezy grove of cottonwoods. With its mast up, sails furled, and a bundle of setting poles near at hand, the boat seems ready for the Corps to break camp and come aboard. Visitors are welcome to step on deck, handle the tiller, sight along one of two mounted blunderbusses, or duck into the captains' cabin at the aft end.

The boat's obvious weight, bargelike lines, and sluggish buoyancy convey what a towering chore it must have been to wrestle such a craft upriver. Even so, on many days the keelboat outpaced the pirogues. Visitors are also welcome to board reproductions of the red and white pirogues— long boats, with graceful lines and space for several oarsmen. Knowledgeable volunteers are often on hand to talk about the boats and the expedition.

Downriver, near present **Little Sioux,** Lewis stood spellbound on deck as the keelboat followed a lane of white feathers, 60 to 70 yards wide, that extended upriver as far as he could see. The feathers glided toward the boats for 3 miles before Lewis identified the source, a huge flock of pelicans resting on a sandbar. As the birds rose, Lewis shot one. Spreading its wings, he held its bony webbed feet in his hands, counted its toes, and perhaps held its head while the men poured five gallons of water into the curious pouch on the underside of its bill.

Back in Nebraska, 3 miles north of Decatur on US 75, you'll find **Blackbird Scenic Overlook,** named for a powerful Omaha chief who died four years before Lewis and Clark's visit. Poised at the edge of a high bluff, it offers a grandstand vista of the Missouri River Valley and a brief sketch of traditional life among the Omaha Indians, whose territory Lewis and Clark entered as they moved through what is now northeastern Nebraska.

Not far from this overlook, the captains and ten men climbed to the top of the bluffs—grassy and wide open in their day—to visit the grave of Blackbird, who had died of smallpox along with hundreds of his people. From the bluff, Clark wrote, the party could see 60 to 70 miles of "verry Crooked" river.

Crooked indeed. Earlier in the week, Clark recorded one particularly dramatic example of the river's meandering course when he set off from camp to hunt turkeys. After walking just a few hundred yards into the forest, he emerged again on the banks Missouri—12 river miles below camp. The river had nearly doubled back on itself. Today, most of those hairpin turns have been ironed out by the Army Corps of Engineers.

AUGUST 13, 1804

Tonwontonga

◆ 1 MILE N OF HOMER, VIA US 75

A forlorn historical marker overlooking farm fields and railroad tracks identifies the site of Tonwontonga, the large Omaha village where Lewis and Clark hoped to contact the tribe and negotiate a peace settlement between them and the Oto.

Farmers and hunters, the Omaha arrived along the Nebraska-Iowa border around 1700 after migrating west from the Ohio River Valley. They lived as extended families in large circular earth lodges, planted corn and other crops in the spring, hunted the plains all summer, and returned to their lodges for the fall harvest. They built several villages, the most important being Tonwontonga, or "Big Village," established in 1775. Led by Chief Blackbird, who befriended white traders, the Omaha rose to prominence on the eastern plains. During the 1790s, they tried to prevent French traders from ascending the Missouri to trade with the Arikara and Mandan.

The expedition's advance party found the village deserted and in ruins. The Omaha had apparently burned their earth lodges in an attempt to control the smallpox epidemic that had decimated them during the winter of 1799-1800, and those who remained were out on the plains for the season, hunting bison. Today, there is no apparent trace of the village.

"After paying all the honor to our Decesed brother we Camped in the mouth of floyds river about 30 yards wide, a butifull evening."

WILLIAM CLARK,
AUG. 20, 1804

AUGUST 18–20, 1804

Dakota City

At this small town's riverside park, a National Park Service platform faces a long, wooded stretch of the Missouri. Though jet noise detracts from the setting, plaques here map Lewis and Clark's progress through the area, marking expedition campsites from Kansas to South Dakota.

Just a few miles downriver, the expedition laid up for nearly a week at a place the captains dubbed "Fish Camp" after they caught and carefully cataloged more than 1,100 fish in a nearby creek.

Unable to contact the Omaha, they remained at Fish Camp waiting for a squad of men who had been sent on a distasteful errand: Bring back Pvt. Moses Reed, a deserter, dead or alive. On August 18, the squad returned with Reed and a few principal Oto chiefs who had not been at Council Bluffs.

Though they could have had Reed shot, the captains sentenced him to run the gauntlet four times, the equivalent of 500 lashes, and expelled him from the permanent party. After inflicting punishment, the mood in camp brightened. The men were issued an extra gill of whiskey, the fiddle played, and the men danced until 11 p.m.—all in celebration of Lewis's 30th birthday.

The following day's formal meeting with the Oto did not go well. The Oto were unimpressed with the gifts of tobacco, beads, and face paint. The captains were irritated by the chiefs, who seemed to care more about presents than peace with their neighbors.

Peace was vital to Lewis and Clark's plan to bring all the Missouri River tribes into an American trading network. Though eager for trade, the Oto did not care whether it was with Americans or not. And peace conflicted with the endless cycle of intertribal raid and revenge—a fact of life difficult to overcome, since it was by raid that young Indian men proved themselves worthy of leadership.

Both parties left the meeting disgruntled. Lewis and Clark broke camp the following morning and passed present Dakota City.

AUGUST 20, 1804

Sioux City

As the boats approached what are now the southern outskirts of Sioux City, Iowa, every man aboard worried about Sgt. Charles Floyd, whose strange illness had taken a bitter turn during the night. "I am Dull & heavy," Clark wrote that morning, "been up the greater Part of last night with Serjt. Floyd, who is a[s] bad as he can be to live."

The men thought a warm bath might comfort Floyd, so they pulled over, built a fire, and fetched water.

"Before we could get him in to this bath," Clark wrote, "he expired, with a great deel of composure, haveing Said to me before his death that he was going away and wished me to write a letter."

Floyd, the expedition's only fatality, probably died of a burst appendix, a condition unknown to medical science until 20 years after the expedition and not operated on successfully until 1884.

They buried him "with all the honors of War" at the top of a high round hill overlooking the river and surrounding country. Lewis read the funeral service. Today, Floyd's grave is marked by a tall obelisk, the **Sergeant Floyd Monument** *(Follow signs off I-29),* which still overlooks the river in Sioux City. Plaques here identify the approximate site of his death and of the expedition's next camp.

Sergeant Floyd Monument

Sioux City is also home to the **Lewis and Clark Interpretive Center** *(900 Larson Park Rd. 712-224-5242. Closed Mon. Oct.–Mem. Day),* an imaginative, first-rate facility that immerses visitors into the Corps of Discovery's daily routine along this stretch of the Missouri. Floor-to-ceiling murals of the 1804 landscape combine with interactive exhibits and convincing sculptures to offer a vivid, hands-on impression of what it was like to travel and camp with the expedition.

Two of the center's six galleries focus on Floyd's death and the state of medical knowledge in 1804. Others explore the scientific and military aspects of the expedition and sum up the results of the journey. Throughout, you'll find interesting opportunities to get involved. Identify plants, for instance, with Lewis. Take a compass bearing with Clark. Compare Lewis's medicines and remedies with modern treatments.

Just up the road, the **Sergeant Floyd Riverboat Museum** *(1000 Larson Park Rd. 712-279-0198)* displays 19th-century photographs of Floyd's grave, copies of Clark's maps and charts of the area, and a sculptured reconstruction of Floyd's face rendered by a forensic artist who studied his skull.

Great Plains

**August 22, 1804 –
April 6, 1805**

This portion of the route covers Lewis and Clark's voyage across the heart of the Great Plains, their encounters with various Plains and Missouri River tribes, and their cheerful winter among the Mandan and Hidatsa north of present Bismarck, North Dakota. Though roads here stick mainly to the plains, they often drop to the banks of the Missouri and its meandering trough of rumpled hills. The land grows wilder the farther north and west you travel, opening up into the grand and rolling topography that Lewis and Clark grew to love for its beauty and abundant bison. The river, though, has been dammed and most of the bottomlands inundated. Even so, this is richly rewarding country. There's a first-rate museum devoted to the expedition, full-scale reproductions of earth lodges and Fort Mandan, ancient village sites, and even a few stretches of wild river.

New Town
FT. BERTHOLD
INDIAN RES.
Lake Sakakawea
Garrison Dam
Ft. Mandan
Reconstruction
KNIFE RIVER
INDIAN VILLAGES N.H.S.
Stanton
Washburn
CROSS RANCH S.P.
Knife
FT. MANDAN
OVERLOOK S.H.S.
Cross Ranch
Nature Pres.
DOUBLE DITCH
INDIAN VILLAGE
S.H.S.
NORTH DAKOTA
Mandan
Bismarck
FT. ABRAHAM
LINCOLN S.P.
HUFF INDIAN
VILLAGE S.H.S.
Huff
N
Ft. Yates
STANDING
ROCK
Kenel
INDIAN
RESERVATION
Lake Oahe
Grand
Mobridge
CHEYENNE RIVER
INDIAN RESERVATION
WEST WHITLOCK
S.R.A.
Cheyenne
Gettysburg
SOUTH DAKOTA
Triple U
Bison Ranch
Oahe
Dam
Pierre
FARM ISLAND
S.R.A.
WEST BEND
S.R.A.
Ft. Pierre
FT. PIERRE
NAT.
GRASSLAND
Bad
LOWER
BRULE
I.R.
CROW
CREEK I.
Lower Brule
Ft.
Thompson
Oacoma
White
Chamberlain
SNAKE CREEK
S.R.A.
Winner
Lake
Franc
Cas
Niobrar

0   40 km
0   60 km

Bear attacking canoe, from painting by John Clymer, circa 1970

AUGUST 22, 1804

Ponca State Park

◆ 2 MILES N OF PONCA OFF NEBR. 12 ◆ 402-755-2284
◆ ADM. FEE ◆ CAMPING

After laying Sgt. Charles Floyd to rest in present-day Sioux City, Iowa, the expedition logged more than 40 miles in just two days of sailing under strong winds that filled the air with sand and blew so hard the men had to reef in the sails. They passed the site of **Ponca State Park** August 22, and landed for the night near present-day **Elk Point,** South Dakota. There, in the first American election west of the Mississippi, the enlisted men chose Sgt. Patrick Gass as Floyd's successor as commanding sergeant.

While the men voted, Lewis struggled to recover from the toxic effects of a curious material he'd found among the bluffs near today's state park. Clark described it as a clear, soft substance, which could be molded and became pliant like wax.

"Capt. Lewis in proveing the quality of those minerals was near poisoning himself by the fumes and tast," Clark wrote. He thought it might be arsenic or cobalt, but modern geologists can not identify the substance. Whatever it was, it left Lewis feeling weak for several days.

Wooded, rugged, and laced with 20 miles of hiking trails, Ponca State Park overlooks the downstream end of a relatively untamed, 59-mile section of the Missouri River called the **Missouri National Recreational River** (402-336-3970). Unchanneled by wing walls, levees, or dredging, this stretch takes on a noticeably wilder character than what lies beyond and feels a lot more like the living river Lewis and Clark navigated.

For a close look, you can poke along the open, grassy banks above the park's boat ramp, where the roiling brown water rushes between small islands and gravel bars. Or drive to the **Three-State Overlook,** poised at the crest of the park's oak-laden bluffs, and take in a breezy vista of the Missouri winding across the plains. Paths for guided horseback trips (Park office. June-Aug.; fee) hug the riverbanks and climb the bluffs to another overlook.

Paddlers can run the entire stretch from Yankton to Ponca in two easy days. Daylong and half-day trips are also possible from several intermediate access points. **Missouri River Tours** (402-985-2216. April-Sept.) rents canoes and runs a shuttle service.

The park will soon open a new interpretive center, the **Missouri National Recreational River Resource and Education Center,** which will focus on the ecology and history of the Missouri. Several exhibits deal specifically

> *"The Wind blew hard West and raised the Sands off the bar in Such Clouds that we Could Scercely See this Sand being fine and verry light Stuck to every thing it touched, and in the Plain for a half a mile every Spire of Grass was covered with the Sand or Dust"*
>
> WILLIAM CLARK, NEAR PRESENT-DAY VERMILLION, S. DAK., AUG. 23, 1804

with Lewis and Clark, offering details from their maps and journals, describing relations with local tribes, listing scientific discoveries, and sketching the immense challenges they faced simply navigating the river.

Other exhibits may not tie in directly with Lewis and Clark, but they enhance our understanding of what the expedition experienced. Here, for instance, you'll find an entire section that presents the Missouri as the Corps of Discovery knew it—as a wild and ever changing watercourse of sandbars and snags, marshes and wetlands, shifting channels and cutoff meanders. In short, it profiles a natural river, rich in waterfowl and flowing through a landscape of floodplain forest and prairie. Elsewhere, the center describes native peoples who lived along the river, Euro-American settlement, and construction of the dams that have converted much of the Missouri into a series of large reservoirs.

As Lewis and Clark approached present-day **Vermillion,** one of the expedition's hunters hailed the party and proudly announced that he had shot a buffalo. Lewis and 12 men hurried out onto the plain to haul the animal back to the river. That night, they feasted for the first time on the totem animal of the Great Plains.

AUGUST 24, 1804

Ionia Volcano

◆ 3 MILES NE OF PONCA

As the expedition's boats continued upriver in the rain, Lewis and Clark noticed steam rising from the eroded flanks of a rounded hill. "Those Bluffs," Clark wrote, "appear to have been laterly on fire, and at this time is too hot for a man to bear his hand in the earth at any debth."

For more than 70 years after the expedition, some scientists believed the hill, called Ionia Volcano, was a true volcano that erupted when Missouri River floodwaters poured onto subterranean molten rock. But others later proved that the heat and steam were caused by the oxidation of freshly exposed, damp shale.

Since most of the hill collapsed during the 1870s flood, it no longer "erupts." Still, the site opens up a terrific view of the Missouri River and surrounding plains, and the short drive from Newcastle leads through a beautiful landscape of rolling prairie hills interspersed with copses of trees. Intimate yet boundless, the topography squares with the expedition's journals and offers modern travelers a true sense of having arrived on the Great Plains.

To reach Ionia Volcano, take the gravel road off Neb. 12 from the Congregational church and head north.

View across the plains from the top of Spirit Mound

Go 2 miles and turn right at the fork in the road. Go another mile to a hilltop cemetery, which lies across the road from an overlook and the top of Ionia Volcano.

AUGUST 25, 1804

Spirit Mound

◆ 6 MILES N OF VERMILLION ON S. DAK. 19 ◆ 605-232-0873

A few days before reaching Calumet Bluff, Lewis and Clark took several men and hiked a few hours north of the river. Their goal was to investigate an isolated hill on the prairie rumored to be inhabited by fierce spirit people 18 inches tall, who had remarkably large heads and "Sharp arrows with which they Can Kill at a great distance."

The party saw nothing of the kind, but what Clark recorded in his journal may seem nearly as far-fetched to modern eyes. "From the top of this Mound we observed Several large gangus of Buffalow & Elk feeding upwards of 800 in number." There were no trees, but the stream courses they saw running through the plain were loaded with shrubs bearing ripe fruit—grapes, currants, and two kinds of plums.

Today, Spirit Mound is one of the few sites along the entire route where one can stand precisely where Lewis and Clark did 200 years ago. It is still a prominent knob of grass rising unobscured from the surrounding landscape, and the view from the top still extends for many miles. But now the vista takes in a patchwork of farm fields and homesteads—the sort of settlement that would have pleased Jefferson. The site, recently acquired by South Dakota, is being restored. Farm buildings that once cluttered its base have been removed, along with fences, roads, and trees. Prairie grasses and other native plants will be reintroduced, an interpretive kiosk will be built, and a wide trail will lead from a parking area to the top of the mound.

As you drive back through Vermillion, you may want to drop by the **W.H. Over Museum** (*Follow signs off S. Dak. 50 Bus. to 1110 Ratingen St. 605-677-5228*), which exhibits a wide variety of traditional Sioux clothing, musical instruments, pipes, and utensils from Lewis and Clark's era. Here, too, are Stanley Morrow's revealing portraits of Plains Indians, circa 1870.

AUGUST 28–31, 1804

Gavins Point Dam

◆ 4 MILES W OF YANKTON ON NEBR. 121

One of several major dams along the Missouri, Gavins Point looms over the spot where Lewis and Clark held councils and feasted with the Yankton Sioux. Vastly altered by the dam's thundering jets of white water and busy parking lots, this important site retains little of the flavor of 1804.

The expedition camped on the south bank just downstream of the dam beneath Calumet Bluff (most of which was torn down during dam construction). Late the following afternoon, about 70 Yankton appeared on the opposite bank, brought in by Sgt. Nathaniel Pryor and Pierre Dorion, Sr., a Frenchman who had lived with the Sioux. Pryor told the captains he had been warmly received, had feasted on fat dog, and had slept among handsome shelters "of a Conic form Covered with Buffalow Roabs Painted different Colours"—tepees.

Lewis and Clark sent gifts of tobacco, corn, and cooking kettles across the river and told the Indians they would speak with them the following morning.

From the captains' point of view, the impending council was vitally important. If Jefferson's scheme for establishing an American trade empire on the Missouri was to succeed, they had to obtain the blessing and cooperation

The Sioux

Lewis and Clark usually referred to the numerous and powerful Indians they met along the plains as the Sioux. Calling themselves the Dakota, Lakota, or Nakota, meaning "friends" or "allies," the Sioux can be divided into three major regional groups from east to west: the Santee, Yankton (or Yanktonai), and Teton. During the 1700s, the Teton and Yankton moved west, gradually leaving the woodlands and prairie for a nomadic existence as High Plains buffalo hunters. When Lewis and Clark encountered them they lived in western Minnesota, the Dakotas, western Nebraska, eastern Wyoming, and Montana.

In Lewis and Clark's day, the many different bands often had competing interests. Some even warred against tribes that other bands considered close friends. This complex and fluid political situation was just one of several among Plains peoples that would undermine Lewis and Clark's efforts to establish a comprehensive peace among the tribes.

> *"The water Shoots in to the Missiouri verry Swift, & has thrown the Sand out, which makes a Sand bar & Sholes from the mouth a considerable distance we Saw 2 Deer, & large flocks of geese up the mo [mouth] of this river"*
>
> SGT. JOHN ORDWAY, DESCRIBING THE NIOBRARA RIVER, SEPT. 4, 1804

of the powerful Sioux bands. The stakes were also high for the Yankton. They wanted a more reliable supply of trade goods, and needed protection from their neighbors, the Teton.

The two sides met with as much pomp and circumstance as each could muster. The Yankton delegation paraded through camp behind four colorfully painted musicians, while the captains wore their dress uniforms, ran up the flag, and fired the keelboat's swivel gun. Lewis delivered a four-hour speech urging them to make peace with the Oto and Missouri and to form a delegation of chiefs to visit Jefferson.

Afterward, the captains smoked the pipe with the Yankton and handed out medals and gifts, including fancy clothes and an American flag. As the chiefs withdrew to talk among themselves, the expedition's men hobnobbed with the other Yankton, admired their bear claw necklaces and tough bison-hide shields, and handed out prizes to young boys shooting bows and arrows.

"After dark," wrote Sgt. John Ordway, "we Made a large fire for the Indians to have a war dance…the Band began to play on their little Instruments, & the drum beat & they Sang. the young men commenced dancing around the fire. it always began with a houp & hollow & ended with the Same, and in the intervales, one of the warries at a time would rise with his weapen & Speak of what he had done in his day."

The next morning, the chiefs told the captains they would help form a delegation to visit Jefferson, that trade and peace were desirable, but that what they needed immediately were guns and ammunition.

Lewis and Clark had not come as traders and could not spare any firearms, powder, or ball. But they did agree to leave Dorion with them to help arrange peace with neighboring tribes. Unfortunately, Dorion was the expedition's only competent Sioux interpreter. He would be sorely missed upriver during the expedition's tense, nearly disastrous encounter with the Teton.

In the meantime, though, the captains patted themselves on the back. They had befriended a powerful band of Sioux who eagerly joined the American trading system and earnestly desired intertribal peace. Or so it seemed.

From the dam's **visitor center** (*Access from Nebr. 121. 402-667-7873 ext. 3246. Mem. Day–Labor Day daily, March-Nov. Mon.-Fri., closed Dec.-Jan.*) atop Calumet Bluff, you'll get a good view of **Lewis and Clark Lake,** a vast reservoir lined with wooded limestone bluffs and flecked with speedboat wakes. You'll also find a small exhibit devoted to the expedition and maps of the many campgrounds, picnic areas, and beaches that dot both shores of the reservoir. Leading from the visitor center is an interpretive trail spotlighting plants that Indians used during Lewis and Clark's era.

For a pleasant stroll to a more secluded vista of the lake, head for the **Gavins Point Nature Trail** in South Dakota's **Lewis and Clark State Recreation Area** (*Cross the dam, turn left, follow signs. 605-668-2985. Adm. fee*). The trail loops through wooded bottomlands pocked with deer tracks and leads to the top of the **White Bear Cliffs,** an expedition landmark.

SEPTEMBER 4, 1804

Niobrara State Park

◆ 1 MILE W OF NIOBRARA ON NEBR. 12 ◆ 402-857-3373
◆ ADM. FEE ◆ CAMPING

Set among rolling grass hills peppered with redcedar trees, this expansive state park overlooks the confluence of the Missouri and Niobrara Rivers and opens up grand vistas of the plains as Lewis and Clark saw them: smooth, undulating, nearly bare, stretching forever beneath a magnificent sky full of gleaming thunderheads.

The expedition camped just above the mouth of the Niobrara beneath steep, cedar-covered hills that can still be seen today. Now well out on the semiarid plains, Clark remarked that ink thickened noticably after just a couple of days in the inkwell. New plants and animals began to appear: the plains cottonwood, yucca, the bull snake, a curious black-tailed deer with large ears (mule deer), and a wild goat (pronghorn) that streaked across the distant plains so quickly that Lewis could not even determine what color it was.

Today, white-tailed deer browse the park's shrubs, wild turkeys strut through its campgrounds, and, during spring and fall migrations, ducks, geese, and other waterfowl clog the wetlands, marshes, and backwater sloughs along both rivers.

Pick up a map at park headquarters and check out the view from one of several high points along the loop road. Then head for the footbridge that spans the Niobrara's marshy delta for a closer look at the Missouri and the complex of islands, sandbars, and backwaters of the confluence. Like Ponca State Park (see pp. 44-45), Niobrara lies along a wild stretch of the Missouri. The park has three boat landings, making it easy to float a short section of the Missouri or to poke around in the quiet side channels. If you don't have a boat, the park runs 8-mile guided float trips during summer (*fare*) on the Missouri.

"He Shot away what fiew Bullets he had with him, and in a plentifull Country like to have Starvd."

WILLIAM CLARK, ON PVT. GEORGE SHANNON, SEPT. 11, 1804

SEPTEMBER 8, 1804

Fort Randall Dam

◆ SCENIC OVERLOOK ON US 18

As Lewis and Clark floated past the prairie hills beneath Fort Randall Dam, a new passenger was getting used to life on board the boats—a live prairie dog the men had caught several miles down the Missouri River.

It had been easy to shoot a specimen, which was grilled later for the captains' dinner, but catching one alive proved quite an undertaking. They tried digging, but quit after shoveling to a depth of 6 feet and seeing no sign of the burrow. They poured five barrels of water down another hole without filling it, but finally they hauled enough water to flush out their new companion.

Now solidly into bison country themselves, the expedition's men had no trouble satisfying their voracious appetite for meat. During three days of hunting above today's dam, Lewis, Clark, York, and others killed nine bison, one elk, and five deer.

SEPTEMBER 11, 1804

Snake Creek Recreation Area

◆ W OF PLATTE, SOUTH DAKOTA, VIA S. DAK. 44 ◆ 605-337-2587 ◆ ADM. FEE ◆ CAMPING

It was raining hard as the expedition's boats made halting progress beneath the beautiful prairie hills that reach downstream from this shady recreation area. As the drenched men struggled against the current, they saw a figure on horseback riding toward them through the mist. They must have whooped with joy when they saw it was Pvt. George Shannon, 18, the expedition's youngest member. He had been missing for 16 days.

The captains knew he'd been ahead of the boats and that he wasn't much of a hunter. They had sent men after him several times. But Shannon, who thought he was behind the boats, had scrambled far upstream. Hungry and unable to catch up, he finally turned downriver,

Golden Notebook

Lewis's entries for the days the expedition spent near Chamberlain are extensive, fluent, detailed, beautifully written—and rare. Except for astronomical observations and natural history notes, they are virtually the only words we have from Lewis between May 20, 1804, and February 3, 1805.

The entries offer a snapshot of a busy, freely flowing pen and an active, intensely engaged mind. But they also convey the quality of being cut off in midstream, as if they were a fragment of something larger. They surface suddenly and end abruptly in midsentence.

Historian Stephen Ambrose believes these entries may indicate that Lewis did indeed keep a journal during this leg of the voyage, but that it was lost.

hoping to meet up with a trading party.

Clark wrote, "He had been 12 days without any thing to eate but Grapes & one Rabit, which he Killed by shooting a piece of hard Stick in place of a ball."

SEPTEMBER 14–17, 1804

Chamberlain Area

After several chilly days of persistent drizzle and rain, the expedition halted near present-day **Oacoma** and camped in what Clark described as "a butifull Plain Serounded with Timber…in which there is great quantities of fine Plumbs." Today, the site is believed to lie under Lake Francis Case.

The men needed a break. They had spent much of the preceding week in the water, dragging the keelboat through shallows and over sandbars. With autumn coming on, the river was bound to get even shallower. Here, the men stopped to dry out their gear and to lighten the keelboat by transferring cargo to the pirogues.

Though travel had been frustrating, the weather gloomy, and the mosquitoes as bad as ever, spirits remained high. While out looking for a nonexistent volcano on September 14, Clark finally shot one of those fleet, mysterious "wild goats" and rendered the first scientific description of the pronghorn. The same day, Lewis penned a detailed description of the white-tailed jackrabbit, another first. While camped here, he added to the expedition's list of scientific firsts by describing the black-billed magpie, mule deer, and coyote.

On September 17, Lewis walked through the present site of Oacoma, occupied then by an immense prairie dog town, and climbed the ramp of rumpled hills that still rise to the west. Atop the hills, he paused to look back on the river and gaze across the endless plains.

"This senery," he wrote, "already rich pleasing…was still farther hightened by immence herds of Buffaloe deer Elk and Antelopes which we saw in every direction feeding on the hills and plains."

Lewis was hunting pronghorn, which, he observed, were not only swift and agile, but also possessed of an acute sense of smell, sharp eyesight, and an uncanny knack for choosing terrain impossible to approach under cover. Eventually, he put the sneak on seven pronghorn that he was forced to approach from upwind.

They spooked, and he ran to the top of an intervening hill, but by then the small herd was 3 miles away. "I doubted at ferst that they were the same that I had just surprised, but my doubts soon vanished when I beheld the rapidity of

"We rested our selves about half an hour, and regailed ourselves on half a bisquit each and some jirk of Elk which we had taken the precaution to put in our pouches in the morning before we set out, and drank of the water of a small pool which had collected on this plain from the rains"

MERIWETHER LEWIS, HUNTING PRONGHORN, SEPT. 17, 1804

their flight…it appeared reather the rappid flight of birds than the motion of quadrupeds."

Birchbark canoe, Akta Lakota Museum

Today, you can get a grandstand view of the terrain Lewis hunted from the **Lewis and Clark Information Center** *(Chamberlain Exit off I-90, May-Sept.),* which stands atop high bluffs south of Chamberlain and offers a long-range vista of the river's course and the seemingly endless expanse of the Great Plains. Oacama, the approximate site of the expedition's 4-day encampment, lies across the river.

Inside, exhibits dealing with the expedition's daily routine and its diplomatic efforts among the Indians have been arranged around a suspended wooden boat hull suggestive of the Corps's keelboat. The hull offers a sense of scale, and its stern extends through the side of the building to form a balcony that overlooks the river. Boat lockers, barrels, and trunks contain examples of cargo and personal items such as powder horns, pipe tomahawks, gunflints, and trade beads—each with the price Lewis paid for it. Other displays describe the expedition's boats, summarize the Corps's scientific achievements, and provide brief cultural profiles of the Yankton Sioux, Teton Sioux, and Arikara.

For a deeper presentation of Lakota culture, head for the north end of Chamberlain and visit the **Akta Lakota Museum** *(N. Main St. 605-734-3452. Mem. Day–Labor Day daily, Mon.-Fri. rest of year)* located on the St. Joseph Indian School Campus in Chamberlain. One of the best Plains Indian museums on the Lewis and Clark route, it tracks the life, art, and crafts of the Lakota from 1800 to the present.

Lewis and Clark would have admired these lavish displays and learned much from the accompanying inscriptions. Among the treasures: beautiful dresses adorned with cowrie and dentalia shells, a sinew-sewn bison hide tepee, elegant horn and gourd utensils, various trade goods, weapons, and a poignant case of tiny moccasins lovingly sewn in the late 1800s for toddlers.

SEPTEMBER 18–23, 1804
Chamberlain to Pierre

After lightening the keelboat at Chamberlain, the expedition made excellent progress to the mouth of the Bad River opposite present-day Pierre, logging an average of 18.5 miles each day under fair skies and generally favorable winds. Today's roads pull away from the Missouri and lead across the High Plains, offering just a handful of opportunities to see the river corridor until you get within about 20 miles of Pierre.

Two days beyond Chamberlain, the expedition arrived at the neck of a huge bend of the Missouri River known as the Grand Detour, or **Big Bend,** which is still conspicuous on highway maps. Clark sent several men across the bend to hunt until the boats came around, then hopped out himself to explore. He walked just 2,000 yards in crossing the neck of the bend and estimated that the boats would have to travel 30 miles in order to work around the bend and reach the same point. While he waited for the boats, Clark rambled and saw bison, pronghorn, deer, elk, and "great quantites of the Prickly Piar which nearly ruin my feet." This was Clark's first nasty encounter with that small, ground-hugging cactus, which still grows among the hills and plains surrounding Big Bend.

If you travel to Pierre along the west bank of the river, you might consider driving out to the **Narrows Overlook** from Lower Brule (*Continue 4.5 miles beyond turn for Pierre on gravel road. Turn left at the sign*). Though often littered by partyers, the site offers good views and a chance to wander the same grass-and-cactus hills Clark saw.

Travelers on the east bank can get a distant view of Big Bend from the **West Bend State Recreation Area** (*35 miles SE of Pierre off S. Dak. 34*). The rich bottomlands that Clark saw are gone, inundated by the present reservoir, but the low, rounded hills of grass and prickly pear are still here, as well as room to wander.

The expedition made quick work of Big Bend, covering roughly 25 miles in one long day of sailing. That night, the men spread their bedrolls on a sandbar several miles beyond the West Bend boat ramp, but they didn't get much sleep. "At a half past one oClock the Sand bar on which we Camped began to give way," Clark wrote, "I got

Teton Fault Lines

There are two key reasons why Lewis and Clark ran into trouble with the Teton. First, their goal of establishing St. Louis trade connections with all tribes on the Missouri threatened a vital Teton food source—crops grown by Arikara farmers to the north. As middlemen, the Teton controlled the flow of trade goods to the Arikara. If St. Louis merchants gained direct access to the Arikara, how could the Teton pay for corn? Their interests called for either blockading the Missouri, or exacting heavy tribute from passing vessels—including the expedition's flotilla. Second, the captains walked into a political hornets nest: The two principal chiefs they dealt with were in the midst of a power struggle with each other.

up and by the light of the moon observed that the Sand was giving away both above & beloy and would Swallow our Perogues in a few minits, ordered all hands on board and pushed off we had not got to the opposit Shore before pt. of our Camp fel into the river."

Continuing west from Stephan, S. Dak. 34 slants down from the plains through an embankment of rumpled hills and begins to hug the Missouri, which looks more like a river and less like a reservoir the closer you get to Pierre. Extensive wetlands surface, along with back channels, wide beds of cat-tails, and timbered islands.

SEPTEMBER 24, 1804

Farm Island State Recreation Area

◆ 4 MILES E OF PIERRE ON S. DAK. 34
◆ 605-224-5605 ◆ ADM. FEE

As the boats of the expedition glided slowly toward this big, tree-covered island, Lewis and Clark prepared gifts for the Teton chiefs they knew they would meet at the mouth of the Bad River. They also made sure the men's weapons were ready in case the meeting soured. But before they reached that point, they got off to a rocky start with the Teton here.

From the island, John Colter hailed the boats and asked for a pirogue to come pick up several elk he had shot. While the keelboat continued upriver and the men butchered and loaded the meat, several Indians stole Colter's horse and a bit of salt from his bag.

Colter ran up the bank and alerted the captains, who soon met several horseless Teton walking along the river. Speaking through a weak interpreter, the captains told them what had happened and said they wanted to remain friends, but were not afraid of any Indians.

Today, Farm Island is an inviting nature preserve where you can get a sense of how things looked along the river in 1804. One trail leads through stands of cottonwood and past marshes and bogs to a breezy grove of cedars beside the Missouri. From there, you can gaze upstream along the line of low, dome-shaped hills to **Fort Pierre,** where Lewis and Clark anchored for the night and met the following morning with the Teton.

"On that nation we wish most particularly to make a friendly impression, because of their immense power, and because we learn they are very desirous of being on the most friendly terms with us."

PRESIDENT THOMAS JEFFERSON ON THE TETON SIOUX, IN A LETTER TO MERIWETHER LEWIS, JAN. 22, 1804

Cottonwood-
lined Missouri
River, near Pierre

The park also serves as a trailhead for the **Lewis and Clark Bicentennial Trail,** a riverside trail that leads north through Pierre. The route, which will be dotted with interpretive signs, runs past the **Pierre Native Plant Arboretum** and connects with trails to LaFramboise Island (see p. 58) and Lilly Park (see p. 56), at the mouth of the Bad River. Still under construction, the trail is scheduled to reach Oahe Dam by 2004, for a total distance of 12.5 miles.

SEPTEMBER 24–28, 1804
Pierre Area

Site of the expedition's bitter face-off with the Teton Sioux, Pierre and its immediate surroundings offer more than a chance to stand close to the spot where Clark drew his sword and the Teton their bows. An excellent museum exhibit focuses on the Sioux, and visits to natural areas beside the river and up on the plains offer the opportunity to walk the landscapes Lewis roamed.

The confrontation with the Teton spanned several days, beginning with a formal council that degenerated into a nearly disastrous quarrel at the mouth of the Bad River, in

"These are the vilest miscreants of the savage race Unless these people are reduced to order, by coercive measures, I am ready to pronounce that the citizens of the United States can never enjoy but partially the advantages which the Missouri presents."

WILLIAM CLARK, ON THE TETONS, WINTER 1804-05

present-day Fort Pierre. It moved upriver to a village for a second, much friendlier session, then ended with another tense standoff as the expedition finally departed.

The stakes for these negotiations were high. Lewis and Clark knew Jefferson considered it essential to establish good relations with the Teton, both because of the tribe's military power and because of the vast potential wealth and political advantages of wresting its fur trade from the British.

The first council took place at the present site of Fort Pierre's **Lilly Park** *(310 Casey Tibbs St.)*, where the Bad River joins the Missouri amid shade trees and clipped lawns. If you had been here in 1804, you would have shared this bank with a crowd of Teton warriors, women, and children, all of them facing a sandbar in the mouth of the Bad River where their chiefs were meeting with the white strangers. Beyond the sandbar stood the keelboat, anchored 70 yards offshore, fully manned and ready for trouble.

Out on the sandbar, the captains soon felt the absence of a competent interpreter. Lewis had to cut his usual speech short. The captains resorted to trying to impress the Teton by parading the troops, handing out gifts, shooting Lewis's air gun, and giving them a tour of the keelboat.

The Teton were unimpressed. Worse, one of the principal chiefs, whom the captains called the Partisan, felt he'd been slighted. After a dram of whiskey on board the keelboat, that chief feigned drunkeness and got troublesome. As the situation deteriorated, the captains somehow managed to persuade the Indians to board a pirogue and return with Clark to the bank.

There, three warriors seized the pirogue's bow cable, another its mast, and the Partisan moved directly against Clark—jostling him, insulting him, demanding that he turn over the pirogue and its cargo. Instead, Clark drew his sword. The men with him picked up their rifles. Lewis ordered the keelboat's guns ready for action. Warriors strung their bows and cocked muskets.

Then, suddenly, the other principal chief, Black Buffalo, relieved the tension by grabbing the pirogue's cable and ordering the warriors back. He tried to detain Clark, and they got into a shouting match until reinforcements arrived from the keelboat.

When Clark's pirogue finally pulled away, the mood shifted again. Black Buffalo and several others waded into the river and asked to be taken aboard. Clark complied. They all spent the night on the keelboat, anchored about a mile upstream, next to the timbered island across the water from present Lilly Park.

"I call this Island bad humered Island," Clark wrote, "as we were in a bad humer."

The following day, the expedition continued upriver, slowly passing hundreds of anxious Teton who had assembled on both banks. The boats anchored off Black Buffalo's village, a cluster of about one hundred large tepees that stood on the west bank about 2 miles below today's **Oahe Dam** *(Visitor center, S. Dak. 1806. 605-224-5862. Mem. Day–Labor Day)*. The chief had asked them to stop, Clark wrote, in order "to let their Squars & boys See the Boat and Suffer them to treat us well."

Treat them well they did. For two days, the expedition feasted with the Teton on roast dog, bison, and pemmican. They watched elaborate firelit dances, smoked the pipe, and listened to a much friendlier statement of the Teton position—trade with us, not with the tribes upriver.

Though all seemed well on the surface, Lewis and Clark suspected treachery. Recently, the Teton had attacked an Omaha village, killing 75 people, destroying 40 lodges, and carrying off dozens of women and children. Those prisoners told Pvt. Pierre Cruzatte, himself half Omaha, that the Teton meant to wipe out the expedition.

As Clark returned to the keelboat after the second night of dancing, his pirogue severed the big boat's anchor cable. His shouted orders and the hustle of men to their oars alarmed the Teton, who were expecting an Omaha reprisal. About 200 warriors ran to the banks before realizing it was a false alarm.

Lewis and Clark, though, took the rush of armed men as an indication of hostile intent, a misreading that probably exacerbated tensions the following morning, when three warriors seized the keelboat's bowline just as the expedition tried to cast off. The situation quickly escalated, with Clark ready to fire the swivel gun and 200 Teton poised at the bank with guns, spears, cutlasses, and bows and arrows. Again, Black Buffalo defused the crisis by shaming the captains into giving them a twist of tobacco. With this face-saving gesture, the Teton released the bowline and the expedition proceeded on.

Clearly, Lewis and Clark had not made the friendly impression Jefferson desired. But if their diplomatic mission had failed, the captains did succeed in fending off a serious threat to the expedition's primary objective, which was to continue exploring the Missouri.

Once you've visited Lilly Park and taken in the beautiful drive north along the river on S. Dak. 1806 to Oahe Dam (look for pronghorn and prairie dogs), double back to Pierre and make your way to the **Museum of the South Dakota State Historical Society** *(900 Governors*

Dr. 605-773-3458. Adm. fee). Here you'll find a major exhibit on Lakota life. Packed with fascinating artifacts, and enriched by incisive commentary, the exhibit starts with the Lakota creation story, depicts nomadic life on the plains, and stresses the cardinal Lakota virtues of gen- erosity, wisdom, fortitude, courage, and responsibility to a large, extended family. Step into a partially furnished tepee. Heft a bison scapula. Ponder a hide painting. Study the migration of various tribes across the plains, and gawk at the lead plate buried near Fort Pierre by French explorers 60 years before Lewis and Clark met the Tetons.

Also at the museum, a new Lewis and Clark exhibit (*Observation Gallery*) highlights the expedition's journey across South Dakota and offers a sweeping vista of Pierre and the western plains.

Next, look for white-tailed deer on **LaFramboise Island Nature Area** (*Off Poplar Ave.*), the big timbered island between Pierre and Fort Pierre. The trail that skirts the western perimeter of the island offers a fine view across the river to the mouth of the Bad River, where Lewis and Clark had their first nearly disastrous confrontation with the Teton.

Paddlers can launch canoes from several sites along the river, starting from the west bank below the dam and including Pierre's Steamboat Park, Fort Pierre's Lilly Park (see p. 56), and Farm Island (see p. 54).

Farther afield and all alone, you can roam the plains at **Fort Pierre National Grassland** (*Maps available from Forest Service, 124 S. Euclid Ave., Pierre. 605-224-5517. Travel restrictions Sept.-Nov.*). The grassland takes in sec- tions of native prairie and supports sharp-tailed grouse, greater prairie chickens, howling coyotes, prairie dogs, pronghorn, mule deer, and white-tailed deer. To see bison, you have to drive north, to the **Triple U Bison Ranch** (*35 miles NW of Fort Pierre on S. Dak. 1806. 605-567-3624. Adm. fee*), where more than 3,500 of the shaggy beasts graze on the rolling plains.

SEPTEMBER 29–OCTOBER 8, 1804

Pierre to Mobridge

The roads between Pierre and Mobridge cut across the open plains and tend to steer clear of the Missouri corri- dor, making it difficult to track Lewis and Clark along this leg of the journey. Even if the roads hugged the water, you wouldn't see much of what Lewis and Clark saw because **Lake Oahe** has inundated the bottomlands they camped on, hunted in, and wrote about for nearly a month. Still, the many access points that dot the shore offer welcome relief from the summer's heat.

The warmth of summer had passed by the time the expedition traveled through this area. The air was cold, the wind often bitter, the plains golden brown. Above the Cheyenne River, the men began seeing abandoned Arikara villages along the banks. "Passed a village of about 80 neet Lodges covered with earth and picketed around," Clark wrote, "those loges are Spicious of an Octagon form as close together as they can possibly be placed and appear to have been inhabited last Spring, from the Canoes of Skins Mats buckets & found in the lodges."

Today, you can step into one of these commodious dwellings at **West Whitlock State Recreation Area** *(22 miles W of Gettysburg via US 212 and S. Dak. 1804. 605-765-9410. Camping)*, where an unfurnished reproduction overlooks Lake Oahe. Roomy, warm, unshakable even in a Great Plains windstorm, this lodge is a smaller version of the typical Arikara homes that were 30 to 60 feet in diameter and often housed 20 people and a horse or two.

OCTOBER 8–12, 1804

Mobridge Area

Across the bridge west of town, you'll find a weathered boat ramp overlooking the mouth of the Grand River and the long line of low hills flanking the Missouri. Just a few miles north of this point, the expedition's boats drew abreast an occupied Arikara village of dome-shaped earth lodges, built on a large, open island now submerged by Lake Oahe.

It was the first of three large Arikara villages above the mouth of the Grand. These communities were all that remained of more than 30 that existed before a shattering smallpox epidemic killed roughly 75 percent of the Arikara population in 1780-81.

The expedition coasted past the village and pitched

The Arikara

The Arikara whom Lewis and Clark met were the descendants of a prehistoric people who built square-shaped earth lodges in what is now eastern Nebraska. Beginning after 1400, and perhaps pushed along by drought, these early Arikara migrated to the Big Bend area south of Pierre, settling in what was then Mandan territory.

The Mandan tried pushing the Arikara out; having failed, they gradually withdrew to the north. In the mid-17th century, tensions resurfaced. By then, the Arikara were living in more than 30 fortified villages of dome-shaped earth lodges along the mouths of the Bad, Cheyenne, Moreau, and Grand Rivers.

Using hoes made from animal scapulas, Arikara women grew corn, beans, squash, pumpkins, watermelons, and tobacco in family-owned plots of about an acre. During the winter, many Arikara took extended hunting trips on the plains, camping in tepees in the style of their nomadic neighbors.

Before smallpox devastated the tribe in 1780-81, the Arikara numbered between 20,000 and 30,000 people divided into dozens of different bands that spoke a wide variety of dialects.

The friendly relations between whites and the Arikara that Lewis and Clark nurtured did not last. The death of an Arikara chief who had visited Washington, D.C., antagonized them, and they blocked an American delegation trying to return a Mandan emissary to his village in 1807. During the fur trade era of 1820-1840, they were openly hostile to whites.

By 1845, disease and war with the Sioux forced the Arikara north to live with the Mandan and Hidatsa. Today, the three tribes live together on the Fort Berthold Reservation east of Williston, North Dakota (see p. 78).

Sunset over Fort Yates, North Dakota

camp just above the island. As Clark and most of the men prepared "both for Peace or War," Lewis met with a St. Louis trader, Joseph Gravelines, who was living among the Arikara. With this fluent interpreter in tow, Lewis crossed to the island and invited the Arikara from all three towns to a council the next day.

After their rough treatment by the Teton, Lewis and Clark regarded the Sioux as the bullies and the prime obstacle to setting up a trade network based in St. Louis. They wanted to isolate and weaken the Teton by forging an alliance between the Arikara and the other earth-lodge dwellers to the north, the Mandan and Hidatsa.

Although the Arikara-Teton relationship was often uneasy and sometimes antagonistic, it was also based on a deeply embedded, mutually beneficial business relation ship. The Arikara saw the Teton less as bullies than as valuable customers. The Teton bartered European goods and meat for Arikara corn and horses. The Arikara, in turn, swapped corn and Teton trade goods for Cheyenne horses, meat, and beautifully decorated buckskin clothing.

Lewis and Clark proposed to disrupt these strong economic ties and replace them with a system the Arikara viewed as untried and perhaps unreliable. As for an alliance with the Mandan, the Arikara had been at war with that tribe for many years.

Cold, windy weather delayed talks for a day, but on October 10 the captains made their usual presentation. In the days that followed, each of the Arikara villages told the captains what they wanted to hear. There would be no interference with the expedition's progress. Peace with the Mandan was desirable, trade with St. Louis possible. But the Arikara replies amounted to a polite brush-off. They really just wanted the Americans to move on.

Though Arikara diplomacy remained murky, Arikara hospitality proved genuine, lavish, and warm. The men were fed cornbread, beans, and squash. They traded for moccasins and buffalo robes, played with Arikara children, sampled Arikara tobacco, and admired the construction of the Arikara lodges and bullboats (see sidebar p. 62).

After four days at the villages, the expedition headed upriver with horns blaring and Private Cruzatte sawing merrily away at his fiddle.

OCTOBER 12–19, 1804
Mobridge to Huff

Roads along this part of the route skip across the plains, occasionally skirting the edge of the Missouri Valley and opening up pleasant vistas of knobby grass hills rising between the water and a sky full of puffy white clouds.

As the men threaded the boats upstream, the captains took turns walking the plains and marveling at the vast herds of grazing deer, pronghorn, elk, and bison—52 herds of bison at a glance, Clark said. Here, too, the Corps's pleasant interlude with the Arikara continued. They met several hunting parties returning to the villages with bull-boats laden with fat meat. The hunters spent a couple of evenings with the expedition, singing and carrying on.

But all was not pleasant. Northeast of present **Kenel,** the men stopped at a sandbar to flog Pvt. John Newman 75 lashes for "having uttered repeated expressions of a highly criminal and mutinous nature." They also kicked him out of the permanent party, stripped him of weapons, and transferred him from the keelboat to the relative ignominy of the red pirogue.

Near present **Fort Yates,** the expedition came across an Arikara hunting party that had trapped a large herd of pronghorn swimming the Missouri.

OCTOBER 19, 1804
Huff Indian Village State Historic Site

◆ 1 MILE S OF HUFF, OFF N. DAK. 1806

Easy to miss, hard to forget, this ancient Mandan village site occupies a broad field of grass facing the Missouri and a large, timbered island. Occupied between 1485 and 1543,

"I observe near all large gangues of buffalow wolves and when the buffalow move those Anamals follow and feed on those that are killed by accident or those that are too pore or fat to Keep up with the gangue."

WILLIAM CLARK, OCT. 20, 1804

it was once a busy community of more than a hundred houses enclosed by a fortification ditch.

Besides reading the interpretive sign, you can walk among the low, grass-covered mounds and shallow depressions that trace the outlines of those homes and gaze downriver at the same two prominent hills the Mandan looked at every day. Perhaps most fascinating, though, is what lies in the small piles of debris that burrowing animals have flung from their holes—marrow bone fragments crushed by Mandan women 500 years ago.

Bullboats

Used by many of the western tribes, bullboats were small, circular boats made by stretching a bison hide over a frame of willow branches. Easily built from available materials, exceptionally buoyant and portable, bullboats were just the thing for floating heavy loads down shallow rivers.

Lewis and Clark first saw the boats paddled by Arikara women.

"I saw at Several times to day 3 Squars in single Buffalow Skin Canoes loaded with meat Cross the River," Clark wrote. "At the time the waves were as high as I ever Saw them in the Missouri."

OCTOBER 20, 1804

Fort Abraham Lincoln State Park

◆ 8 MILES S OF MANDAN ON N. DAK. 1806
◆ 701-663-9571 ◆ ADM. FEE ◆ CAMPING

At the end of a fine autumn day spent walking the plains west of the Missouri, Clark toted his rifle through the riverside hills of this beautiful state park and came upon the "old remains of a villige on the Side of a hill."

He had little else to say about **On-A-Slant Village,** an abandoned Mandan town of some 88 earth lodges built on a grass hill overlooking the river. Today, a small but impressive remnant of that village has been reconstructed on its original location, just a short stroll from the park's visitor center.

Before heading up to the lodges, drop by the museum for an overview of Mandan history and culture, beginning with the tribe's migration up the Missouri around A.D. 900. Copies of Bodmer and Catlin paintings portray the full extent of bustling villages such as On-A-Slant and bring you face to face with Mandan leaders. Exhibits illustrate Mandan agriculture, hunting practices, earth-lodge construction, and the tribe's matrilineal clan structure. A small Lewis and Clark display includes a copy of the war hatchets that the expedition's blacksmiths fabricated to trade for Mandan corn during the winter of 1804-05.

At the village site, three family-size lodges stand beside a mammoth council lodge. At its height, On-A-Slant contained dozens of the smaller dwellings, built closely together, and it was fortified on three sides by a palisade. Though these grassy domes may seem rather humble from the outside, they feel spacious inside, and the cathedral-like interior of the ceremonial lodge can take your breath away.

One of the lodges, adorned with reproductions of period artifacts, provides a vivid glimpse of what Lewis and

Clark saw when they visited Mandan homes. Here, you'll find bison robes and beds, backrests and mats, pottery and cooking utensils, ceremonial rattles, children's toys, paddles, and stone-pointed weapons. A magnificent bison hide painting hangs behind the functioning fire pit, and animal skins dangle from an overhead beam. The smell of wood smoke and dressed leather adds to an already convincing setting. A lodge like this would have housed an extended family of roughly 12. Outside, in the village plaza, stands a small circle of vertical logs called the Ark of the Lone Man, a feature unique to Mandan villages

In the future, the park plans to reconstruct a portion of the village's original log palisade, which stood between the lodges and today's road. The park also plans to use a second lodge for an in-depth exhibit focusing on Mandan agricultural practices.

After Clark paused at On-A-Slant, he angled upriver a short distance to where the boats had tied up for the night. The hunters had killed ten deer that day, and Cruzatte had wounded and then been chased by a grizzly bear. The following morning, the boats set off as snow began to fall.

OCTOBER 21, 1804
Bismarck Area

North Dakota's capital offers little pertaining directly to Lewis and Clark, who camped in snow and roasted fresh bison meat across the river in present **Mandan**. However, the **North Dakota Heritage Center** *(612 E. Boulevard Ave. 701-328-2666)* presents a lavish interpretation of the region's Native American peoples, with special emphasis on Mandan, Hidatsa, and earlier lodge dwellers. Among the riches: Mandan baskets, antler adzes, gaming pieces, stone points, and a George Catlin original of a lodge interior showing ten people with plenty of room to spare.

If you'd like to get on the river for a couple of hours, consider booking a cruise on Bismarck's *Lewis & Clark Riverboat (Just N of I-94 on River Rd. 701-255-4233. Fare. Reservations suggested),* which runs trips to Fort Abraham Lincoln during summer. Or, if you prefer riding the rails, try the **Fort Lincoln Trolley** *(S of Main St. on N. Dak. 1806. 701-663-9018. Fare),* which departs hourly from Mandan on summer afternoons.

OCTOBER 22, 1804

Double Ditch Indian Village State Historic Site

◆ 12 MILES N OF BISMARCK ON N. DAK. 1804

Perched on a high, grassy bluff overlooking the swift waters of the Missouri River, this lumpy terrace of open grassland was one of three deserted Mandan villages that Lewis and Clark noticed as they made their way upstream from present Bismarck. Like On-A-Slant, Double Ditch was abandoned after a catastrophic smallpox epidemic killed almost 90 percent of the tribe in 1780-81.

Now on the National Register of Historic Places, Double Ditch ranks as one of the most spectacular prehistoric earth-lodge villages on the Missouri. Here, the circular mounds and depressions left by the dwellings are especially vivid, and the river wilder than it's been for hundreds of miles. Interpretive signs erected throughout the site sketch Mandan history, offer a clear concept of what the town looked like at its height, and commemorate Lewis and Clark's passage. It is a deep pleasure to crouch here on land rumpled by prehistoric hands and to imagine the expedition's big wooden boat creeping upriver.

OCTOBER–NOVEMBER 1804

Lewis and Clark Interpretive Center

◆ JCT. OF US 83 AND N. DAK. 200A, WASHBURN
◆ 701-462-8535 ◆ ADM. FEE

Clever, focused, and bountifully supplied with artifacts and reproductions, this outstanding facility covers all the major themes of the Lewis and Clark Expedition: its route, people, equipment, travel logistics, Indian relations, diplomacy, and scientific achievements. It also offers some interesting bits of trivia and displays an extensive collection of Karl Bodmer prints that lavishly illustrate village life and landscapes along the Missouri River just 30 years after Lewis and Clark's voyage. The exhibits start with a huge copy of Clark's masterpiece, his map of the West, which makes an interesting comparison with the pre-expedition map of North America you'll find nearby.

Though the museum sketches the entire course of the expedition, it pays particular attention to the winter of 1804-05, which the men passed among the Mandan just 15 miles upriver. A diagram of Fort Mandan and renderings of Mandan earth lodges set the scene. A small blacksmith forge and antiquated medicine chest serve as reminders of how the expedition paid for Mandan corn, beans, and meat. Recordings of Mandan songs and period fiddle tunes recall the winter's festive cross-cultural gatherings. Read up on Sacagawea, and rest your forearms on the gunwales of the museum's centerpiece—a massive, full-scale reproduction of one of the dugout canoes the Corps hacked from 10-ton cottonwood logs during the spring of 1805.

In a second exhibit hall focusing on Fort Clark (established in 1830), you'll find more Bodmer prints depicting Mandan life, modern murals of the land as Lewis and Clark saw it, and an account of the 1837 smallpox epidemic that nearly wiped out the Mandan.

Just a few miles downstream of this point, Lewis and Clark met the Mandan for the first time. Groups of them kept emerging along the banks to hail the boats and watch the expedition pass. By then, the river was shallow and full of sandbars. The boat crews had trouble finding the channel. The weather was cold, at times snowy, and several of the men, including Clark, had rheumatism. It was time to stop for the winter. Fortunately, they did not have far to go.

Portrait of the Mandan and Hidatsa

In 1804 the Mandan and Hidatsa lived in five villages strung along the Missouri and Knife Rivers near present Stanton. Lewis and Clark wintered across the Missouri from the Mandan village of Mitutanka, and several miles downriver from a second, Ruptare. Both were built in 1787 after smallpox and raids

by the Sioux and Arikara forced the Mandan north from their ancestral homes near present Bismarck.

The Mandan settled on wary terms with their new neighbors, the Hidatsa, who lived in three villages—one in Stanton, the others within today's Knife River Indian Villages N.H.S. The oldest Hidatsa town was established around 1600, or about 300 years after the first recorded presence of the tribe in the area. By the mid-19th century, another wave of smallpox and Sioux raids forced both tribes farther north to the vicinity of present New Town (see p. 78), where they were joined in 1862 by their former enemies the Arikara. Fort Berthold Reservation, which surrounds New Town, is the home of the three tribes today.

Winter at Fort Mandan

"I line my Gloves and have a cap made of the Skin of the Louservia (Lynx) (or wild Cat of the North) the fur near 3 inches long the weather is so Cold that we do not think it prudent to turn out to hunt"

WILLIAM CLARK, AFTER A NIGHT OF -38°F, DEC. 12, 1804

After about a week of scouting the river from present-day **Washburn** to **Stanton,** the captains decided to build Fort Mandan about 14 miles west of Washburn, on the north side of the Missouri, and across the water from a large Mandan village.

It took just six weeks to complete Fort Mandan, but construction was difficult. Sometimes it was so cold the men had to work in one-hour shifts. To gather chimney stones, they had to push a pirogue upriver among flowing sheets of ice. When they finally set aside their tools on Christmas Eve, the Corps could relax in 1,600 square feet of snug living space—the rough equivalent of two family-size Mandan lodges. They had also constructed a large meathouse and a blacksmith shop, both apparently built against the gated wall, with a sentry's platform atop the meathouse.

"Our Rooms are verry close and warm," wrote Sergeant Ordway during one cold snap, "but the Sentinel who Stood out in the open weather had to be relieved every hour."

During that winter, the weather was often brutally cold, the rations sometimes short, and there was no possibility of hearing from loved ones back home. Despite these hardships, the expedition passed a light-hearted, often gleeful winter at Fort Mandan. There were no fistfights, no incidents of insubordination, and little of the boredom that had marred the previous winter at Wood River.

And no wonder. The men had bonded as a tight and efficient team of comrades. Around them lay a vast, wild, and exceedingly foreign land ripe for exploration. There was the immediate challenge of surviving an exceptionally brutal North Dakota winter. And, of course, there were the fascinating Mandan, with their games, dances, music, food, and beautiful women—who proved as accommodating as the expedition's men could wish.

Hunting not only fed the men, it kept them fit. They roved up and down the frozen river and ventured far out onto the plains. Sometimes, they stayed out for more than a week, camping in subzero weather, struggling to keep the wolves from devouring all they'd shot, then hauling back what was left on sleds and borrowed horses. Occasionally, they returned empty-handed.

But there were also fat times. When huge herds of buffalo streamed into the river bottoms in early December, the men turned out with the Mandan, scrabbling around on foot while the Indians glided into the herds on horseback. After four days the expedition had killed more than 30 bison.

Mandan earth lodge in winter

> *"The Plains are on fire in view of the fort on both Sides of the River, it is Said to be common for the Indians to burn the Plains near their villages every Spring for the benifit of ther horse, and to induce the Buffalow to come near to them."*
>
> WILLIAM CLARK, MARCH 30, 1805

To carry them through lean times, Pvt. John Shields set up his blacksmithy and mended Indian hoes, guns, and other metal objects in exchange for corn, beans, squash, and meat. Later in the winter he fashioned small hatchets that were so popular among the Indians, the fort's larder ran a surplus.

At Christmas, the men celebrated with three blasts of the swivel gun, three generous snorts of brandy, small arms volleys, and a feast. Then everyone crammed into one of the huts for several hours of dancing. The frivolity continued on New Year's, but this time the men carried the celebration to the Mandan, where they went from lodge to lodge, like carolers, kicking up their heels to a fiddle, tambourine, and horn. The Mandan cheered them on—especially the Frenchman who could dance on his head.

Throughout the winter, Lewis and Clark kept the men busy with military duties and routine chores. But their most onerous task concerned the boats, which lay in the frozen river. To no avail they tried axes, pry bars, and heated stones. Finally, during a late February thaw, they managed to hack them out with pikes and to winch them onto the bank with a nine-strand elk-skin rope. Soon after, the ice gave way in a huge sheet and careened down the river.

The captains spent much of their winter preparing an extensive report on the upper Louisiana Territory for Jefferson. They worked long hours, poring over Clark's map, flipping through their voluminous notes, and rummaging through specimens of plants, rocks, animal skins, bones, and Indian items that lay about. They also interviewed dozens of Indian visitors and traders from the Northwest and Hudson's Bay Companies, who filled them in on vast areas of country they had not seen.

From this amalgam of sources, they produced a book-length document that summarized the geography of the Missouri River and its tributaries, offered concise assessments of the region's Navive American peoples, and described its plants, animals, climate, and suitability for settlement. It also included Clark's magnificent map of the United States west of the Mississippi, which accurately laid out the Missouri's course to the Mandan villages and reflected the captains' best guess about what lay beyond.

Besides preparing their report, the captains routinely dosed the men for venereal disease and dealt with pleurisy, frostbite, and snowblindness. They amputated the toes of a Mandan boy who had frozen his feet, and Lewis acted as midwife for Sacagawea (see sidebar p. 69), the Shoshone wife of French fur-trader Touissant Charbonneau, as she gave birth to Jean Baptiste Charbonneau. The baby would accompany the expedition to the Pacific and back.

There were also some alarms. In late November, a Sioux and Arikara war party jumped some Mandan hunters, killed one man, and stole nine horses. Clark immediately took 21 soldiers up to the Mandan village expecting to help avenge the raid, but the Mandan hadn't stirred. It was too cold, they said, the snow too deep, the raiders too far ahead. In February, the Sioux attacked an expedition party of four men sent downriver to retrieve meat. No one was hurt, but the men lost two horses and some knives. This time, Lewis turned out with 24 men and tracked the Sioux for more than 30 miles before giving up. His group hunted for several days and returned with 2,400 pounds of meat.

In March, as geese and swans flew north along the river and grass sprouted on the plains, the expedition prepared for the next leg of the voyage. Six enormous dugout canoes were built to replace the keelboat, which would set off for St. Louis with the captains' report, four live magpies, a live prairie dog, and many other specimens. Other work parties shelled corn, dried meat, sewed moccasins, made elk-skin ropes, and prepared the boats for departure.

Soon, the Missouri broke into a mix of slush and ice chunks. The Mandan began hopscotching across the cakes of ice to retrieve drowned bison. When the river cleared, temperatures pushed into the 60s, and the men danced nearly every night. By the afternoon of April 7 everything was set. Two pirogues and six canoes lay in the water, packed to the gunwales, ready to head upstream with 32 men, a woman, and a baby boy.

"We were now about to penetrate a country at least two thousand miles in width, on which the foot of civillized man had never trodden," Lewis wrote, "and these little vessells contained every article by which we were to expect to subsist and defend ourselves."

Sacagawea's Story

Born around 1788, Sacagawea was a Lemhi Shoshone who had been kidnapped by the Hidatsa during a raid at the Three Forks of the Missouri in present Montana. Probably 12 at the time, she lived for about four years in Hidatsa villages before becoming a wife of French fur-trader Toussaint Charbonneau. Both moved into Fort Mandan when Lewis and Clark hired Charbonneau as an interpreter.

While living at Fort Mandan, Sacagawea gave birth to Jean Baptiste Charbonneau, nicknamed "Pomp" by Clark. The presence of Sacagawea and her baby reassured many of the various tribes Lewis and Clark encountered as they voyaged to the Pacific and back. Her language skills proved invaluable among the Shoshonean-speaking peoples of the Rockies. And though her services as a guide are often overblown, she did help navigate the party in southwestern Montana, where she had lived as a child.

Little is known of her life after the expedition. The best evidence indicates that she died in 1812 at Fort Manuel, on the Missouri in present South Dakota.

FORT MANDAN RECONSTRUCTION

You'll find a terrific, fully furnished reproduction of Fort Mandan *(701-462-8535)* on County Road 17, 1.5 gravel miles west of the Lewis & Clark Interpretive Center (see pp. 64-65). Set back from the river in a grove of cottonwood, the modest triangular enclosure of shed-roofed huts presents a thoughtfully executed representation of the expedition's winter quarters for 1804-05. The actual fort was built closer to the water, about a dozen miles upriver on a site believed to have been washed away by the Missouri.

Like the original, the reproduction contains two rows of log rooms that form two sides of a rough triangle and face a log palisade that forms the third. Stone chimneys protrude from the roofs of the huts. An operating blacksmithy occupies one of the huts near the gate, and a storehouse for meat, provisions, tools, and other items stands at the far end of the fort. Inside the huts, you'll find rough-hewn bunks and buffalo robes, lofts over the rooms, and period reproductions of the sorts of guns the men carried, along with many personal items, such as hats, knives, mugs, leather clothing, lanterns, and candles. The captains' quarters have been furnished with even greater care to reflect their busy winter of preparing maps, reports, and specimens for Jefferson.

**Cross Ranch
Nature Preserve**

All this helps set the stage for volunteers in period garb who, during the summer, reenact various tasks that members of the expedition would have performed, such as molding bullets, sewing moccasins, manning the blacksmithy, chopping wood, cooking, or just passing the time with visitors.

The original fort bustled with activity all winter long. Groups of Indians regularly dropped by to trade, organize hunting trips, or just visit and share a meal with the men. There would have been chitchat and laughter, sometimes a little fiddle music, the clang of the blacksmithy, and the smell of wood smoke, roasted meat, and boiled corn.

Beyond the gates lay the expedition's boats (more or less where the picnic tables now stand), and beyond them the Missouri: 500 yards wide and frozen bank-to-bank all winter. Today, you have to walk through the cottonwoods to see the water. In autumn, huge flocks of migrating geese, ducks, and other waterfowl still hurry past, just as they did while the expedition heaved the beams of Fort Mandan into place.

During construction of the fort the captains were visited by Touissant Charbonneau, whom they hired as a translator. His wife, Sacagawea (see sidebar p. 69), joined the party as well and contributed to its success.

FORT MANDAN OVERLOOK

Continue north from the reconstruction on County Road 17 to this open river terrace. It offers a pleasant vista of the Missouri Valley and the rim of the Great Plains, and of what is believed to be the actual site of Fort Mandan. Only a vague identification of the fort site is possible from this elevated point, but the general terrain (with the exception of the coal-fired electric plants) remains suggestive of the grand landscape that surrounded and obscured the tiny outpost.

It takes little imagination to envision these rumpled hills dusted with snow and picture large herds of bison filing down through the ravines and hollows. Elk, deer, and sometimes pronghorn would have moved across the flat bottomlands, and the expedition's hunters would have paused at a place like this to scan the country for game.

CROSS RANCH STATE PARK AND CROSS RANCH NATURE PRESERVE

One of the most rewarding natural history stops in the region, Cross Ranch (*15 miles SW of Washburn off N. Dak. 200A. 701-794-3731. Adm. fee. Camping*) takes in a slope of mixed-grass prairie hills overlooking the Missouri River and its curving border of cottonwoods and flat grassy bottomlands. You might see bison amble across the open hills, swatting at flies with their quirtlike tails. Deer leap for cover in the cottonwoods, and coyotes trot daintily among the buckbrush and yucca.

Here, you can walk through an expansive landscape that has changed little since Lewis and Clark's day. A ramble among the prairie hills offers the chance to bone up on native grass species, go toe-to-toe with prickly pear cactus, and have a look at buffaloberries—an expedition favorite. Perhaps most tempting, though, is a float trip down this beautiful stretch of river. The park rents canoes in summer.

STANTON VICINITY

Before building Fort Mandan, Lewis and Clark had pushed upriver between October 27 and November 1, 1804, to the vicinity of present-day Stanton and invited Mandan and Hidatsa leaders to a formal council on the Missouri's east bank. By then, the men had spent several days among the Mandan, who had flocked to the expedition's camps to meet the white strangers and to ogle their fascinating gadgets and weapons. Some had even hitched a ride upriver on the keelboat.

"the huts were in two rows, containing four rooms each, and joined at one end forming an angle. When rasied about 7 feet high a floor of puncheons or split plank were laid, and covered with grass and clay; which made a warm loft."

PATRICK GASS,
DESCRIBING FORT
MANDAN LIVING
QUARTERS,
NOV. 3, 1804

Delegations from all five villages gathered on a raw, blustery day under the expedition's awning and settled in for five hours of speeches, ceremony, and the all-important gift-giving. Like the Arikara, these villagers were savvy, corn-rich brokers at the crossroads of a vast trading network. From the west, they took in horses, meat products, and elegant leather clothing. From the north came a dependable supply of guns, kettles, knives, blankets, beads, and other manufactured goods delivered mainly by the Cree and Assiniboin.

The captains understood that much, but mistook the Cree and Assiniboin for nomadic rogues preying on hapless farmers. They thought the Mandan and Hidatsa would welcome an alliance with the Arikara so they could turn safely away from the piratical northern tribes and embrace St. Louis as their new source for manufactured goods.

But the Indians had little to gain by talking peace with the Arikara, and much to lose by dumping their traditional suppliers in favor of St. Louis—an unproven source more interested in fur than in corn.

After the council, Lewis and Clark lingered on the floodplain opposite present Stanton for several days waiting for the chiefs to reply. Groups of Indians mingled informally with the men, and spirits soared. Cruzatte broke out the fiddle. Everyone danced, sang, and drank. The men traded for corn, beans, and squash.

Soon, Lewis and Clark heard from the Mandan. The chiefs said little about St. Louis trade, but agreed to send a delegation to the Arikara, assured the captains of their friendship, and invited them to winter near their villages.

It was a promising start for the winter, and seemed a promising start for diplomacy. But as the expedition dropped back downriver to start building Fort Mandan, the captains had heard nothing from the Hidatsa.

KNIFE RIVER INDIAN VILLAGES
NATIONAL HISTORIC SITE

This magnificent history park (*Off N. Dak. 31, 0.5 mile N of Stanton. 701-745-3309*) preserves the intriguing remains of three Hidatsa communities, examines the intermingled culture and history of the Mandan and Hidatsa peoples, and presents a splendid, meticulously furnished full-scale reproduction of an earth lodge.

Lewis and Clark spent very little time here, and were never welcomed with the enthusiasm shown by the Mandan. In fact, when Lewis visited in late November, he was snubbed, and the expedition insulted, even threatened.

The Mandan were partly to blame. In an attempt to monopolize trade with the Corps, they had told the

Hidatsa that the expedition would kill any Hidatsa who visited Fort Mandan. The captains tried to patch things up when they heard about that, and many Hidatsa did visit the fort. But sour feelings lingered.

Today, the **visitor center** shows an excellent film that sketches the history of both tribes and describes the fulfilling routine of village life. Exhibits explain the villages' role as the central marketplace of the Northern Plains and show the layout of a typical earth-lodge interior. A wealth of fascinating artifacts is also on display—from sports equipment and toys to a bison bladder bucket.

Outside stands the smooth dome of the **earth lodge** (*Accessible only in summer*). Within it lie the comfortable trappings of everyday Hidatsa life arranged as if the family had just walked out to visit friends. There are warm canopy beds, a sweat lodge, a small corral for horses, decorative animal skins, a bison skull shrine, tools, weapons, painted parfleche boxes, and more. Add the enlightened patter of a park interpreter, and the experience feels a bit like walking into a Bodmer painting with Meriwether Lewis as your guide.

From the reproduction, a 1.5-mile round-trip walk leads to the remains of two village sites. Only the farthest—**Awatixa,** or Metaharta—was occupied in Lewis and Clark's day. It was there that Charbonneau is said to have lived with Sacagawea before they joined the expedition. Two miles north of the visitor center lie the remains of the third and largest village, **Big Hidatsa,** or Menetarra.

Upper Missouri

April 8–July 13, 1805

Beginning in central North Dakota and heading west to the foot of the Rocky Mountains, this chapter covers Lewis and Clark's first plunge into lands that were entirely unknown to European civilization in 1805 and follows their grueling portage around the Great Falls of the Missouri. Much of their winding route through the badlands, cliffs, and canyons of the upper Missouri lies far from any major highway, making it difficult to retrace their course except on foot or by boat. But this has its advantages: These remote areas are among the few virtually unchanged landscapes that remain on the entire Lewis and Clark Trail. Few who visit them regret the extra time, effort, and expense required. And even the main roads lead to rewarding stops, including an extraordinary interpretive center in Great Falls, Montana, devoted to the expedition and the magnificent spectrum of native peoples that the Corps encountered between St. Louis and the Pacific coast.

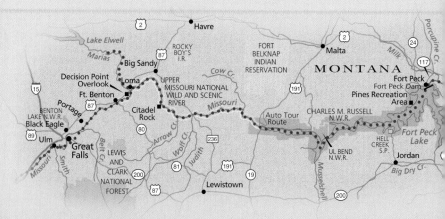

Detail from "Lewis' First Glimpse of the Rockies," Olaf Seltzer, 1934

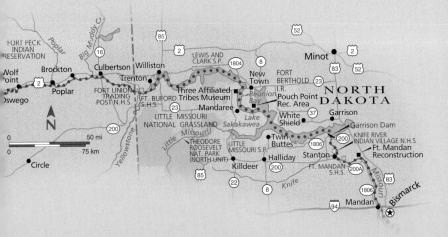

**Little Missouri
State Park**

APRIL 8–22, 1805

Lake Sakakawea

In the warmth of early spring, Lewis and Clark shoved off from Fort Mandan and pushed their flotilla of canoes and pirogues up the bending course of the Missouri River, passing bottomland prairies, copses of trees, and a continuous embankment of grassy, dome-shaped hills. Most of what they saw for two weeks now lies submerged beneath Lake Sakakawea, which floods the Missouri River trench for 180 miles. Though spur roads lead to dozens of boat ramps and shoreline campgrounds, the sites bear little resemblance to the riverine landscape Lewis and Clark knew.

For a rewarding drive along the lake, take N. Dak. 1806, which skirts the southern shore, then dip south on N. Dak. 8 to Halliday, head west on N. Dak. 200 to Killdeer, and north on N. Dak. 22 toward New Town. This course opens up some good lake vistas and explores the same topographical transition Lewis and Clark noted in the region—a general shift from smooth rolling grass plains to a rugged and angular landscape of buttes, knobs, gulches, and coulees vividly represented at **Little Missouri State Park** (*Off N. Dak. 22. 701-794-3731. May-Oct.; adm. fee. Camping*).

As the expedition headed upriver from present **Stanton**, Lewis and Clark took turns wandering over the awakening land—grass sprouted, wildflowers bloomed, and a host of birds built their nests and filled each dawn with chatter.

While the captains explored on shore, most of the men worked the boats and logged roughly 20 miles a day—excellent progress. But the big dugout canoes, which measured more than 35 feet in length, took some getting used to, especially in crosswinds. On the second day out, the boat crews swamped one and had to dry its cargo that night at camp, a mile south of **Garrison Dam.**

By now, camp had taken on a different look from the previous season. Gone was the big keelboat, which had always stood nearby as a sort of mobile fortress. Fewer people (33) stood in the smoke of the fires, and they wore more leather clothing. In addition to tents, there now stood a large, bison-hide tepee that the captains shared with Drouillard, Charbonneau, Sacagawea, and her infant son. Meals were a little different too, thanks to Sacagawea, who often collected wild vegetables such as Jerusalem artichokes, breadroot, and wild onions.

As they pushed beyond modern **Garrison,** they began running into Hidatsa hunting parties. Some were headed for home, their horses and dogs loaded with meat. Others waited for the huge herds of antelope that would soon begin to migrate across the river. They also overtook a party of three French trappers who planned to ascend the Yellowstone that summer.

Above the **Little Missouri River,** Charbonneau nearly capsized the white pirogue by turning it broadside to a gale. Other hands quickly saved the situation, but if the boat had overturned several nonswimmers might have drowned in the high waves, and the captains probably would have lost their papers, instruments, medicine chest, and much of their remaining stash of trade goods—crucial items they would need to buy horses later in the summer.

Near **Pouch Point Recreation Area** *(16 miles S of New Town. Camping),* the men began seeing drowned bison lying along the riverbanks, with fresh grizzly bear tracks all around. To Lewis, the presence of the "white bear" was a tantalizing prospect. He knew that the Mandan and Hidatsa regarded grizzly hunts as seriously as they did raids, that they attacked the bear in parties of six to ten, and that the

North Dakota Powwows

The Arikara, Mandan, and Hidatsa peoples dance, sing, and feast at four public powwows each summer *(701-627-4781)*: at Twin Buttes on the third weekend in June; at White Shield the second weekend in July; at Mandaree the third weekend of July; and—one of the largest—at Little Shell *(W of New Town)* the second weekend in August.

bear often killed one or more of them. But, Lewis noted, the Indians were poorly equipped with bows, arrows, and indifferent muskets. Surely Americans armed with long rifles would have little to fear from such a beast. "The men," he wrote, "as well as ourselves are anxious to meet with some of these bear." That attitude would change.

APRIL 15, 1805

New Town Area

As the Corps approached the vicinity of New Town, Lewis described the river as wide, with a moderate current, and with upland areas of high scabrous knobs devoid of timber but peppered with sagebrush, dwarf cedar, and juniper. Pronghorn browsed amid the sagebrush. Prairie dogs basked in the sun. Geese nested in bottomland trees, and black bears, bison, elk, and deer appeared along the river.

From **Crow Flies High Historic Site** *(2 miles W of New Town),* you can still spot the occasional pronghorn or deer and take in a grandstand vista of the Missouri River trench with its buttes, bluffs, badlands, and brush.

South of town you can visit **Reunion Bay** *(Primitive camping),* where Lewis and Clark met for their return journey in 1806, after each had finished exploring the Marias and Yellowstone Rivers respectively. It's also the approximate site of the Corps's campsite of April 14, 1805, where Clark watched two grizzly bears lope up a steep hill "with Supprising ease & verlocity."

That same day, Lewis noted that the party had now traveled up the Missouri as far as "any whiteman had ever ascended; except two Frenchmen who having lost their way had straggled a few miles further, tho' to what place precisely I could not learn." The Corps of Discovery had finally paddled off the map and into country unknown to European civilization. The captains had learned a little about what lay ahead from conversations with the Mandan and Hidatsa, but the information they had gleaned was sketchy at best.

Much of the area around New Town lies within the Fort Berthold Reservation, home to the Arikara, Mandan, and Hidatsa (see sidebars pp. 59 and 65). West of town and across the bridge, the tribes run a casino and the **Three Tribes Museum** *(5 miles W of New Town on N. Dak. 23. 701-627-4477. April-Oct.; adm. fee).* There, you'll find the "Way to Independence" and "Forebearers Bridge" exhibits as well as scapula hoes, tobacco pouches, lovely beaded buckskin clothing, and other reminders of the traditional earth-lodge way of life that extended into the 20th century.

Outside near the museum, the tribes have constructed one full-scale earth lodge. Future plans also call for the construction of an earth-lodge village.

APRIL 18–19, 1805

Lewis and Clark State Park

◆ OFF N. DAK. 1804 ◆ 701-859-3071 ◆ ADM. FEE
◆ CAMPING

Nestled among buttes and badlands overlooking Lake Sakakawea, this small state park offers the chance to roam through one of North Dakota's largest intact native prairies, with its characteristic grass species of little bluestem, western wheatgrass, and buffalo grass. If your timing is right, you might also see mule deer, white-tailed deer, grouse, or pheasants poking around in the rugged hills.

Slowed by strong winds and high waves, the expedition towed its boats to the vicinity of this park, then laid up for a day to let the blustery weather pass.

APRIL 20–26, 1805

To the Yellowstone River

It took the expedition six hard days of fighting headwinds to log the 62 miles between their windbound camp near today's Lewis and Clark State Park and the mouth of the Yellowstone River. High waves splashed into the canoes, wetting the gear and forcing layovers to dry out and to wait for the wind to ease. Mornings were chilly, sometimes so cold that the water froze to the oars as the men rowed. Windblown alkali dust filled the air with clouds so thick the men sometimes could not see the opposite bank. The dust irritated their eyes and got into everything. "We are compelled to eat, drink, and breath it very freely," Lewis wrote.

By now, the wild rose, plum, and chokecherry bushes had blossomed, the cottonwoods were leafing out, and game was abundant. Herds of bison, elk, deer, and pronghorn were everywhere, but the adult animals were too lean to satisfy the men's voracious appetites. So they supplemented with fat beaver and bison calves—as good, Lewis wrote, as any veal he had ever tasted.

On April 22, the captains walked through the site of present **Williston** and described the valley as beautiful but treeless and covered with bison, elk, and pronghorn. Near **Trenton,** the expedition lost another day to the wind. The next morning they pulled onward, but the wind kicked up again and by mid-morning they had to stop. Lewis decided he would walk to the Yellowstone and fix its position for their maps while Clark got the boats up the river.

He set off with four men and hiked for several miles along the south bank before climbing into the hills visible across the river. From the upland crest, he could trace the wooded and meandering courses of both the Yellowstone and Missouri for many miles. The vast grasslands surrounding the rivers teemed with bison, elk, and pronghorn so gentle, Lewis wrote, "that we pass near them while feeding, without appearing to excite any alarm among them." As the men descended from the hills, they shot several bison for supper and camped on the Yellowstone, 2 miles south of the confluence.

Bourgeois House, Fort Union Trading Post N.H.S.

The confluence lies just off today's **Fort Buford State Historic Site** *(N. Dak. 1804. 701-572-9034. Mid-May–mid-Sept.; adm. fee. Camping)* and looks much the same as it did in 1805, when the Corps of Discovery landed on the point between the rivers. Beginning in 2003, the history of this major expedition landmark will be presented at the park's **Confluence Area Interpretive Center.** Exhibits will focus not only on Lewis and Clark, but also on the area's subsequent history, Native American cultures, and natural history. A 3-mile nature trail may also link the site with the re-created **Fort Union Trading Post National Historic Site** *(701-572-9083),* which stands upriver and offers tremendous vistas of the Missouri and Yellowstone Rivers.

The view from Fort Buford is also exceptionally rewarding. From the park's grassy banks, you can gaze across the swift current of the Missouri and trace the Yellowstone's wooded course as it bends into the distant plains beneath a low brow of broken cliffs. As in Lewis and Clark's day, the bottoms and marshy backwaters are tangled with shrubs, including willow, serviceberry, chokecherry, and honeysuckle. Gravel bars stretch far out into the Yellowstone, and hawks glide overhead.

The boats arrived here at noon. Clark measured the

widths and depths of the rivers while Lewis remained above on the Yellowstone, aiming his sextant at the sun until 7 p.m. before walking down to rejoin the party.

"Found them…much pleased at having arrived at this long wished for spot," Lewis wrote. "We ordered a dram to be issued to each person; this soon produced the fiddle, and they spent the evening with much hilarity, singing & dancing."

Both captains recommended the confluence area as a likely fort site. There was plenty of stone for building, and plenty of game for food. In later years three forts were built, all of them on the north bank of the Missouri: Fort Union, 1828; Fort William, 1832; and Fort Buford, 1866.

APRIL 28–MAY 8, 1805

Fort Union to Fort Peck Dam

Along this leg of the journey, US 2 bounds over a broken High Plains landscape, dipping occasionally to the edge of the crooked Missouri and rarely diverging from its course by more than a few miles. The river flows freely here, meandering beneath dry bluffs, buttes, and bare hills that stand 200 to 300 feet above the water. Several major spur roads and dozens of ranch roads cut south from the highway and lead to primitive but often beautiful river landings.

The expedition moved swiftly through this area, often sailing under favorable winds and logging more than 20 miles a day. Wind and bitter weather slowed them occasionally. The rudder irons broke on both pirogues. Canoes shipped water and gear got wet. But these fleeting discomforts and delays didn't add up to much. The country, Clark said, was beautiful beyond description, the animals fatter, and the game so plentiful the men could afford to be choosy about their meat.

Here, too, they began to gain some of the respect the Indians had for the ferocity of the plains grizzly bear. Lewis got first crack at the "white bear." Near **Culbertson,** he and another hunter wounded two of them. One ran off. The second grizzly, a small male, chased Lewis for 70 yards before he and his partner could reload and kill it. "It is asstonishing to see the wounds they will bear before they can be put to death," Lewis wrote.

Meanwhile, Clark began seeing another animal new to their experience: bighorn sheep. During their winter among the Mandan, the captains had seen the horns and skins of bighorn, but never the living animal. Clark watched them cavort on the steep hills near Culbertson and admired their agility. He wrote, "Those animals run & Skiped about with great ease on this declivity & appeared to

"The flesh of the beaver is esteemed a delecacy among us; I think the tale a most delicious morsal, when boiled it resembles in flavor the fresh tongues and sounds [air bladders] of the codfish, and is usually sufficiently large to afford a plentifull meal for two men."

MERIWETHER LEWIS,
MAY 2, 1805

Fort Peck Reservoir at Charles M. Russell National Wildlife Refuge

prefur it to the leavel bottom or plain."

On May 1, heavy winds separated the boats and forced a halt under the prominent bluff southwest of **Brockton.** One canoe load of men was stranded on the north bank all night without blankets, which they sorely missed since it snowed that night and for most of the following morning.

On May 3, with the weather still cold, the captains ambled up the Poplar River, remarking on the unusual number of porcupines trundling about at its mouth and the remarkable clarity of its water. By now, herds of migrating pronghorn were swimming across the Missouri—easy prey for grizzly bears and wolves who waited for them on the north bank.

Near **Wolf Point,** it was Clark's turn to test his mettle against a grizzly. He and George Drouillard came upon an enormous bear, "a turrible looking animal, which we found verry hard to kill." They put five bullets through the bear's lungs, five more elsewhere, yet it swam halfway across the river to a sandbar and roared for 20 minutes before it died. It weighed 500 to 600 pounds, stood more than 8 feet tall, and unnerved most of the men.

When another grizzly swam ahead of the boats the following day near **Oswego,** no one pursued it. "I find that the curiossity of our party is pretty well satisfyed with rispect to this anamal," Lewis wrote. "The formidable appearance... added to the difficulty with which they die when even shot through the vital parts, has staggered the resolution several of them, others however seem keen for action with the bear."

MAY 8–24, 1805
Charles M. Russell N.W.R.

◆ 406-538-8706 ◆ CAMPING

Reaching far back into the Missouri River Breaks country of northeastern Montana, this wild swath of tightly packed hills, eroded bluffs, and gravelly headlands straddles the length of the Fort Peck Reservoir. Immense, remote, largely inaccessible to casual travelers, the refuge spans territory that took Lewis and Clark more than two weeks to cross and that still provides a home for many of the animals they saw while in the area, including pronghorn, deer, bighorn sheep, and elk.

Gone, though, are the plains grizzly bears who gave the expedition such a dramatic comeuppance here. Gone, too, are most of the rich river bottoms where the men hauled their canoes, roasted their buffalo tongues, and watched the shadows lengthen among the crush of knobby hills. What remains are the upland areas bordering the reservoir—vast stretches of prairie cut apart by thousands of crooked coulees and side canyons that converge on the Missouri trench like veins to a leaf stem.

This water-carved landscape, called the Missouri Breaks, is nearly as wild and beautiful as when Lewis and Clark saw it, but it is difficult to visit. Its network of rugged back roads is literally impassable when wet. None of the handful of dependable gravel roads follow the lakeshore for more than several miles. Strong winds and high waves often stymie the most determined paddlers and even keep small motorboats from venturing onto the lake. However, auto tours at both ends of the refuge offer a fair sampling of the terrain and a good chance to see the major animals. Maps are available from the refuge headquarters in Livingston, the Sand Creek Wildlife Station on the west end, the Jordan Wildlife Station, or at the Corps of Engineers' **Power Plant Museum** below the dam.

As the expedition pushed beyond present-day **Fort Peck,** Lewis kept his pen flying, noting among other things that the bison were now so numerous and gentle that the men had to throw sticks and stones to move them out of the way. He wrote a long description of the mule deer and made extensive observations on sagebrush, wild licorice, breadroot, greasewood, dwarf cedar, chokecherry, the quality of the soil, the lay of the land—even Charbonneau's method for making 6-foot bison sausages.

On May 11, Lewis inspected ponderosa pine branches that Clark had cut in the vicinity of the **Pines Recreation Area** (5 miles W of Fort Peck, then 26 miles SW on gravel roads), a beautiful spot where you can still watch elk graze.

Nearby, Pvt. William E. Bratton weighed in against a grizzly and shot it through the lungs. The bear chased him for a half mile, then gave up, walked another mile, dug a hole for itself, and was "perfectly alive" when Lewis and seven others found and killed it with two carefully placed shots.

Upper Missouri River Rides

Maps and other planning information for trips on the Upper Missouri are available from the Bureau of Land Management (*Lewistown Field Office, P.O. Box 1160, Lewistown, MT 59457. 406-538-7461*). The packet includes a list of outfitters who rent boats, provide shuttle service, and run guided trips on the river.

One of these, Missouri River Outfitters (*P.O. Box 762, Fort Benton, MT 59442. 406-622-3295*), offers canoe or pontoon boat trips leavened with historical commentary.

"I must confess that I do not like the gentlemen," Lewis wrote, "and had reather fight two Indians than one bear."

Still eager for a bout with a grizzly, but more prudent now, six of the party's best hunters crept to within 40 yards of a dozing bear near **Hell Creek State Park** (*26 miles N of Jordan. 406-232-0900. Camping*). According to plan, four took aim, fired, and hit the bear, which charged immediately. Two reserve hunters followed with a volley of their own, but the bear kept coming. The men scattered and ran, two pushing off in a canoe. Four men hid in the brush and fired again. The bear rousted them out, drove two over a 20-foot cliff into the river, and plunged in after them. Finally, one of the hunters ran to the cliff and killed the bear in the water.

On the river the same day, Charbonneau panicked during a windstorm and flipped the white pirogue on its side. The crew righted the foundering boat and got it to shore while Sacagawea calmly retrieved papers and other valuable items that washed overboard. Lewis and Clark, on shore at the time, could only watch and then calm everyone down that night with grog and a gill of whiskey.

Today, you can catch a glimpse of the Missouri River as it was in 1805 by taking a 20-mile auto tour (*Begins 1 mile N of US 191 bridge*) that runs east along the Missouri bottomlands before climbing to jaw dropping vistas of the Missouri Breaks. It offers good chances for seeing deer, pronghorn, sharp-tailed grouse, and elk. It also opens the way to Lewis and Clark's camp of May 23, which lies on the north bank just below the mouth of Rock Creek, and within a 30-minute walk of the tour route's big hairpin curve.

MAY 24–JUNE 13, 1805

Upper Missouri National Wild and Scenic River

Isolated, pristine, and achingly beautiful, this 149-mile stretch of the Missouri River (*US 191 to Fort Benton*) sweeps past fulsome prairie hills and riparian bottoms and

Fort Peck Dam

glides under towering sandstone pinnacles. A scenic gem, it is also a priceless historical thoroughfare now protected by the **Upper Missouri Breaks National Monument.**

Nowhere else on the entire Lewis and Clark Trail can you travel so far through a landscape so lightly altered since their voyage.Night after night for a week, you can pull your canoe into the very same campsites where the captains slept in their bison-hide tepee. Day after day you can read descriptions of terrain in expedition journals that seem to match today's surroundings rock for rock. You can hike to the spot where Lewis first saw the Rockies, or simply amble among the prickly pear and shortgrass.

There are differences, of course: fences here and there, cattle, a scattering of ranch buildings, two bridges, and a couple of ferries. You will see neither bison, wolf, nor grizzly, and the Audubon bighorn sheep the expedition saw are now extinct. But there are Rocky Mountain bighorn, loads of deer, elk, pelicans, great blue herons, songbirds, rattlesnakes, and the plants Lewis described in the area.

Though a handful of roads approach the river, the only meaningful access is by boat. It takes roughly seven days to float the entire stretch, but shorter trips are also possible. Local outfitters rent canoes, rafts, and drift boats and run guided trips (see sidebar p. 84). Backcountry camping experience is necessary if you plan to make the trip on your own, but the river is manageable for those with little paddling experience.

As the Corps of Discovery muscled its way beyond what

is now the US 191 crossing, the current swiftened, and rocky bars extended far out into the channel. The men had to tow the boats with elk-skin ropes that kept breaking. Still they made excellent time, rarely fewer than 18 miles a day.

Near **Cow Creek,** Lewis climbed into the hills and saw a few glittering summits of the Rockies poking over the horizon. His joy, he wrote, was counterbalanced by the thought of "the difficulties which this snowey barrier would most probably throw in my way to the Pacific."

Farther along, Clark named the Judith River after a young woman he would marry shortly after returning from the Pacific. At Arrow Creek, they found the rotting carcasses of more than a hundred drowned bison, attended by dozens of "fat and extreemly gentle" wolves.

By May 31, they had reached the **White Cliffs Area,** a gorgeous stretch of river studded with oddly shaped rock columns, great brows of white sandstone cliffs, and jagged bands of creamy pinnacles jutting from the grassy hills.

JUNE 2–11, 1805

Marias/Missouri Confluence

By the time the expedition reached the yellowish badland bluffs around present **Loma,** the brutal labor of towing the boats upriver had taken its toll: Many of the men could barely walk or stand. Fortunately, the boat crews got a chance to rest here for several days while Lewis and Clark scratched their heads over a puzzling fork in the river route. Today you can gaze down on the confluence from **Decision Point Overlook**, located on a high grassy bluff near the Loma Bridge Fishing Access. Their camp lay about a mile downriver, where the Missouri makes a fairly sharp bend to the south.

Today, we know the Marias flows into the Missouri from the north. But the captains had no idea which fork was the Missouri. None of their Indian sources had mentioned a tributary anywhere near this point. The north fork was deeper and looked like the Missouri they had known so far: whitish brown, turbid, roiling, with a muddy bed. The south fork was nearly twice as wide, but looked entirely different: clear, swifter, with a stony bed.

Lewis and Clark suspected the south fork was the correct route. The true Missouri, they reasoned, ought to run clearer here because it should soon lead them into the mountains, where clear water was the rule. Its transparency and southerly course also squared with Indian accounts of the river near the Great Falls. Still, they decided to explore both forks, hoping to turn up some conclusive evidence. Clark's party hiked up the Missouri and got within

**Moonrise over
Missouri Breaks**

25 miles of the falls before looping back.

Meanwhile, Lewis's party hiked nearly 80 miles up the Marias before returning in cold rains over treacherous muddy bluffs like those you can still see from the overlook reaching off to the northwest. At one point, Lewis slipped and nearly slid over a 90-foot drop, but managed to save himself by jamming his spear-like espontoon into the mud. Shortly after, he heard a voice behind him cry, "God, God, Captain—what shall I do?" Pvt. Richard Windsor was clinging to the edge of the precipice, his right arm and leg dangling over the drop-off. Lewis calmly instructed him to use his knife to dig a foothold in the face of the bluff and crawl to safety.

It was a wet, grim slog back down the Marias River gorge. "Continued our rout down the river," Lewis wrote, "Sometimes in the mud and water of the bottom lands, at others in the river to our breasts and when the water became so deep that we could not wade we cut footsteps in the face of the steep bluffs with our knives and proceded."

Hole-in-the-Wall, White Cliffs

But not all was misery. On the fourth day out, the skies cleared and Lewis found himself in a wooded bottomland "filled with innumerable little birds." There were goldfinches, wrens, redpolls, purple finches, brown thrushes, turtle doves, and robins. "When sun began to shine today these birds appeared to be very gay and sung most inchantingly."

Back at Loma, the captains decided to leave the red pirogue behind, store a heavy load of gear in a cache pit, and follow the south fork. Every other member of the party, including the best boatman, thought they should go the other way. It's a measure of the men's respect for the captains that they said they would cheerfully follow Lewis and Clark up what they considered the wrong fork. Lewis went ahead of the boats on foot. If he didn't strike the Great Falls of the Missouri soon, they would know they had chosen the wrong course and could more quickly correct their error.

JUNE 13–15, 1805

Fort Benton

Lewis skirted the site of Fort Benton as he hiked up to the Great Falls, but Clark and the boat crews pushed right through, moving slowly past what is now the town's park.

The night before, they had camped just beyond the line of eroded gray bluffs you can see curving downriver from Fort Benton's boat landing.

Clark noted that one of the men, when grabbing a bush, had seized the neck of a rattlesnake, but no harm done. Clark was more worried about Sacagawea who had been sick for three days despite his best efforts to bleed and dose her (see sidebar this page). In the days ahead, she would get much worse. So would navigation. It would take four days of grueling effort to drag the boats from Fort Benton to the expedition's portage camp below the Great Falls.

"The fatigue which we have to encounter is incretiable," Clark wrote on June 15, "the men in the water from morning untill night hauling the Cord & boats walking on Sharp rocks and round Sliperery Stones which alternately cut their feet & throw them down, not with Standing all this dificuelty they go with great chearfulness, aded to those difi- cuelties the rattle Snakes inumerable & require great caution to prevent being bitten."

Fort Benton offers little by way of Lewis and Clark inter- pretation. There are some small exhibits and a good slide show at the **Bureau of Land Management visitor center** *(1718 Front St. 406-622-5185. May-Sept.)*, and a fine statue of the captains with Sacagawea. But this old river town is worth a visit just to amble the banks of the Missouri and take in the expansive downstream vista of cottonwoods and grassy bottoms, cutbanks and bare gray hills.

It took Lewis and his party of four men just two days to reach the Great Falls from the mouth of the Marias. They followed the Missouri's north bank, sometimes climbing the bluffs, sometimes shortcutting across the plains. They shot elk, bison, deer, even a couple of grizzlies, and hung what they didn't eat beside the river for Clark and the struggling boat crews. On the first day out, and not far east of Fort Benton, Lewis was overcome by dysentery.

"Having brought no medecine with me I resolved to try an experiment," he wrote. He boiled chokecherry twigs to make "a strong black decoction of an astringent bitter tast," then drank two pints. "By 10 in the evening I was entirely relieved from pain and in fact every symptom of the disorder forsook me."

Sacagawea's Illness

By the time Clark and the boat crews reached the Great Falls area, Sacagawea seemed near death. She was in great pain, sometimes deranged, had a nearly imperceptible pulse and twitching fingers. Lewis thought she suffered from "an obstruction of the mensis" brought on by a cold, but modern scholars believe she had pelvic inflammatory disease brought on by gonorrheal infection.

Both captains had a high personal regard for her, but also recognized, as Lewis put it, that she was their "only dependence for a friendly negociation with the Snake Indians on whom we depend for horses" to get over the Rockies.

Lewis treated her with sulphur water from what is now called Sacagawea Spring, along with poul- tices of Peruvian bark and opium. After several days, she recovered.

Great Falls Area

Brutal, arduous, inspiring, Lewis and Clark's epic portage around the Great Falls robbed them of a solid month of prime midsummer travel days just as they reached the foot of the Rocky Mountains. Menaced by grizzly bears and flash floods, mauled by hailstorms, their feet mercilessly jabbed by prickly pear cactus, the men had to drag six enormous dugout canoes and tons of gear nearly 18 miles to bypass five major waterfalls that roared northeast of the present-day city of Great Falls.

Even though the Great Falls have been dammed and the surrounding plains paved with wheat and barley fields, this is one of the most rewarding sections of country anywhere on the Lewis and Clark Trail. Within the city itself, you'll find several important expedition landmarks, and many opportunities to walk or bike along the Missouri.

Nearby, you can stroll the same shortgrass hills that Lewis hurried across to catch his first glimpse of the Great Falls of the Missouri. You can also dip a finger into the same sulphur spring he tapped to restore Sacagawea to health, or dodge rattlesnakes along the same creek where the expedition wrestled its canoes up onto the plains. Downriver, you can float a stretch of the free-flowing Missouri right past one of the Corps's most important campsites. Or, you can follow the expedition upriver through one of Montana's most beautiful, and accessible, Missouri River canyons.

Your first stop, though, should be the **Lewis and Clark National Historic Trail Interpretive Center** (*4201 Giant Springs Rd. 406-727-8733. Mem. Day–Labor Day daily, Tues.-Sun. rest of year; adm. fee*). Built into steep bluffs overlooking a swift and relatively undeveloped stretch of the Missouri, this intriguing facility covers the entire Lewis and Clark journey and pays special attention to the rich spectrum of native cultures the expedition encountered along the way. Across the lobby, three lean figures in tattered buckskin stand frozen in the act of dragging an enormous dugout canoe up to the floor. Beyond them flows the living Missouri, with its crumbling rock bluffs, birdlife, and a view of Black Eagle Falls.

Start with the excellent introductory film, then follow the exhibits, which artfully sketch Lewis and Clark's voyage. In addition to maps, portraits, landscape paintings, and convincing reproductions of expeditionary and Indian items, you'll find some clever hands-on exhibits. Pull on the rope attached to the Missouri River Mile-O-Meter, and you'll soon learn how difficult it was to haul the boats upriver. Elsewhere, you can listen to Lewis bargain for horses with the Shoshone through a four-language translation chain, or step into a partial reproduction of a Mandan earth lodge.

The center also offers various interpretive programs: short presentations every hour; daylong workshops on such crafts as decorative quillwork; and multiday field trips.

Outside, get a whiff of sage, dried grass, and mud as you amble from the center to **River Camp.** There, interpreters offer direction in activities directly related to Lewis and Clark, such as making moccasins, tanning hides, or navigating with period instruments. Botanical signs along the center's paths help visitors identify native plants and link them to the expedition.

For a longer jaunt, look for the **Lewis and Clark Natural History Walk,** which leads from the interpretive center through **Giant Springs Heritage State Park** (*4800 Giant Springs Rd. 406-454-5840. Adm. fee*). There, you can take in the park's namesake springs, an enticing pool of clear cold water that Lewis and Clark visited on separate excursions.

Beyond the park, **Rivers Edge Trail** continues for several miles along the rim of the bluffs to overlooks of **Rainbow Falls** and **Crooked Falls** before continuing out onto the shortgrass prairie. The trail also leads upriver from the interpretive center for several miles, hugging the Missouri as it passes through the heart of town. Several major loop routes branch from the trail and head north and south across the dams.

Next, head for **Ryan Dam** (*N on US 87 to Ryan Dam Rd.*) and the remains of the Great Falls of the Missouri, which Lewis's party reached on June 13 after hiking two days from the Marias River. South of present **Portage**, Lewis had begun to hear "the agreeable sound of a fall of water" and soon saw "the spray arrise above the plain like a collumn of smoke." By noon, he'd clambered down into the gorge "to gaze on this sublimely grand specticle"—a thundering

The Grueling Portage around the Great Falls

The expedition's route began at Belt Creek, northeast of the city of Great Falls, and rambled across the plains, skirting the gulches and ravines that feed into the gorge. They crossed the present Malmstrom Air Force Base then angled across the city's southern outskirts to the White Bear Islands, south of 40th Avenue South.

The men made the passage four times, hauling the canoes and gear on flimsy chassis they had cobbled together. After laying out the route and accompanying the first load across, Clark returned to the Lower Portage Camp to cache some of the baggage and organize the rest for transport. Lewis remained at the Upper Portage Camp at White Bear Islands, receiving the goods, reviving the portage crew, and futilely assembling his iron-frame boat.

cascade of explosive white water plunging over cliffs at least 80 feet high and 300 yards wide.

Today, the dam's parabolic rim stands above and behind the cliffs, controlling the Great Falls like a faucet (maximum flow in spring and early summer). Though the falls have changed, the downstream canyon looks pretty much the way it did in 1805. So do the rolling hills along its rim—steep, fulsome swells of knee-high grass, prickly pear, and yucca.

Lewis camped beneath the falls, then hiked the north bank from waterfall to waterfall before turning downstream to rejoin Clark on June 16.

To retrace Lewis's downstream path and to get an outstanding view of the lower end of the portage route, drive to **Morony Dam.** On the last switchback leading down to the dam, you'll find an unmarked turnout with a heavy cable strung across what was once a road. From there, you can pick your way along the bluff tops for about a mile to **Sacagawea Spring** (look for the pipeline valve), which Lewis tapped to treat Sacagawea (see sidebar p. 89).

From the high knob at the edge of the bluffs, you can look across the Missouri to the mouth of **Belt Creek** and then trace the Missouri's gentle south bank downriver to a high point of land studded with crumbling rock and juniper. Just beyond the point, Lewis and Clark established their **Lower Portage Camp** *(On private property),* where the expedition emptied its dugouts, pulled them upstream along the north bank, and sent them across to Belt Creek (see sidebar p. 91). There, the boats were left to dry while the men sorted through the heaps of cargo at Lower Portage Camp, stashed extra gear, hid the white pirogue, and cobbled together four wheeled chassis to fit beneath the canoes. When all was ready for the first leg of the portage, the men walked their loads up the south bank to Belt Creek and hauled both canoes and baggage up onto the plains.

To retrace what you can of the route, return to the city of Great Falls and drive to Belt Creek *(via US 89 and Highwood and Salem Rds.),* which cuts through a scrubby little side canyon of crumbled rock, buffalo grass, and prickly pear. **Salem Bridge** crosses the creek where the expedition pulled the canoes from the water and began lugging them up onto the plain. In fact, the gravel road climbs the very same slope the crew followed and offers a chance to walk the portage route for roughly 2 miles.

That short stretch, though, is just about the only section of the portage modern travelers can follow. The rest crosses wheat fields, the Air Force base, or Great Falls itself and rarely parallels a road. Still, the drive back to the city

"The men has to haul with all their Strength wate & art, maney times every man all catching the grass & knobes & Stones with their hands to give them more force in drawing on the Canoes & Loads, and notwithstanding the Coolness of the air in high presperation and every halt [the men] are asleep in a moment, maney limping from the Soreness of their feet"

WILLIAM CLARK, AT THE GREAT FALLS OF THE MISSOURI, JUNE 23, 1805 conveys a sense of the distance involved and opens up vistas of surrounding mountains rising from the plains.

For the expedition, the overland trip was a grinding ordeal. Empty, the canoes averaged roughly one thousand pounds. On the portage they were piled high with gear. The burden, Lewis said, was as much as the men could possibly move. The plains were hot, water scarce, and the soil underfoot pockmarked with innumerable bison hoofprints, which were sharp and nearly as painful underfoot as the prickly pear thorns. Even so, the portage crew made excellent time.

It usually took them one day to reach the **Upper Portage Camp,** and one day to return and stage for the next push. On the second and third trips they hoisted the sails of the canoes and got a boost from the incessant plains wind. But the final one-way trip took four days. Thunderstorms filled the gulches with rushing water and stranded the crew on the plains. While the unprotected men waited to proceed, a hailstorm beat them bloody, knocked many down, and, Clark said, nearly killed some. The same day, Clark himself was nearly killed—along with York, Sacagawea, Pomp, and Charbonneau—when a flash flood swept through a ravine where they had taken shelter.

Great Falls of the Missouri

Despite these and other hardships, it took just 11 days to move everything to the Upper Portage Camp. For an overview of its approximate location, drive south on Upper River Road to 40th Avenue South. The islands below are what remain of the White Bear Islands. There, the men celebrated Independence Day by drinking the last of the liquor and dancing to Pvt. Pierre Cruzatte's fiddle. There, too, Lewis's frustrating experiment with the iron-frame boat came to its disappointing end. He and Clark had hoped the boat, capable of carrying four tons of gear and men, would replace the white pirogue. But after covering the frame with the skins of 28 elk and 4 bison, Lewis could find nothing to seal its seams. There were no pine trees for pitch, and attempts with charcoal and beeswax failed.

On July 10, Clark and several others headed upriver to build two more dugouts. Lewis remained at the Upper Portage Camp until July 13, while the canoes ferried baggage up to Clark's camp near modern **Ulm.**

Detail from "Lewis and Clark in the Bitterroots," John Clymer, 1969

The Rockies

July 10 – October 7, 1805

This chapter follows the Corps of Discovery's trek through southwest Montana and over the Rocky Mountains to the banks of the Clearwater River in northwest Idaho. Nowhere else will you find such a vast, deeply satisfying landscape that is so tightly woven with expedition experiences and so easily reached on good roads. Here are the rivers, still cold, swift, and full of fish, where the men hauled their canoes. Here are the broad, flat-floored valleys, still hopping with game. And here are the mountains themselves—range after range of cold, hard fact that buried the myth of the Northwest Passage and nearly buried Lewis and Clark.

Along this stretch, the expedition anxiously searched for horses, finally purchasing some from the Shoshone Indians. They stashed their canoes, crossed the Continental Divide, and made a starvation trek across the Bitterroot Range, collapsing along the Clearwater River in Nez Perce territory.

JULY 10–15, 1805

Ulm Area

"The prickly pear is now in full blume and forms one of the beauties as well as the greatest pests of the plains."

MERIWETHER LEWIS, JULY 15, 1805

It takes just a few minutes on I-15 to reach this small river town, where Clark and his crew of rough-hewn boatmen added two dugout canoes to the expedition's flotilla. But a more rewarding drive follows County Road 226 south from Great Falls and heads west on Wilson Butte Road, a fine ribbon of gravel that hugs the placid Missouri, bounds over grassy riverside hills, and offers several access points for fishing, paddling, or just dangling a toe in the water.

Clark's crew hollowed and shaped the canoes in a buggy cottonwood grove a few miles east of the present town. It was a maddening task. "We ar much at a loss for wood to make ax [handles]," Clark wrote. The best wood they could find, chokecherry, snapped so easily that the party's four wood choppers made and broke 13 of them in less than a day. Also, the large cottonwoods they felled were cracked inside, which required the men to build what they considered short boats: one 25 feet long, the other 33, and both about 3 feet wide. While the carpenters hacked away, the rest of the men brought the other canoes upstream from White Bear Islands.

Lewis joined Clark on July 13, after walking up from the Upper Portage Camp. Along the way, he passed the frame of "a very extraordinary Indian lodge." Built like a giant tepee from 50-foot cottonwood logs, it measured 216 feet in circumference, had a large fire pit in the center, and was surrounded by 80 tepee rings. "It was most probably designed for some great feast," Lewis wrote, "or a council house on some great national concern." He was very nearly right. The structure was probably a medicine lodge built by the Piegan Blackfeet for their annual sun dance, a vitally important ceremony involving the whole tribe.

The expedition shoved off again on the morning of July 15. "We now found our vessels eight in number all heavily laden," Lewis wrote. Despite the addition of two canoes, the boats were so crowded that the captains got out and walked to lighten the load. "We find it extreemly difficult to keep the baggage of many of our men within reasonable bounds," Lewis griped. "They will be adding bulky articles of but little use or value to them."

North of town, you might visit **Ulm Pishkun State Park** *(Off I-15. 406-866-2217)*. Raked by strong winds, the park takes in a high, rimrocked bluff that forms what is thought to be the largest buffalo jump in the state.

An interpretive center at the base of the bluff describes how small bands of Indian families lured herds of bison over the edge using little more than their own wits and swift

feet. More to the point for Lewis and Clark, the place conveys a deeper understanding of the peoples whose land the Corps of Discovery was now traveling through. Here, you'll find a bison-hide tepee furnished with buffalo robes, and exhibits that describe the bison's central role in Northern Plains Indian life. Here, too, are panels briefly sketching the lives of present-day Indians on Montana's six reservations. One includes a picture of a Blackfeet sun dance lodge similar to what Lewis described in 1805.

Outside, a half-mile interpretive trail stretches along the base of the bluff, where archaeologists have found compacted deposits of bison bones 12 feet deep. Another trail, accessible by road, explores the top of the bluff, where you can pick out the ancient drive lines that funneled bison to the brink.

Though it's interesting to saunter among the scattered bone fragments, the top of the bluff also opens up a panoramic vista of the Missouri's course, and thus the expedition's route from the Great Falls into the broken range of mountains visible to the southwest.

Though Lewis never saw Ulm Pishkun, the site would have fascinated him. He understood how buffalo jumps worked and penned a description on May 29, 1805. His account correctly dwells on the critical—and perilous—role of the buffalo runner who dashed ahead of the stampeding herd and jumped to a safe spot just beneath the edge of the cliff.

"The part of the decoy I am informed is extreamly

dangerous," he wrote. "If they are not very fleet runers the buffaloe tread them under foot and crush them to death, and sometimes drive them over the precepice also, where they perish in common with the buffaloe."

JULY 16, 1805

Pelican Point Fishing Access

◆ 6 MILES SW OF CASCADE, OFF I-15 ON MISSOURI RIVER RECREATION RD.

The coarse, volcanic ridges that converge on the Missouri just beyond this pleasant river landing mark the spot where the Corps of Discovery finally entered the main body of the Rocky Mountains. It was—and is—a dramatic passage, which leads to a magnificent canyon of steep grassy slopes, forested glens, lush meadows, and towering outcrops of scabby rock that bulge from the hillsides and rise straight from the water. Pelicans and cormorants squat at the heads of gravel bars. Bald eagles and ospreys roost in the trees. Deer nibble at the brush.

The **Missouri River Recreation Road** (*Old US 91*) is a two-lane heartbreaker that parallels the interstate, hugs the riverbanks, and makes it possible to trace the expedition's route to the upper end of present-day Holter Lake. Dozens of pullouts and boat landings offer enticing stops for admiring the land, wading, or launching a canoe.

Lewis, who had walked out ahead of the boats, was the first to reach this point. He camped a couple of miles downstream, and in the evening climbed a singular pinnacle called **Tower Rock,** which still looms above the Missouri where the Missouri River Recreation Road crosses the interstate at Hardy Creek.

From there, he could gaze back over the plains and the abundance of bison they were about to leave behind. The Indians had said that game would be scarce in the mountains, so the Corps had put up a large stock of grease and dried meat against hard times. For now, though, there were still elk and deer to shoot, as well as ripe currants and berries to pick along the river.

JULY 18, 1805

Dearborn Fishing Access

◆ 20 MILES SW OF CASCADE, OFF I-15 ON MISSOURI RIVER RECREATION RD.

This boat landing lies just across the Missouri from the Dearborn River, where the canyon opens onto a gentler landscape of rolling hills and flat river bottoms. The expedition passed this point on the morning of the 18th, after

---

"here for the first time I ate of the small guts of the buffaloe cooked over a blazing fire in the Indian stile without any preperation of washing or other clensing and found them very good."

MERIWETHER LEWIS, NEAR CASCADE, MONTANA, JULY 16, 1805

camping just a few miles downstream, more or less where I-15 crosses to the south bank. The previous evening, the men had threaded the canoes up the canyon, gaping at bighorn sheep that trotted casually among the cliffs.

Here, the captains decided to send Clark ahead on foot to contact the Shoshone Indians, who they feared might flee from the gunfire of the expedition's hunters. Meeting the Shoshone was crucial. They would know the best route over the Rockies, and could sell them the horses they had to have to cross the alpine barrier.

Clark took York and two other men, but left behind Charbonneau and Sacagawea—the party's best hope for fluent translation with the Shoshone. Why he left them is anyone's guess. He stuck close to the river as far as present **Holter Dam,** then followed an "Indian rode" into the dry, gravelly hills to the west, pulling well ahead of the canoes.

Explorer's Heaven

In 1805 the braided channels of the Missouri River formed a rich riparian corridor that ran the length of the Helena Valley in place of the present Canyon Ferry Reservoir. Lewis estimated that the outermost channels were separated by as much as 3 miles. He described bottomlands and banks crowded with shrubs and low trees including willow, box elder, wild rose, sumac, honeysuckle, chokecherry, serviceberry, and four types of currant. Trumpeter swans, geese, sandhill cranes, mergansers, sandpipers, and songbirds dwelled there, along with beavers, otters, and many different snakes—including the western hognosed variety, which Lewis first chronicled for science on July 23, 1805.

JULY 18–20, 1805

Holter Lake Recreation Area

◆ 10 MILES SW OF CRAIG, ON MISSOURI RIVER RECREATION RD. ◆ 406-494-5059 ◆ ADM. FEE ◆ CAMPING

Nestled against grassy, broad-backed ridges flecked with ponderosa pine, this reservoir of the Missouri River starts off as a roomy lake, but soon flows into a narrow, deep, serpentine gorge that eventually leads to what Lewis called the "gates of the rocky mountains." That craggy landmark, as well as the gorge itself, is accessible only on foot or by boat. Still, it's worth visiting the upper end of the lake to amble over the billowing shortgrass hills and maybe spot a mountain bluebird.

Lewis and the men beached their canoes in a grove somewhere along the eastern shore of the present lake and dined on elk amid the usual swarm of mosquitoes. Clark camped beyond the crest of the high, thinly forested mountain at the southwest end of the lake. The next morning, both parties moved on, the canoes fighting a strong current as the men pushed into the narrows beyond the present **Departure Point** boat ramp and campground.

From Departure Point, you can paddle in the expedition's wake to **Gates of the Mountains** (11 water miles) and camp along the water's edge. Limestone cliffs, pockmarked by caves and coves, rise a thousand feet or more from the water, and bighorn sheep and mountain goats are common. If you prefer a good walk, drive to the top of the knob above Departure Point and wander out into the knee-high grass and undulating terrain of the **Beartooth Wildlife Management Area,** a prime birding spot frequented by elk, deer, and bighorn sheep. There, you can roam the land as Lewis often did—freely, off trail, following whatever hillside, swale, or ravine that appeals.

Farther south, a pleasant, two-hour cruise *(Gates of the Mountains Boat Tour, 18 miles N of Helena off I-15. 406-458-5241. Mem. Day–Labor Day; fare)* leads through the awesome limestone chasm that Lewis called "gates of the rocky mountains." His "gates" probably did not refer to any particular set of cliffs, but rather to the exceptionally narrow, exceptionally deep gash in the mountains that begins across the lake from the boat dock and continues downriver for nearly 6 miles.

Step aboard one of these large, rumbling boats and before long, you'll be gliding past 1,000-foot cliffs, steep forested ridges, eroded pinnacles, arches, and great brows of limestone rising directly from the water. Mountain goats, deer, ospreys, and bald eagles are often seen. Near the turn-around, you can get off and catch a later boat back, which makes it possible to spend the day—or a few days—roaming the backcountry or just sunning yourself on a stony beach.

Lewis, of course, approached the gates from the north. As the cliffs closed in around the boats, the men began to see bighorn sheep. River otters were so plentiful and swam so close to the boats that one of the men managed to kill one with his setting pole. Late in the day the boats reached the depths of the chasm, but the men were forced to keep moving until well after dark because they could not find a place to land among the cliffs.

"These clifts rise from the waters edge on either side perpendicularly to the hight of 1200 feet," Lewis wrote. "Every object here wears a dark and gloomy aspect. the tow[e]ring and projecting rocks in many places seem ready to tumble on us."

Clark, meanwhile, continued his search for the

> *"We entered much the most remarkable clifts that we have yet seen.... the river appears to have forced it's way through this immence body of solid rock for the distance of 5¾ miles.... nor is ther in the 1st 3 miles of this distance a spot except one of a few yards in extent on which a man could rest the soal of his foot."*
>
> MERIWETHER LEWIS, GATES OF THE ROCKY MOUNTAINS, JULY 19, 1805

Shoshone, hiking about 30 miles in moccasins to a camp on the west side of present **Hauser Lake**. "My feet," he wrote, "is verry much brused & cut walking over the flint, & constantly Stuck full Prickley pear thorns, I puled out 17 by the light of the fire to night."

That camp, for July 19, lay a mile or so to the south of today's **Clark's Bay Day Use Area** *(Airport exit off I-15. Follow signs for York)*, a pleasant boat launch and picnic area that lies along a narrow bend of Hauser Lake. If you follow the road a little farther, you'll come to **Devils Elbow Campground** and a highway bridge. Lewis and the boat crews camped July 20 in the bend upstream of the bridge. For a terrific vista of both sites, drive to the top of the hill between Clarks Bay and Devils Elbow. There, a short trail leads to an overlook that takes in the sinuous shoreline of Hauser Lake, the upper Helena Valley, and the mountains to the west. The ground under your feet closely matches Clark's description—gravelly, sparsely covered with grass, and bristling with prickly pear cactus. This narrow section of the lake, with its high rock walls and convenient boat landings, makes a terrific spot to launch a canoe and paddle in the expedition's wake.

JULY 20–27, 1805

Helena Area

From Gates of the Mountains, I-15 descends onto the broad, grassy floor of the Helena Valley, which lies between the forested peaks of the Continental Divide to the west and the Big Belt Mountains to the east. Beneath the Big Belts, Canyon Ferry Reservoir reaches south for nearly 25 miles. Spur roads lead to some moderately rewarding sites along this leg of the expedition's journey, but the reservoir has inundated the lush bottomlands and braided river channels where Lewis observed trumpeter swans, sandhill cranes, and river otters (see sidebar p. 99).

Northeast of town near **Black Sandy State Park** *(Off Cty. Rd. 453 E. 406-444-4720. Camping),* high rocky knobs scattered with ponderosa pine frame yet another canyon of the Missouri. There, you can stroll down from **Hauser Dam** along a free-flowing stretch of the river where Lewis picked blackcurrants and where one of the hunters shot an elk.

As the canoes emerged from the canyon, Lewis saw smoke rising in the southwest. Clark, walking far to the south, also saw the smoke. Weeks later, they learned that the fires had been set by Shoshone who had heard the party shooting, had mistaken them for Blackfeet, and had fled over the mountains. Too bad. If Lewis and Clark had been able to buy horses here, they could have crossed the Continental Divide above Helena and followed the Clark Fork River down to the Missoula area, thus cutting off some 400 miles of arduous travel.

But it was not to be. The boat crews continued upriver and camped on the east bank, north of today's County Road 280 crossing.

Clark, meanwhile, decided to wait for the canoes at Beaver Creek, which flows into Canyon Ferry Reservoir northeast of present-day **Winston.** His feet were blistered, and the other men's "So Stuck with Prickley pear & cut with the Stones that they were Scerseley able to march at a Slow gate." Today, you'll find the **White Earth Campground** and boat ramp *(7 miles E of Winston, along Beaver Creek Rd.)* in the general vicinity of Clark's bivouac. Though the reservoir and its shoreline look nothing like the river did in 1805, the surrounding mountains do.

Clark and his men rested here two days while Lewis and the boat crews labored upriver through myriad channels, islands, and gravel bars that once occupied the bed of Canyon Ferry Reservoir. The weather was hot, the men greatly fatigued. But they cheered up when Sacagawea began to recognize the surrounding country and said

Three Forks could not be much farther ahead. On July 23, Clark again set off in search of the Shoshone. This time, his party included Charbonneau, but not Sacagawea.

South of Helena, US 287 parallels the expedition's route as far as **Toston,** then breaks away from the Missouri and heads across the plains to the Three Forks vicinity. Heading south, stop by **York's Islands Fishing Access** (5 miles SE of Townsend, off US 287), a breezy oasis of tall cottonwoods where the Missouri retains something of its 1805 character and where you can launch a canoe (bring your own) for a casual, 5-mile float back to Townsend. The site takes its name from Clark's own map, which named the cluster of islands across from the present boat ramp in honor of York, Clark's slave since boyhood.

The float trip to Townsend passes another expedition landmark, **Crimson Bluffs,** a striking cliff of brick red shale that rises directly from the river. Sacagawea recognized the bluff and told the men that her people used the shale to make red paint and dye.

Another nice detour leads 5 miles to **Toston Dam** (2 miles SW of Toston, off US 287), where the Missouri rushes through a beautiful desert canyon.

As Lewis and the increasingly weary boat crews labored upriver to Three Forks, they averaged about 18 miles a day, hauling on tow ropes, shoving on setting poles. "Their labour is excessively great," Lewis wrote. "I occasionally encourage them by assisting in the labour of navigating the canoes, and have learned to *push a tolerable good pole* in their fraize." On July 23, Lewis's party camped at the south end of what is now Canyon Ferry Reservoir, and just above Toston Dam on the 25th. They reached Three Forks the morning of the 27th, the men beginning "to weaken fast from this continual state of violent exertion."

Clark, meanwhile, had skirted the west side of the river, reaching the forks on July 25, and then scouting more than 20 miles up the Jefferson River before turning back to wait for the canoes. Despite his blistered, punctured feet and debilitating fatigue, he covered well over 100 miles in just five days, during which he saved Charbonneau from drowning and helped kill two grizzly bears.

JULY 27–30, 1805

Missouri Headwaters S.P.

◆ CTY. RD. 286, OFF I-90 ◆ 406-994-4042 ◆ ADM. FEE
◆ CAMPING

At this important expedition landmark, three pristine rivers join to form the Missouri amid a soothing landscape of verdant riverbanks, cottonwood groves, gravel bars, low

" We have a lame crew just now, two with tumers or bad boils on various parts of them, one with a bad stone bruise, one with his arm accidently dislocated but fortunately well replaced, and a fifth has streigned his back by sliping and falling backwards on the gunwall of the canoe. "

MERIWETHER
LEWIS,
JULY 31, 1805

Three Forks, headwaters of the Missouri River

cliffs, and semiarid grasslands. The Jefferson flows in from the southwest, the Madison from the south, and the Gallatin from the southeast. These swift clear waters converge here after crossing the floor of a large, open valley surrounded by mountain ranges.

Lewis first saw it at 9 a.m., July 27, 1805, after emerging from the stony hills north of the park. "The country," he wrote, "opens suddonly to extensive and beatifull plains and meadows which appear to be surrounded in every direction with distant and lofty mountains."

So little has changed since Lewis penned his description that you can almost see the expedition's dugouts pulled up in a distant bend of the Jefferson, a wisp of wood smoke rising from the cook fires. White-tailed deer, just like those the men feasted on, still browse the riverbanks, sandhill cranes still chuckle in the bottomlands, and the rich willowy scent of mountain wetlands still permeates the chilly morning air.

At the north end of **Fort Rock** (a broad promontory of elevated limestone that Lewis described as "a handsom site for a fortification"), you'll find a small expedition exhibit and a scenic 1-mile trail that starts in the picnic area and loops the edge of Fort Rock. At this end, the trail overlooks the lush mouth of the Gallatin River, the drier Madison/Jefferson confluence, and the narrow gap in the hills where Lewis and the canoes emerged the morning of July 27. Signs also identify **Lewis Rock,** the very knob of limestone Lewis climbed to map the area. Just north of

Fort Rock, the park's boat ramp lies close to the spot where the expedition paused for breakfast before continuing upriver to the confluence.

Next, head for the south end of Fort Rock, which opens up terrific vistas of the valley floor, the converging river courses, and the surrounding mountain ranges. While on the rock, look for yellow pincushion cactus and the small pyramids of sand and gravel built by western harvester ants. Both caught Lewis's eye.

For a closer view of the confluence, park at the **Headwaters Viewpoint** and stroll through the grass to the riverbank. There, the glassy waters of the Madison and Jefferson glide together and officially form the headwaters of the Missouri. The view can make you ache for a boat. If you have one, consider an afternoon float on the Jefferson from the **Drouillard Fishing Access** (*Off US 287, 1 mile S of I-90*) back to the park. Other landings make similar trips possible on the Madison and Gallatin. For information on outfitters and boat rentals call the Three Forks Chamber of Commerce (*406-285-4753*), or stop by the visitor center (*Main St., Three Forks*).

Lewis and the boat crews passed the confluence shortly after breakfast and camped about 2 miles up the Jefferson on "a handsome level smooth plain." In the afternoon, they were joined by Clark, who had seen no Indians, was nearly exhausted, and had a high fever, chills, and aching muscles. Lewis comforted him with a warm bath and a thundering dose of laxative pills.

Clark wasn't the only man in rough shape. During the morning Lewis had noted that the swift waters of the Missouri had taken a toll on the men. "The current still so rapid," he wrote, "that the men are in a continual state of their utmost exertion to get on, and they begin to weaken fast." He decided to halt for a couple of days to give them a rest, "which seemed absolutely necessary."

During the two days the expedition passed here, Lewis nursed Clark back to health. He got the men to build Clark a shade bower to rest under, dosed him with Peruvian bark, and fed him fat venison. Meanwhile, the men gathered strength as they made and mended moccasins and did other light chores. They amused themselves fishing for trout, which, Lewis wrote, would "not bite at any bate we

Survival Instinct

In the years following the Voyage of Discovery, two expedition members were killed by the Blackfeet near Three Forks: George Drouillard, in 1810, and John Potts, in 1808. Most memorable, though, is how Potts's trapping partner, John Colter, survived his harrowing run-in with the Blackfeet. After killing Potts, the Blackfeet stripped Colter and told him to run for it—barefoot— across a broad plain full of prickly pear between the Jefferson and Madison Rivers. He kept ahead of the Indians for 6 miles, pausing only to kill their front-runner with his own spear. He then dove into the Madison and hid beneath a jam of driftwood until nightfall. After walking naked and weaponless for seven days, he finally reached a fur-trading post on the Bighorn River.

can offer." They chased and caught a young sandhill crane, which Lewis examined with his customary thoroughness and then released, remarking that it "strikes a severe blow with his beak." They also listened to Sacagawea's tale of her abduction by Hidatsa raiders five years previously, when she and her band of Shoshone had camped at the very same spot.

While the men relaxed, Lewis fixed the position of the confluence, described its advantages as a fort site, and made notes about kingfishers, mallard, grasshoppers, crickets, and various plants. He also worried.

"We begin to feel considerable anxiety with rispect to the Snake [Shoshone] Indians," he wrote. "If we do not find them or some other nation who have horses I fear the successful issue of our voyage will be very doubtfull …we are now several hundred miles within the bosom of this wild and mountanous country, where game may rationally be expected shortly to become scarce and subsistence precarious without any information with rispect to the country not knowing how far these mountains continue, or wher to direct our course to pass them."

AUGUST 1, 1805

Lewis and Clark Caverns S.P.

◆ 17 MILES SW OF THREE FORKS ON MONT. 2
◆ 406-287-3541 ◆ ADM. FEE ◆ CAMPING

Lewis and Clark never saw this park's immense limestone cave system, but on July 31 they camped just a few miles downstream from the turnoff, and Lewis probably trudged right through as he took a turn ahead of the canoes, looking for the Shoshone.

"Our rout," he wrote, "lay through the steep and narrow hollows of the mountains exposed to the intese heat of the midday sun without shade or scarcely a breath of air."

Their hike led them over the rocky highlands that stand to the north and west of the park. Lewis, usually a tireless walker, found the going difficult.

"To add to my fatieque in this walk of about 11 miles," he wrote, "I had taken a doze of glauber salts in the morning in consequence of a slight disentary…being weakened by the disorder and the operation of the medicine I found myself almost exhausted before we reached the river."

The park offers the chance to explore the same sparsely timbered hills, take in marvelous vistas of the Jefferson River, and see many of the same plants and animals that Lewis and Clark saw nearby: limber pine, needle and thread grass, deer, pronghorn, blue grouse, and pinyon jays. Visitors can also take guided tours of the caverns

(May-Sept.; adm. fee), which begin from an entrance high in the park's mountains.

As you approach the area from Three Forks, the road shadows the Jefferson across rolling grass plains toward the northern spur of the Tobacco Root Mountains. The river looks much as Lewis described it in 1805: "crooked and crouded with islands, it's bottoms wide fertile and covered with fine grass from 9 inches to 2 feet high and possesses but a scant proportion of timber, which consists almost entirely of a few narrow leafed cottonwood trees distributed along the verge of the river." As the dry foothills converge on the river, you're likely to see pronghorn and deer, but not black bears, which Lewis and Clark saw in abundance eating currants along the riverbank.

Beyond the park, the road plunges through a spectacular canyon of high slanting cliffs and steep grass slopes peppered with sagebrush and juniper. Somewhere along these cliffs, Clark shot a bighorn, which provided a welcome meal for the boat crews, who had not eaten fresh meat in two days. As the men towed the canoes through the "Swift & very Sholey" waters of the canyon, one of the boats broke free of its tow rope, swung on the rocks and nearly capsized in a rapids. Clark's party camped near present **La Hood**, across from the mouth of the Boulder River. Lewis, meanwhile, camped on the north bank, west of present **Cardwell**. For a general sense of what their camp looked like, drop by the boat ramp south of Cardwell on County Road 359.

AUGUST 2–6, 1805

Whitehall to Twin Bridges

From Whitehall, Mont. 55 and 41 follow the Jefferson south through an expansive grass valley lying between the Tobacco Root Mountains to the east, and the Highland Mountains to the west. Lewis's party hiked beneath the steep, tree-blackened slopes of the Tobacco Roots, preferring to walk through prickly pear on the upland slopes rather than take the "risk of falling down at every step" among the potholes and thick grass of the river bottoms.

"The tops of these mountains are yet covered partially with snow," Lewis wrote, "while we in the valley are nearly suffocated with the intense heat of the midday sun; the nights are so cold that two blankets are not more than sufficient covering."

Lewis, healthy again and covering dozens of miles a day, camped just once—near **Waterloo**—before reaching the vicinity of Twin Bridges. Clark and the boat crews, meanwhile, had to camp three times as they fought their way

"After passing the river this morning Sergt. Gass lost my tommahawk in the thick brush and we were unable to find it, I regret the loss of this usefull implement, however accedents will happen in the best families"

MERIWETHER LEWIS, NEAR PRESENT-DAY WHITEHALL, MONT. AUG. 2, 1805 upstream. The Jefferson was fast and shallow, with stony rapids barring their progress every few hundred yards or so. "At those places," Lewis later wrote, "they are obliged to drag the canoes over the stone there not being water enough to float them, and betwen the riffles the current is so strong that they are compelled to have cecourse to the cord; and being unable to walk on the shore for the brush wade in the river along the shore and hawl them by the cord…their feet soon get tender and soar by wading and walking over the stones. these are also so slipry that they frequently get severe falls. being constantly wet soon makes them feble also." In many places, they had to double man the canoes to drag them over the shallows.

For a taste of their labor, consider wading in the river at the **Silver Star Fishing Access** *(15 miles S of Whitehall on Mont. 55)*, which lies in the general vicinity of Clark's August 4 camp. By the time Clark reached that point he could barely walk, thanks to a large boil on one ankle.

The previous day, while hobbling along the banks, Clark had discovered a set of fresh Indian footprints. He followed the tracks to the top of a hill, from which he could see his August 2 campsite. Clark concluded that the Indian had seen their fires and had run off. The event may indicate that the expedition had missed another opportunity to contact the Shoshone and buy horses.

Beyond Silver Star, you'll see a gap opening up at the south end of the Tobacco Roots. Through that gap, the Ruby River flows toward **Twin Bridges,** where it joins the Beaverhead to form the Jefferson. Just north of town, the Big Hole River kicks in from the west. Lewis and Clark called the confluence the "Forks of the Jefferson."

AUGUST 3–8, 1805

Twin Bridges Area

Nestled in the open valley floor with high, broad-backed mountain ranges rising in all directions, the Twin Bridges area presented Lewis and Clark with yet another set of river forks. Lewis arrived in this area the evening of August 3 and spent the next two days scouting the meandering branches of the Jefferson's forks while Clark and the boat crews continued their grim upstream pull.

Lewis made a broad loop south of town, taking in the Ruby and Beaverhead Rivers, and then walked about 15 miles up the Big Hole before returning to the confluence. Thanks to a network of lazy gravel roads, you can approximate his route by car or, better yet, by mountain bike (if you've brought one). With the scent of the rivers and the buzz of insects, you can pedal the open country and spot deer, hawks, great blue herons, and many other birds Lewis would have seen in the area. From Twin Bridges, follow US 287 south about a mile, turn right on East Bench Road and proceed for 4.5 miles. Then turn right on Silver Bow Lane and right on Mont. 41, back to town.

Beaverhead Rock

Lewis left Clark a note at the mouth of the Big Hole recommending the canoes ascend the Beaverhead. The Big Hole, he concluded, was unnavigable. Still, he explored it. Unfortunately, Clark never got the note—a beaver swam off with it! So, the boat crews stumbled up the Big Hole, hacking a quarter mile passage through the willows at one point, and, on August 5, camping in mud not far below the **High Road Fishing Access** *(3 miles SW of town off Mont. 41)*. The next day, one of Lewis's party, descending the Big Hole, met Clark and turned him around.

As the canoes headed downriver, one capsized and two swamped. Pvt. Joseph Whitehouse was thrown into the water and nearly crushed to death as one of the massive dugouts pinned him to the riverbed and scraped over him. Some of the expedition's most valuable stores, including the medicine chest, provisions, and Indian presents, were soaked.

The party dried out at the mouth of the Big Hole, ditched one canoe, and headed up the Beaverhead the following afternoon. So crooked was the river that they had to camp twice within a half dozen straight-line miles of Twin Bridges.

AUGUST 9, 1805
Beaverhead Rock

◆ 12 MILES SW OF TWIN BRIDGES ON MONT. 41

As the expedition pressed on from Twin Bridges, Sacagawea recognized this abrupt hunk of limestone rising from the plains and told the captains they would find her people farther up the Beaverhead, or perhaps on another river west of the Continental Divide.

With Clark still suffering from "the rageing fury of a tumer on my anckle musle," the captains decided Lewis should travel ahead with a small party, find a route over the divide, and contact the Shoshone.

From the north, Beaverhead Rock may not look much like its namesake. But drive south past it about 2.5 miles and look back from the historical marker. The bluff and the long, velvety ridge that reaches back from it look very much like the head and body of a swimming beaver. Before continuing south, you might drive back to the fishing access right beneath the rock just to imagine hauling seven canoes, each as long as a motor home, around the tight bends of the narrowing river.

As Lewis rocketed ahead, covering 20 to 30 miles a day, Clark and the boat crews crept forward, rarely logging more than 5 miles. After slipping, falling, and dragging the dugouts over stones most of the day, many of the men were barely able to walk by evening. And yet, every morning in the chill of dawn, they splashed back into the cold water, shouldered the tow ropes, braced their swollen feet against the sharp rocks, and proceeded on.

AUGUST 13, 1805

Clark's Lookout

◆ NW EDGE OF DILLON VIA OLD US 91 N

One of the few spots on the trail where you can stand exactly where Clark did in 1805, this 40-foot knob of limestone offers great views of the Beaverhead and its vibrant riparian corridor stretching off to the distant south. Clark climbed it on the afternoon of the 13th and took compass bearings on Beaverhead Rock, the Big Hole River, and, among the dry southern mountains, the mouth of what is today called Clark Canyon.

To find Clark's Lookout, turn west on Old US 91 N (*Next to Town Pump gas station*), go under the overpass, and take the left turn immediately beyond the river crossing. The cliff is on the right. Go around the fence and amble to the top.

AUGUST 10 & 14, 1805

Rattlesnake Cliffs

◆ 8 MILES SW OF DILLON, BARRETTS DAM EXIT OFF I-15
◆ CAMPING

As you coast to a stop from the Barretts exit off I-15, the Rattlesnake Cliffs rise directly ahead as a great hulking mound of rock, grass, and sagebrush. On August 10, Lewis sat beneath these cliffs, making notes about the abundant rattlesnakes he found here while Hugh McNeal and John Shields kindled a fire. Meanwhile, George Drouillard slipped around to the right to make a grocery run.

"He arrived," Lewis wrote, "at noon with three deer skins and the flesh of one of the best of them, we cooked and eat a haisty meal and departed."

Four days later, Clark and the canoe party camped across the interstate from these cliffs, near present-day **Barretts Dam.** The river for most of the day had been "one continued rapid." So many of the men were now lame that Clark himself had had to push a setting pole. Morale was low. Over supper, Charbonneau struck Sacagawea and got a severe reprimand from Clark.

Their spirits would have lifted considerably had they known that at that very moment Lewis was camped with the Shoshone on a tributary of the Columbia River, admiring a herd of several hundred horses.

AUGUST 15–17, 1805
Clark Canyon

It took Clark nearly three days to get the canoes up this 12-mile canyon of velvety shortgrass hills between the Rattlesnake Cliffs and Clark Canyon Dam. A quick stop at **Grasshopper Creek Fishing Access** (*Off I-15*) shows why it took so long. Here, the Beaverhead—rocky, swift, very cold—narrows almost to creek status. It's nice water for fly-fishing from drift boats, but hell for lugging ponderous, slab-sided dugouts upstream.

"The men," Clark wrote near Grasshopper Creek, "complain much of their fatigue and being repetiedly in the water which weakens them much perticularly as they are obliged to live on pore Deer meet which has a Singular bitter taste."

Their luck was about to change.

AUGUST 10 & 16–24, 1805
Clark Canyon Reservoir

◆ 20 MILES SW OF DILLON VIA CTY. RD. 324
◆ 406-683-6472 ◆ CAMPING

Lapping beneath the flanks of nearly treeless mountains, this reservoir marks the spot where Lewis and Clark's long boat journey up the Missouri and its tributaries finally came to an end. Here the Beaverhead split into two unnavigable streams (site now submerged), and the Corps of Discovery happily stashed its canoes. From this point to northwestern Idaho, the men would depend on their own feet and the backs of horses.

> *"men much fatigued and weakened by being continually in the water drawing the Canoes over the Sholes... complain verry much of the emence labour they are obliged to undergo & wish much to leave the river. I passify them."*
>
> WILLIAM CLARK, NEAR DILLON, MONT., AUGUST 12, 1805

As you cross the dam, pause to look at the Beaverhead's winding downstream course. Somewhere among those bottomland meadows on the morning of August 17, Clark and the boat crews looked up to see several Indians riding toward them. Only when they got closer did Clark recognize one as Drouillard, dressed as a Shoshone. Clark left the boats and hurried on to the forks, where he found Lewis camped with 16 Shoshone and their horses.

The Lemhi Shoshone

The Lemhi Shoshone are a division of the Northern Shoshone, who lived in the Rocky Mountains and also were known as the Snake Indians. They migrated to Montana and Idaho from the Great Basin of Nevada and Utah during the 1600s. After acquiring the horse after 1700, they became nomadic bison hunters on Montana's northern plains. By Lewis and Clark's day, the Blackfeet and other tribes had driven them west of the Continental Divide. Their culture combined traits of both the Great Basin and Great Plains peoples. They traded extensively with neighboring tribes west of the divide, and obtained Spanish goods through the Ute. But because the Spaniards did not trade for firearms, the Shoshone had just a few captured guns among them. This put them at a disadvantage against their enemies—the Hidatsa, Blackfeet, and Atsina—who could buy guns from Canadian traders.

Today, the Lemhi live in central Idaho, on the Shoshone-Bannock Reservation around Fort Hall.

The site of Lewis and Clark's reunion and their subsequent camp lies between **Camp Fortunate Overlook** *(1 mile past the dam, off Cty. Rd. 324)* and Armstead Island. If you could have stood here in 1805, you would have looked down on a joyful scene—seven dugouts pulled up in the grass, a large sail rigged for shade, horses grazing nearby, and roughly 50 people dressed in buckskin milling around, slapping each other's backs, hugging, singing, dancing.

Though Clark was delighted to find Lewis among horses and friendly Indians, he soon learned that the overland trip had been no easy trick. Lewis's party had frightened off small groups of Shoshone twice before making successful contact. And he had had great difficulty convincing the Shoshone to accompany him back to the forks. Recently raided by the Atsina, they thought Lewis might be leading them into a trap. The situation had nearly unraveled on August 16 when the group did not find Clark at the forks, as expected. Everyone had spent a tense night, and the Shoshone—along with the precious chance to purchase horses—might have vanished the next day had Clark not arrived when he did.

Even so, the position remained delicately balanced. Most of the tribe, and nearly all the horses, were still on the west side of the divide. The Shoshone were half-starved, subsisting on roots and berries, and they were eager to bug out for the buffalo country near Three Forks. Holding them in place long enough to buy horses and get over Lemhi Pass would be difficult.

For the time being, spirits soared. The men, who had been nagging Clark to go overland for at least a week, were about to get their wish, as well as some time among the Shoshone women. The Shoshone, who were in sad want of

manufactured goods, were delighted to see that their customers had everything they could possibly want—guns, powder, lead, knives, cloth, beads, kettles, and much more.

Then, amid the general merriment, came two bombshells of goodwill. First, one of the Shoshone women recognized Sacagawea and ran to embrace her. Then, as Sacagawea sat translating for the captains, she suddenly realized that the Shoshone chief, Cameahwait, was her brother. She ran to him, hugged him, threw her blanket over him, and wept. Camp Fortunate indeed.

As shadows lengthened across today's Armstead Island, Lewis and Clark settled on a plan. Clark, Charbonneau, Sacagawea, and a party of 11 men with axes would accompany Cameahwait to his village. There, they would leave Charbonneau and Sacagawea to hurry the Indians and horses back over the pass while Clark and his men scouted the Lemhi and Salmon Rivers. If the route looked good, they would build canoes. In the meantime, Lewis and the rest of the men would repack the gear for horse travel, cache the canoes, and follow Clark over the divide.

All started according to plan. The next morning, the captains bought three horses, Lewis wrote, for a "uniform coat, a pair of legings, a few handkerchiefs, three knives and some other small articles the whole of which did not cost more than about 20$ in the U' States." The men bought another for "an old checked shirt a pair of old legings and a knife." Clark took two of the horses and led his party west over the divide with Cameahwait.

"Cameahwa it informed me...that the river [today's Salmon] was confined between inacessable mountains, was very rapid and rocky insomuch that it was impossible for us to pass... down this river to the great lake where the white men lived as he had been informed. this was unwelcome information but I still hoped that this account had been exaggerated."

MERIWETHER
LEWIS,
AUG. 13, 1805

Lewis and the remaining men immediately began making 20 pack saddles, harnesses, and other horse tack. Others made moccasins and buckskin clothing, seined the creeks for trout, hunted, sunk the canoes in a pond, and secretly dug a large cache pit. Lewis wrote extensively about the Shoshone. In the mornings, hard frost whitened the ground. Autumn was on its way.

After five days, Cameahwait returned with about 50 Shoshone, Charbonneau, Sacagawea, and many horses. More Indians arrived the following day, but they were on their way to the buffalo country and were not interested in helping with the portage. Lewis bought nine packhorses and a mule and left on the 24th, heavily laden and assisted by Cameahwait and some of his people. He estimated he would need to buy another 15 horses for the mountains ahead, and prices were rising.

Before you leave Clark Canyon Reservoir, consider a stroll along the **Cattail Marsh Nature Trail** (*Follow gravel fishing access road off Cty. Rd. 324*) below the dam, to get a feel for the thick riverside brush that compelled the expedition's boat crews to wade while towing their dugouts. You might also drive to the south end of the reservoir, where pronghorn, great blue herons, pelicans, gulls, ducks, and bald eagles are seen.

AUGUST 10–13, 1805

Over Lemhi Pass

Except for a few, widely spaced fence lines, one tiny town, and the occasional plume of dust behind a distant pickup truck, this outstanding backcountry route over Lemhi Pass tracks the expedition through country that looks almost exactly as it did in 1805. It starts at Camp Fortunate; tops out at the crest of the Continental Divide, where magnificent vistas spill away to the mountains of Montana and Idaho; and ends on the banks of the Lemhi River.

On the way, you can follow Lewis through the same open valley where he had his first tantalizing encounter with a Shoshone on horseback, straddle what he called "the most distant fountain of the waters of the mighty Missouri," and amble down the same grass hills he descended before making successful contact. It's a great 50-mile trip, half of it on pavement, half of it on good gravel and dirt suitable for trucks and most cars in summer and early autumn (*for road conditions and travel regulations, call the national forest service office in Dillon, 406-683-3900*). You can drive the whole distance in a couple of hours, but the setting is so compelling that you may feel rushed even if you set aside half a day.

From Camp Fortunate, follow County Road 324 along
Clark Canyon Reservoir's north shore. After several miles,
the hills open to the west and the road swings into the gap,
with Horse Prairie Creek hugging the hills to your right.
Lewis's advance party took the same turn on August 10, as
they anxiously sought contact with the Shoshone.

Soon, the hills fall away from the road, and you drive
out onto the expansive floor of **Horse Prairie.** "This plain,"
Lewis wrote, "Is surrounded on all sides by a country of
roling or high wavy plains through which several little
rivulets extend their wide vallies quite to the Mountains
which surround the whole in an apparent Circular manner;
forming one of the handsomest coves [valleys] I ever saw."

Near **Grant,** a gravel road cuts north across the valley.
The turnoff makes a good place to stop and reconstruct
Lewis's first encounter with a Shoshone, which happened
close to where the gravel road crosses the meandering line
of willows that marks Horse Prairie Creek.

Lewis and his men were walking west, widely spaced,
with Lewis and McNeal in the center, Drouillard to the
north, and Shields to the south, close to present County
Road 324. As they approached today's gravel road, Lewis
saw an Indian on horseback about 2 miles ahead.

"His arms," he wrote, "were a bow and a quiver of
arrows, and was mounted on an eligant horse without a
saddle, and a small string which was attatched to the
underjaw of the horse which answered as a bridle."

A Shoshone. Lewis was overjoyed, but worried. He knew
he had to approach the horseman carefully. Unarmed and

bearing gifts, he got within a hundred paces. Despite his cautious advance and reassuring gestures, Lewis could not stop Shields from flanking the skittish horseman. Perhaps suspecting a trap, the Indian "suddonly turned his hose about, gave him the whip leaped the creek and disapeared in the willow brush in an instant and with him vanished all my hopes of obtaining horses for the preasent."

If only Lewis had brought Sacagawea, his quest for the Shoshone might well have ended here. Instead, his party tracked the horse to the base of the hills across the valley, where they lost its trail among the tracks of other horses. From there, they followed the hills northwest, camping beneath the forested peaks that wall off the valley's far end.

To pick up their trail, continue west on County Road 324 for 10.5 miles beyond Grant. If the road is dry, take the turnoff for **Lemhi Pass.** Proceed a mile or two until the road falls in with **Trail Creek,** which Lewis struck August 12 and followed to the Continental Divide. Today's gravel and dirt road follows pretty much the same course.

Despite the disappointments of the previous day, Lewis's party marched triumphantly up this narrow stream. Two miles below the pass, Lewis wrote, McNeal "exultingly stood with a foot on each side of this little rivulet and thanked his god that he had lived to bestride the mighty & heretofore deemed endless Missouri."

As you approach Lemhi Pass, you might resist—as Lewis did—the temptation to rush right to the crest of the divide. Look, instead, for the left turn that cuts across the slope to a shady grove of evergreens. There, just below the picnic area, you'll find a tiny spring welling from the ground—Lewis's most distant fountain of the Missouri, "in surch of which we have spent so many toilsome days and wristless nights." He and the men sat near this place, savoring the moment.

"Thus far I had accomplished one of those great objects on which my mind has been unalterably fixed for many years," Lewis wrote. "Judge then of the pleasure I felt in allying my thirst with this pure and ice cold water."

After a short rest, the men walked up the slope above the pass, an open saddle of sagebrush, grass, and wildflowers that drops sharply to the west and faces a vast and wrinkled land packed to the horizon with deceptively gentle mountain crests. The pass now marks the Continental Divide and the border between Montana and Idaho, but in 1805, it marked the western boundary of the United States.

Lewis and the men paused here, gazing into the mountain barrier that stood between them and the Pacific Ocean, then angled down into the velvety hills to your right, keeping to the heavily traveled Indian road. Within a mile, they struck Horseshoe Bend Creek, where they "first tasted the water of the great Columbia River," and then continued "over steep hills and deep hollows to a spring." There, they ate the last of their 15-month-old pork and camped.

Before continuing into Idaho, consider taking some time to walk. A trail to your left leads down to Agency Creek, but you can also strike off into the open hills to your right. Either way, you'll get a clear sense for why Lewis and Clark longed for Shoshone horses.

Monument to Sacagawea, north of Tendoy

AUGUST 13–15, 1805
Tendoy Area

Cradled amid the Beaverhead Mountains, this small town lies near the site where Lewis finally caught up with the Shoshone and where he spent two hungry days among them before heading back over the pass with Cameahwait to rejoin Clark.

From Tendoy, dawdle north on the dirt-and-gravel road that runs from the Tendoy Store along the east side of the Lemhi River. About a mile from town, you'll find the **Monument to Sacagawea,** a small block of granite indentifying Lemhi Valley as her birthplace. In the dry foothills northeast of this spot, Lewis finally made his pivotal contact with the Shoshone.

Traveling north, he topped a crease in the hills and there, just 30 paces ahead, were two women and a girl. He was able to approach them, give them presents, and paint their cheeks with vermilion as a token of peace. Meanwhile, others had spotted Lewis and alerted the village.

"We had marched about 2 miles," Lewis wrote, "when we met a party of about 60 warriors mounted on excellent horses who came in nearly full speed."

Lewis set aside his gun and walked forward holding an American flag. The women held up their presents, shouted, smiled. Seeing that Lewis was not an enemy, the Shoshone leaders dismounted and embraced him "very affectionately in their way which is by puting their left arm over you wright sholder clasping your back, while they apply their left cheek to yours." Soon, both groups had fallen together "and we wer all carresed and besmeared with their grease and paint till I was heartily tired of the national hug."

AUGUST 13–15, 1805

First Shoshone Village Site

◆ N OF TENDOY AT SANDY CREEK, ON PRIVATE PROPERTY

After a friendly smoke in the hills, Lewis and the Shoshone walked down to the Indians' village, which stood along the river near **Sandy Creek.** The setting has not changed much. Lewis saw the same wandering ribbon of cotton-woods along the river, the same ramp of bare hills and hulking, broad-backed mountains across the valley. And he was very happy to see hundreds of horses grazing on what are still wide meadows of lush grass.

The Shoshone had had a tough year. Raided by the Atsina that spring, they had lost 20 people, many horses, and all of their tepees. They were living in brush shelters, and now that the salmon runs were on the wane they had very little to eat. Still, they did their best for Lewis and the men, who had walked 20 miles on empty stomachs. The Indians gave them cakes of dried berries and danced for them late into the night.

During the evening, Lewis was also served a piece of grilled salmon—which "perfectly convinced me that we were on the waters of the Pacific Ocean." True enough, but, as Cameahwait told him, after the Lemhi joins the Salmon River, the water route quickly becomes impassable, at least for dugout canoes.

Lewis remained the next day, "hungary as a wolf" with nothing to eat but flour paste and berries. His men hunted from borrowed horses, but came back empty-handed. So did the Shoshone, who chased a herd of ten pronghorn back and forth across these hills and gullies at full speed for two hours without getting close enough to draw a bow.

During the day, Lewis asked Cameahwait—through Drouillard's proficient sign language—to return with him to Camp Fortunate with horses and porters in order to help the expedition pack its gear over Lemhi Pass. Cameahwait seemed to comply, but the next morning the Shoshone, leary of a trap, were very reluctant to move. Lewis assured them of his good intentions, threatened to block future trade of guns and ammunition, and, as an extra prod,

> *"Notwith-standing their extreem poverty they are not only cheerfull but even gay, fond of gaudy dress and amuse-ments.... they are frank, com-municative, fair in deal-ing, generous with the little they possess, extreemly honest, and by no means beggarly."*
>
> MERIWETHER LEWIS, ON THE LEMHI SHOSHONE, AUG. 19, 1805

questioned their valor. Finally, Cameahwait and a handful of Shoshone set off with Lewis and his men.

AUGUST 20 & 26–30, 1805

Second Shoshone Village Site

◆ N OF TENDOY AT KENNEY CREEK, ON PRIVATE PROPERTY

After Lewis and Cameahwait departed, the Shoshone moved their village south to the vicinity of Kenney Creek, where on August 20 Clark found the Shoshone after marching west over Lemhi Pass with Cameahwait.

There, Clark spoke with the Shoshone about what lay ahead. Thanks to Sacagawea's presence, he got a detailed and discouraging account of both the Salmon River and an overland route across the deserts of southern Idaho. That left just one unappealing alternative: the Lolo Trail, an arduous route to the northwest used by the Nez Perce to cross over the Bitterroots into buffalo country.

Rather than take anyone's word about the Salmon, Clark hired a Shoshone guide, whom he called Old Toby, and set off the same day to see the Salmon River route for himself. He and the 11 men with him would be gone for nine days.

In the meantime, Lewis and the rest of the men packed the gear over Lemhi Pass, aided by Cameahwait and many of the Shoshone. The Indians came very close to ditching Lewis, and who could blame them? They were starving within a day's ride of abundant game. Still, Lewis managed to shame them into continuing the portage and staying here on Kenney Creek until the end of August while he bought horses, saddles, and pack cords from them.

Clark returned on August 29, "perfictly satisfyed," Lewis said, "as to the impractability of this [Salmon River] rout either by land or water." Set on following the Lolo Trail, they bought 29 horses at constantly escalating prices. The Shoshone knew a captive market when they saw one. As trading drew to a close, the captains paid a musket for one horse; Clark's own pistol, a hundred rounds of ammunition, and a knife for another.

The expedition needed horses not only to pack its gear, but also, perhaps, to eat. Food was on everyone's mind. Clark and his reconnaissance crew had come back skinny. "My party," he had written, are "hourly Complaining of their retched Situation and doubts of Starveing in a

Snagging Salmon

As described by Clark, the Shoshone strapped a sharp bone, about 6 inches long, to the ends of their gigging poles with a cord about a foot long. The fisherman would wade in the river or walk along the bank, probing with his pole. When he felt a salmon, he'd jam the bone right through the fish. The bone would slip from the pole and, because it was tied through their middle, would snag like a button on the far side of the fish. All the fisherman had to do then was haul the writhing salmon to the bank and knock it on the head.

Countrey where no game of any kind except a fiew fish can be found." Things would get much worse in the weeks ahead.

Idaho 28 continues north through **Baker** and the Lemhi Range, bending around the northern spur of the mountains near **Salmon.** As the mountains fall behind, badland foothills close in from either side of the valley, and the meandering tree lines of the Lemhi and Salmon Rivers converge.

Along this stretch, the expedition followed the same course Clark had scouted earlier in the month. As he had descended, Clark had kept running into small groups of Shoshone gigging and trapping salmon (see sidebar p. 119), including one group, northwest of Baker, that had built an elaborate fish weir. The Shoshone gave Clark all the boiled salmon and chokecherries his men could eat, as well as several dried fish for the road. But things had changed by the time the combined party came through. The salmon run was drying up and these same Shoshone could no longer afford to be so generous. The captains bought fish.

AUGUST 31, 1805

Salmon

Surrounded by low, desertlike hills, bands of cream-colored cliffs, and high forested mountains, this town lies at the confluence of the dazzling Salmon and Lemhi Rivers. Clark's reconnaissance crew paused at the confluence, but the combined party hurried down the east side of the valley, passing through on the morning of August 31.

As Idaho 28 approaches Salmon from the east, look for the **Sacajawea Interpretive Cultural and Education Center** *(Idaho 28, 208-756-3214).* This small but excellent facility focuses on Lemhi Shoshone culture, Sacagawea, and the tribe's relations with Lewis and Clark. Exhibits include reproductions of traditional Shoshone clothing, equipment, and weapons, historical photos of Shoshone people, and a large topographic map that pinpoints expedition events from Dillon to the Salmon River.

More than a building, the center faces the Beaverhead Mountains and takes in a wide swath of lush bottomland along the Lemhi River. Interpretive trails ring the property and loop along the river through stands of cottonwood and willow. Lewis and Clark must have walked along stretches of the river that looked very much like this. Also outside, you'll find an interpretive Shoshone tepee village, a stick hut encampment, and a fish weir similar to the one sketched in the captains' journals.

Another rewarding site is the confluence itself, on the north side of town, at the **Lemhi Hole Fishing Access**

(Right turn off US 93). There, the Lemhi spills into the Salmon over a gravel bank lined with cottonwoods, and the combined current rushes north toward the Beaverhead Mountains. Here, Clark's reconnaissance party came upon some Shoshone who gave them five salmon.

Standing here today, with this large, swift, and apparently navigable river coasting past your feet, it's hard to imagine that Clark's hopes for a river route did not rise when he first saw the Salmon. Quick, smooth, pooling to emerald green, the river does in fact provide a fine and steady water route all the way to the town of North Fork that even casual boaters can float in less than a day.

It's beyond North Fork that the river gets hairy—and quite a bit more fun, if you like white water. For a list of outfitters, contact the Salmon Valley Chamber of Commerce *(208-756-2100).*

AUGUST 21 & 31, 1805
Tower Rock Campground

◆ 11 MILES N OF SALMON ON US 93

North of Salmon, the dry hills and low cliffs flanking both sides of the valley approach the river, nearly pinching it off at this prominent knob of rusting sandstone where Clark and his reconnaissance party camped on August 21. Over a supper of venison and salmon, Clark admired Tower Rock, the surrounding hills, cliffs, and, of course, the handsome river.

Before turning in, he wrote, "I shall in justice to Capt Lewis who was the first white man ever on this fork of the Columbia Call this Louis's river."

Later in the month, the combined party walked their horses a mile past this point and turned right, following Tower Creek up into the steep, dry hills. Today, you can trace their route on a gravel road that parallels Tower Creek and dead-ends about a half mile from their camp *(Now private land).* Thickets of chokecherry and serviceberry crowd the banks, just as they did in 1805, when the men trudged beside the stream, picking handfuls of ripe fruit.

Beyond Tower Rock, road and river follow Clark's reconnaissance route through a rugged desertlike canyon. This is what the combined party avoided by ascending Tower Creek and marching northwest to the North Fork Salmon River. You can hike across the same hills by following a 6-mile trail from **Wagonhammer Springs Picnic Area** *(2 miles S of North Fork)* to **Trail Gulch** *(3 miles N of North Fork).* To reach the trail, follow the road beyond the locked gate from the picnic area for 1.5 miles and look for the trailhead. The trail offers tremendous vistas of the river bottomlands, winding like a precious ribbon of green beneath the bare, velveteen slopes of the mountains.

AUGUST 22–24, 1805
North Fork

This small crossroads town stands at the confluence of the Salmon and North Fork Salmon Rivers, where Clark's reconnaissance route turned abruptly west and followed the Salmon into the awesome gorge that closes on the river just a few miles from town. To the north, US 93 picks up the approximate route that the combined party took over the Continental Divide and into the Bitterroot Valley.

It would be a shame to pass up a detour down the Salmon. A good road heads west from the town of North Fork and hugs the river for more than 20 miles, leading past the thundering rapids, soaring cliffs, and steep gravelly mountainsides that dashed Clark's hopes for a water route. The scenery, spectacular from the start, gets better the farther you go, and you can see deer, bighorn sheep, and elk among the bottomlands and forests of ponderosa pine.

Clark got only 8 or 9 miles into the canyon before the horses could go no farther. He, Old Toby, and three others clambered down the banks another 12 miles and climbed a mountain near Shoup before calling it quits. Cameahwait had been right. The river route was out. Each of the five rapids they'd passed since leaving the horses behind would require portaging the loads over slippery rocks and lining the empty canoes down rough water. One portage would demand "Cutting down the Side of the hill" and removing large rocks. What's more, game was scarce along the river. Even if they could force their way through the canyons, they might starve.

As Lewis put it while traveling down the Lemhi, "The season is now far advanced to remain in these mountains as the Indians inform us we shall shortly have snow; the salmon have so far declined that they are themselves haistening from the country and not an animal of any discription is to be seen in this difficult part of the river larger than a pheasant or a squirrel and they not abundant; add to this that our stock of provision is now so low that it would not support us more than ten days."

SEPTEMBER 1–4, 1805
Over Lost Trail Pass

◆ VIA US 93

After making their northwest traverse from Tower Creek, Lewis and Clark halted for the night on the North Fork Salmon River's east bank, somewhere near the mouth of **Hull Creek** *(4 miles N of North Fork)*, where steep grassy slopes rise from a gentle meadow. While some of the men

North Fork Salmon River

pitched sailcloth shelters and turned the horses out to graze, others gigged salmon from the river or rode down to North Fork to buy dried salmon from some Shoshone camped there.

In the morning, they got off to an easy start, following a well-beaten Indian trail through the same meadows and open stands of ponderosa pine that flank today's highway. Then as now, the route steepened, the forests thickened, and the mountain slopes closed in on the river. Near present **Gibbonsville,** the trail they had been following turned east, leaving them without a path as they continued north into the steepest, most rugged country the Corps had encountered so far.

"Proceded on," Clark wrote, "thro' thickets in which we were obliged to Cut a road, over rockey hill Sides where our horses were in pitial danger of Slipping to Ther certain distruction & up & Down Steep hills, where several horses fell, Some turned over, and others Sliped down Steep hill Sides, one horse Crippeled & 2 gave out."

Snowy white-bark pine, Lost Trail Pass

They bushwhacked for about 5 miles and camped in a thicket close to US 93, within a few miles of Gibbonsville, perhaps somewhat south.

To get a general feel for this difficult terrain, stop at **Twin Creek Campground**—or any convenient turnout—and plunge into the woods. Don't bother looking for a trail. Beneath the dense canopy of Engelmann spruce and subalpine fir, you'll find tangles of fallen tree trunks, thickets of prickly brush, mucky depressions, and slopes steep enough to require hands and feet. It's bad enough today without a trail; much worse in moccasins, tugging at the halter of a stumbling horse.

The expedition struggled through more of the same the following day, with snow, rain, and sleet piled on. They camped in the slop, somewhere along the Continental Divide not far from **Lost Trail Pass** (where exactly is in dispute). They had nothing to divide between 34 mouths but nine grouse and a little cornmeal. In the morning, they woke to a hard frost and had to thaw their sailcloth shelters by the fires before they could pack them up. Their moccasins were frozen. The snow was ankle deep. Their fingers ached with cold, and they were beginning to relish the thought of horsemeat.

From the pass, US 93 plunges down into a narrow, heavily wooded chasm. The party stumbled down the prominent, clear-cut mountain to your left, which is called **Saddle Mountain.** As they descended, the hungry men saw several bighorn sheep, but none were close enough to shoot.

SEPTEMBER 4, 1805

Indian Trees Campground

◆ 7 MILES N OF LOST TRAIL PASS, OFF US 93

This beautiful grove of immense ponderosa pines stands at the base of Saddle Mountain, where Lewis and Clark finally set foot again on relatively flat, relatively open ground. They reached the valley floor somewhere between the forks of Camp Creek, which join just below the present campground, and stopped to enjoy their first decent meal in two days, a fine deer that one of the men had killed. Today's highway runs through the same grassy valley, following Camp Creek north to Sula.

The "Flathead" or Salish People

The English name "Flathead" for the Salish-speaking people of western Montana possibly derives from the sign language designation for the tribe, which consisted of pressing both sides of the head in a flattening motion. The Salish did not practice head flattening.

The Salish acquired horses around 1700 and became buffalo hunters on the Montana plains, but pressure from the Blackfeet and other tribes forced them to spend much of their time west of the Continental Divide. They lived in much the same way as the Lemhi Shoshone—fishing the western rivers part of the year, then crossing to the buffalo country in the autumn.

The Confederated Salish and Kootenai Tribes still live on their ancestral homelands in western Montana.

SEPTEMBER 4–6, 1805

Sula

As you approach Sula on US 93, the mountain ridge to your right slants down to a small, semi-circular valley of hay fields and willow thickets surrounded by low, sparsely wooded hills. This pleasant spot, known as **Ross's Hole,** is where Lewis and Clark met a band of about 400 Flathead, or Salish, Indians, who were on their way to the Missouri River buffalo country. They had pitched 33 tepees near the eastern edge of the valley—perhaps a stone's throw from Sula's tiny general store—and their herd of at least 500 horses grazed on the grassy flats beyond. "Those people recved us friendly," Clark wrote, "threw white robes over our Sholders & Smoked in the pipes of peace, we Encamped with them…The Chiefs harangued untill late at night."

If the men had hoped for a feast, they were disappointed. The Salish were down to cakes of serviceberries and chokecherries, which they were happy to share. But times were tough for everyone west of the divide, including the Indians' dogs, who ate several pairs of the expedition's moccasins while the men slept.

"It is hear a handsome stream about 100 yards wide and affords a considerable quantity of very clear water, the banks are low and it's bed entirely gravel. the stream appears navigable, but from the circumstance of their being no sammon in it I believe that there must be a considerable fall in it below."

MERIWETHER
LEWIS, ON THE
BITTERROOT RIVER,
SEPT. 9, 1805

The next day, Lewis and Clark spoke formally with the Salish chiefs, explaining as best they could the purposes of the expedition through a five-language translation chain. Afterward, the captains bought 13 more horses, and the Salish generously exchanged seven of the Corps's worn-out ponies for what Clark called "ellegant horses."

On September 6, both parties broke camp and set off during the afternoon in opposite directions. The Salish headed for the buffalo country, while the expedition crossed the low mountain (Sula Peak) on the west side of Ross's Hole and picked up the East Fork Bitterroot River.

SEPTEMBER 6–9, 1805

Down the Bitterroot River

Beyond Ross's Hole, US 93 follows the East Fork Bitterroot River through a short, narrow canyon crowded with low cliffs and dense thickets of shrubs and trees. No wonder Lewis and Clark detoured over Sula Peak—they'd had their fill of steep, rocky terrain and thick underbrush. The expedition rejoined the East Fork and camped near **Spring Gulch Campground** (*Off US 93*), where you can stroll in the shade of large ponderosa pines and watch the pristine river glide and pool beneath the steep cliffs of Sula Peak.

At **Conner,** the West Fork Bitterroot River joins the East Fork to form the Bitterroot, which the captains called Clark's River. Soon, the valley begins to open up and the high jagged crest of the Bitterroot Range swings into view. This was Lewis and Clark's first daunting sight of the worst the Bitterroots could dish out—vast amphitheaters of gray rock and snow jutting thousands of feet above what they knew to be rugged, densely timbered foothills. They made about 22 miles under a dark, drizzling sky and made another hungry camp on the east bank, 4 miles south of **Hamilton.**

For the best views of the Bitterroots' capacious glacial troughs, cirques, and high cliffs, follow the signs through Hamilton for the Daly Mansion, and continue north on County Road 269.

The expedition traveled on the same side of the river, camping near **Stevensville** in a hard, steady rain. "We are all Cold and wet," Clark wrote. But not hungry. The hunters brought in an elk and a deer.

Continuing north, you might stroll through **Lee Metcalf National Wildlife Refuge** (*2 miles N of Stevensville on Cty. Rd. 203*), where a mile loop trail leads to the Bitterroot River beneath widely spaced ponderosa pines and cottonwoods. White-tailed deer wade the fields of waist-high grass and Canada geese nest in the trees. The expedition shot both while moving through the area September 9.

SEPTEMBER 9–11, 1805

Lolo

♦ 12 MILES SW OF MISSOULA ON US 93

A historical marker just south of town identifies the general area of **Traveler's Rest,** where Lewis and Clark paused to give the men a break and to build up a surplus of meat before setting off on the Lolo Trail. Though the site is now surrounded by residential subdivisions, it's still easy to see how the opening in the mountains to the west would have offered a much better passage than anything Lewis and Clark had seen since crossing Lemhi Pass.

As the party approached Traveler's Rest, Old Toby told the captains about a nearby river that flowed in from the east and joined the Bitterroot River a short distance to the north (today's Clark Fork). He said that it led to the Continental Divide and that by following it on horseback

Raft trip through Idaho-Selway-Bitterroot Wilderness

you could reach Gates of the Mountains in four days. This meant that if the expedition had obtained horses near the gates in mid-July, they could have crossed the mountains near present-day Helena and avoided seven weeks of travel on the upper Jefferson and Beaverhead Rivers.

Lolo Trail Adventures

The folks at Lewis and Clark Trail Adventures (Box 9051, Missoula, MT 59801. 406-728-7609 or 800-366-6246) offer three-day guided mountain bike trips along the Lolo Trail, as well as guided day and overnight hikes. They also run white-water rafting and canoe trips down the Missouri, Yellowstone, Lochsa, and Clark Fork Rivers.

Lewis and Clark would explore alternate routes to the Missouri on their return in 1806. For now, they looked west and got encouraging news from three Nez Perce warriors who had just crossed the Lolo Trail. They said the trip took just six days, and that the expedition would find their tribe living on a navigable tributary of the Columbia River. They were in a hurry, chasing Shoshone horse thieves. Two warriors left after eating boiled venison. "The third remained," Lewis wrote, "having agreed to continue with us as a guide, and to introduce us to his relations." What a stroke of luck that would have been. But, the man had second thoughts the next day and rode off.

SEPTEMBER 11–22, 1805

The Lolo Trail

◆ LOLO TO WEIPPE VIA US 12

This well-established Nez Perce route over the Bitterroot Range would have confronted the Corps of Discovery with great difficulties even under the best circumstances. It crosses some of the most rugged and remote country in the Rockies, where row upon crooked row of dark-forested mountains plunge thousands of feet into a vast and confusing maze of narrow, steep-sided canyons. Difficult at best. But with little game to shoot and weather freezing wet to endure, the Lolo savaged the Corps, turning their 12-day, 170-mile passage over the Bitterroots into an excruciating race against starvation.

Their survival was a triumph over the worst conditions they faced anywhere on the entire journey from St. Louis to the Pacific. Elsewhere—at Great Falls and later along the Columbia River estuary—the expedition contended with exhaustion, illness, danger, cold, and wet. But it was always on relatively full stomachs. Here on the Lolo Trail, the men would add hunger to those hardships—prolonged and intense hunger, which sapped their strength when a herculean effort was required.

The Lolo Trail starts at **Lolo,** follows Lolo Creek to Lolo Pass, and then heads southwest along forested ridge tops of

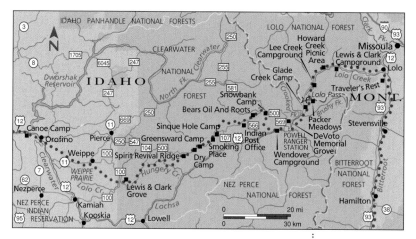

Clearwater National Forest before descending to open country at the tiny Idaho town of **Weippe.** Partway across, Lewis and Clark diverged from that general route for two days, stumbling down to the area around the Powell Ranger Station (known informally as **Powell;** see p. 132) before climbing back to the trail.

Today, US 12 roughly parallels their course from Lolo to Powell. But from Powell to Weippe, primitive back roads offer the only access to the expedition's route.

Heading west on US 12, you can see that Lewis and Clark had good traveling for at least a dozen miles. The valley floor is open and the climb gradual. After camping at the mouth of **Woodman Creek,** though, the men were forced into the wooded hills on what Clark called a "most intolerable road on the Sides of the Steep Stoney mountains."

They reached **Grave Creek** *(US 12)* at noon, lunched on four deer, and picked handfuls of serviceberries (deer and berries are still here). After their meal, they pushed on until early evening and camped about 2 miles northeast of **Lolo Hot Springs.**

To retrace a portion of their march, stop at **Howard Creek Picnic Area** *(3 miles past the Lewis and Clark Campground),* where you can hike a well-marked 0.5-mile round-trip section of the original Lolo Trail through a thick forest to a steep, grassy slope offering vistas of the mountains near Lolo Pass.

The expedition paused at **Lolo Hot Springs** *(25 miles SW of Lolo on US 12. 406-273-2290. Adm. fee),* where the men washed their faces, drank water, and continued on. Sgt. John Ordway noted that "a little dam was fixed and had been used for a bathing place." The dam has been replaced by a large commercial pool, and the bathing is still a pleasure.

" We fell on a Small Creek from the left which Passed through open glades Some of which ½ a mile wide, we proceeded down this Creek about 2 miles to where the mountains Closed on either Side crossing the Creek Several times & Encamped. "

WILLIAM CLARK,
AT LOLO PASS,
SEPT. 13, 1805

A couple of miles beyond the hot springs, you'll get another chance to hike the Lolo, from **Lee Creek Campground.** Clark called this stretch a "tolerabl rout" through "pine Countery falling timber &c. &c." A maintained path, **Wagon Mountain Trail #300,** climbs for 5 miles through thick forest, crossing over a relatively gentle ridge to the upper end of **Packer Meadows** near Lolo Pass.

SEPTEMBER 13, 1805

Lolo Pass Area

◆ VIA US 12

After climbing out of the Lolo Creek drainage, Lewis and Clark followed a series of open meadows, or glades, along this broad and otherwise deeply forested saddle in the Bitterroots. They camped at the lower end of the meadows, within a mile or so of the pass, on a small stream they called Glade Creek (now Pack Creek). Today, their campsite and the meadows they descended look much as they did in 1805. Both lie within easy reach of the revamped **Lolo Pass Visitor Center,** which will open during the summer of 2003 with expanded Lewis and Clark exhibits. Though the expedition's passage of the Lolo is presented here in satisfying detail, the center will cast a much broader net by taking in the entire history of the route's use by Native American peoples, principally the Nez Perce. It also celebrates native cultures and touches on the natural history of the Bitterroot region, settlement, the Nez Perce War of 1877, and modern forestry issues.

A massive, three-dimensional relief map depicting the Lolo Trail corridor is planned to orient visitors to modern roads. It will clearly mark the arduous route followed by Lewis and Clark. Above the exhibits, an extensive mural will wrap around the walls, offering glimpses of landscapes and important Lolo Trail landmarks such as Weippe Prairie, Indian Post Office, and Packer Meadows.

The Lewis and Clark exhibits are scheduled to focus on the expedition's starvation trek over the Lolo in 1805, its relations with the Nez Perce and Salish-Kootenai, and its much easier journey back over the Lolo in 1806. Here, too, a modest assortment of reproduced expedition artifacts, as well as summaries of the captains' accomplishments in

botany, zoology, and mapmaking are expected. But perhaps most interesting for those well versed in Lewis and Clark's story are plans to present the Indian accounts, from oral tradition, that describe meeting the Corps in 1805.

To reach the upper end of **Packer Meadows,** where the expedition topped Lolo Pass, head south from the visitor center on Forest Road 373 (gravel). Within a mile or so, the trees fall away to your right, revealing a broad meadow. Lewis and Clark's long string of packhorses and buck-skinned men entered here in the evening and headed off to your right, following the stream that cuts through the lush bed of grass and camas plants. Double back to the visitor center and pick up Forest Road 5670 to the Corps's **Glade Creek Camp.**

SEPTEMBER 14, 1805
DeVoto Memorial Grove

◆ 10 MILES SW OF LOLO PASS ON US 12

This misty enclave of massive cedar, spruce, and fir trees preserves a remnant of the type of old-growth forest Lewis and Clark encountered after stumbling down from Lolo

Pass. Some of these awesome trees are 3,000 years old, with trunk diameters of 4 to 5 feet. All tower over a short loop trail that leads across a mossy bed of ferns and shrubs to the rushing waters of Crooked Fork.

The Corps struggled along the crest of the steep ridge that rises directly across from the stream. They were having a rough day—rain, hail, snow, and sleet—with men and horses groping over endless tangles of fallen timber. Downstream, they stumbled off the ridge and down to the headwaters of the Lochsa River and an abandoned fishing camp.

Slim Pickings on the Lolo

In the autumn of 1805, game was so scarce in the Bitterroot Range that the Corps's accomplished hunters managed to kill just slightly more than one day's worth of meat from September 11 to 21. To eat well, by Lewis's yardstick of four deer per day, the hunters needed to bag roughly 45 deer while on the Lolo Trail. Instead, they killed five, along with one stray horse, a dozen or so grouse, a duck, a coyote, and some crayfish. The men also slaughtered three colts from their own herd and depleted their meager stores of cornmeal, portable soup, and bear oil.

SEPTEMBER 14, 1805

Powell Ranger Station

◆ 4 MILES SW OF DEVOTO MEMORIAL GROVE, OFF US 12 ◆ 208-942-3113

After eking out 17 arduous miles from Lolo Pass, the Corps camped on the Lochsa River in what is now a residential and staging area for the Forest Service. From the ranger station, you can walk down to the river—a glass-clear sheet of fast water—and stand pretty much where the Corps roasted its first meal of horsemeat.

"[We] had nothing to eat but Some portable Soup," Ordway wrote in his journal. "We being hungry for meat as the Soup did not Satisfy we killed a fat colt which eat verry well at this time."

By now, the captains knew that their guide, Old Toby, had taken a wrong turn and that they would have to climb back out of the Lochsa Valley to regain the Lolo Trail. Before following in their footsteps, be sure to pick up a map of the Lolo Motorway from the ranger station.

SEPTEMBER 15, 1805

Wendover Campground

◆ 4 MILES W OF POWELL OFF US 12

From Powell, the expedition continued downriver for about 4 miles, fighting through what is still thick brush and deadfall, to the vicinity of this pleasant riverside campground and picnic area. Here, they began their 3,000-foot climb into the mountains to the north.

The road up, Clark said, was "as bad as it can possibly be to pass"—steep and crammed with fallen trees. Horses slipped and rolled, slamming into tree trunks. One smashed Clark's writing desk. Two others gave out and were left behind (but not, oddly enough, killed for meat).

You can still hike this important section of the Lewis and Clark Trail, which is marked across the road from the campground entrance. The 7-mile trail climbs through densely wooded terrain that is steep, challenging, and beautiful. Though today's hiker may think of it as a rugged backcountry path, Lewis and Clark would have considered this maintained trail a good highway.

To continue with the expedition through the mountains, double back toward the Powell Ranger Station and the Lolo Motorway.

SEPTEMBER 15–22, 1805

The Lolo Motorway

◆ POWELL TO WEIPPE VIA FOREST ROADS ◆ 208-942-3113

Still wild and often deserted, this backcountry route hugs the Lolo Trail across the lonely country of the Bitterroot Range, passing through deep forests and meadows to astounding vistas and some of the most evocative Lewis and Clark sites anywhere. Check with the Clearwater forest about current road conditions and the need for permits *(208-926-4272)*. The roads are recommended for high-clearance vehicles only, for whom 10 miles an hour still seems a bit reckless. Fallen trees can stop or even trap travelers unequipped with saws. You can explore for a day from either end of the route, but the entire trip takes two or three days, with one relatively easy bail-out point. There are no campgrounds, no toilets, no sources of potable water—just magnificent landscapes and the resonating presence of Lewis and Clark.

Just east of Powell, turn north on Forest Road 569, which climbs steeply for about 9 miles through thick woods and open, clear-cut slopes before striking the Lolo Trail at the junction with Forest Road 109. There, a ten-minute walk through bear grass and huckleberries leads to a panorama of the Bitterroots at **13 Mile Camp,** an open, south-facing saddle where the expedition grazed horses and spent the night during its return trip in June 1806.

Continuing west, pick up Forest Road 500 and bump along for 6 miles to **Snowbank Camp.** This anonymous wooded slope is where the Corps slept after its exhausting climb from the Lochsa on the 15th. (The modern trail approximating their ascent joins the road a quarter mile east of the historical marker.) Here, they found a snowbank for water and made a thin stew from grouse, portable soup, and what was left of the colt. They woke to 4 inches of fresh snow, with more falling. Before setting off, Clark saw several

" We dined & suped on a skant proportion of portable soupe, a few canesters of which, a little bears oil and about 20 lbs. of candles form our stock of provision, the only recources being our guns & pack-horses. the first is but a poor dependance in our present situation where there is nothing upon earth exept ourselves and a few small pheasants, small grey Squirrels, and a bluebird"

MERIWETHER
LEWIS,
AT DRY CAMP,
SEPT. 18, 1805

fat mule deer nearby, but his rifle misfired seven times. And so, Ordway wrote, "we mended up our mockasons and Set out without any thing to eat, and proceeded on."

Forest Road 500 closely follows their grueling route, passing another return trip campsite called **Bears Oil and Roots.** Wet snow fell on the expedition all day and made the trail nearly impossible to follow. Clark went ahead, often guided only by the rub marks left on trees by passing Nez Perce packhorses. Snow sloughed off the branches, soaking them all, and the clouds were so low and thick, Ordway wrote, "that we could not See any distance no way."

The party slogged on to the vicinity of **Indian Post Office,** a string of rock cairns built along the spiny crest of an open ridge top, with a sea of forbidding peaks undulating off in all directions. The Corps camped somewhere in the thick forest that drops off to your right, in 8 inches of fresh snow. "I have been wet and as cold in every part as I ever was in my life," Clark wrote. "Indeed I was at one time fearfull my feet would freeze in the thin mockersons which I wore…men all wet cold and hungary."

Their evening meal? Another colt.

The historical marker for this camp, called **Lonesome Cove,** indicates a trail that leads about a mile to the probable site. There is no such trail today, but staggering down there into the bear grass and deadfall is certainly instructive.

From Lonesome Cove, the road bends south of Lewis and Clark's route of September 17—another wretched day of crashing through deep forest on empty bellies. The weather had warmed and the snow was melting, but with food virtually nonexistent and no end of the mountains in sight, morale was dropping fast.

As you drive this portion, you'll pass a bail out from the Lolo (FR 107) after 8 miles, and soon regain the expedition's route at **Sinque Hole Camp.** There, a brisk, 10-minute walk on a well-marked trail leads to the Corps's camp of the 17th, a rocky knob beside a marshy spring. Here, the captains decided Clark and six others should hurry ahead to good hunting country and send back meat while the rest of the expedition labored on. Clark set off the next morning and sprinted ahead for three days. He never found good hunting, but he did find the Nez Perce,

The Nez Perce

Named for the French words meaning, "pierced noses," the Nez Perce call themselves *nimí pu,* meaning "the real people." After acquiring the horse, their trips across the Rockies to buffalo country became easier, though they continued to fish for salmon on the western rivers. Noted for raising the spotted Appaloosa horse, the tribe enjoyed friendly relations with people of European descent until 1863, when gold on Nez Perce land led whites to demand a 90 percent reduction in the tribe's reservation.

In 1877, as the U.S. government forced the last of the "non-treaty Nez Perce" onto the new reservation, war broke out.

Today, the Nez Perce live on a portion of their ancestral homelands near Lewiston, in northwestern Idaho.

which was even better.

Meanwhile, Lewis and the rest of the party ate the last of the colts and toiled onward, logging 18 miles along the route of the present road to **Dry Camp,** another anonymous site on a steep forested ridge where the men had to fetch water for their portable soup from a ravine a half mile away. This stretch takes in two more return trip sites in June 1806: the **Smoking Place** and **Greensward Camp.**

Beyond Dry Camp, Lewis's party trudged up today's Sherman Peak and got their first view of the end of the trail— open prairies far to the west. Lewis wrote, "The appearance of this country, our only hope for subsistance greatly revived the sperits of the party already reduced and much weakened for the want of food." Today's trail to **Spirit Revival Ridge** on Sherman Peak leads to a similar panorama of vast forests diminishing to a mere wisp of plain. Lewis said the plain looked about 60 miles distant, "but our guide assured us that we should reach its borders tomorrow."

Sinque Hole Camp

Not quite. Lewis's group struggled on for four more days before emerging from the forest near the town of **Weippe.** Most of their route lies well off the present road. The men were getting scrawny, sick, weak. Some had dysentery and many had broken out with boils. With them every step of the way was Sacagawea, tending her infant. But in the midst of this grim ordeal came some welcome relief: Clark had hung part of a horse he had killed beside the trail and thus provided two good meals. By then, the Corps had descended into a warmer, moister climate, where large cedar trees measuring 2 to 6 feet in diameter were common. A remnant of that forest stands at **Lewis & Clark Grove** *(1.5 miles NE of FR 500 on FR 520).* Lewis passed through on the 21st, noting several "sticks" large enough "to form eligant perogues of at least 45 feet in length."

Lewis's party made its last hardship bivouac at **Pheasant Camp** *(1 mile S of jct. of FR 500 and FR 100),* in a small meadow where Lolo Creek runs. They slept across the creek from the road after bolting down what by then passed for a hearty meal: a bit of horsemeat, a coyote, a few grouse, one duck, and a hatful of crayfish.

Fortunately, more relief was on the way. The next morning, one of Clark's men met them on the trail leading a horse heavily laden with dried salmon, camas roots, and berries Clark had bought from the Nez Perce. The party ate, then marched on to the Nez Perce villages near Weippe, where Clark waited.

To reach Weippe, head north on Forest Road 100 for roughly 12 miles and turn west at Peterson Corners.

SEPTEMBER 20–23, 1805

Weippe Prairie

◆ 22 MILES SE OF OROFINO ON IDAHO 11

Three days before Lewis and the rest of the expedition staggered out of the dark mountains that rise behind this broad prairie, Clark arrived here and found the Nez Perce camped in two villages about a mile south of present-day Weippe. The Nez Perce were busy digging camas bulbs and fishing for salmon on the Clearwater River.

The Indians gave Clark and his famished companions plenty of dried salmon and camas bread. They gorged themselves, but the abrupt change in diet produced dire consequences—acute diarrhea, painful lower intestinal gas, and vomiting. When Lewis arrived, Clark warned him about the food, but it was no use. Starving men will eat their fill. Soon, everyone was sick.

With the Corps so vulnerable, the Nez Perce discussed killing them for their trade goods, and for their arsenal of rifles, which the tribe badly needed. But an old woman named Watkuweis argued against it. She had been kidnapped by the Blackfeet and had spent time among white traders who had been kind to her. She asked that the tribe not hurt these men. Her council, as well as a desire for a long range and dependable source of trade goods, carried the day.

After meeting with the Nez Perce on the 23rd, the captains bought as much fish, roots, and berries as their weakened horses could carry. The next day, the men, still ghastly sick, led their horses across Weippe Prairie and into Clearwater Canyon to build canoes. Lewis could barely ride even a gentle horse, and several men fell beside the trail, doubled up in pain.

SEPTEMBER 26–OCTOBER 7, 1805

Canoe Camp

◆ 4 MILES NW OF OROFINO ON US 12

Somewhere near this small riverside park, the expedition's few ambulatory members felled several stout ponderosa pines and set about building five large dugout canoes. As they sweated, they could look across the river and watch Nez Perce fishing for salmon at the fork of the Clearwater

"The pleasure I now felt in having tryumphed over the rocky Mountains and decending once more to a level and fertile country where there was every rational hope of finding a comfortable subsistence for myself and party can be more readily conceived than expressed"

MERIWETHER LEWIS, AT WEIPPE, SEPT. 22, 1805

and North Fork Clearwater Rivers—more or less where the fish hatchery stands today.

Work pro-gressed slowly. Again, as at the Great Falls, they could not obtain wood suitable for ax handles. So, with most of the Corps weakened and nearly all still "Complaining of ther bowels," the carpentry crews soon adopted what Sgt. Patrick Gass called "the Indian method of burning out the canoes." That is, they built a fire on each log and chipped out the charcoal as it burned.

The Smoking Place, a Lolo Trail landmark, prior to vandalization

The hunters occasionally brought in a deer or a coyote, but there was rarely any relief from the debilitating diet of dried fish and roots. "Provisions all out," Clark wrote on October 2, "which Compells us to kill one of our horses to eate and make Suep for the Sick men." Ordway said the horse was eaten as earnestly "as though it had been the best meat in the world."

By October 6, the new dugouts lay along these banks, and the Corps got ready to depart. Their horses had been branded and turned over to the Nez Perce for safekeeping, and all of the saddles and some of the ammunition had been cached nearby.

Though the territory that lay ahead was still unknown to the expedition, a Nez Perce chief had sketched a rough map for the captains that showed the Clearwater, Snake, and Columbia Rivers as far as Celilo Falls, near the present-day town of The Dalles, Oregon.

The next day, Lewis was still so sick he was of little help to Clark, who also felt lousy, but was "obliged to attend every thing."

The men slid the canoes into the water, loaded them, and headed downriver under a cloudy sky at 3 p.m. Despite their late departure, continued illness, and ten "danjerous" rapids, the Corps logged roughly 20 miles. Quite a pace. But of course they now had the force of a major Columbia River tributary at their backs.

Columbia River

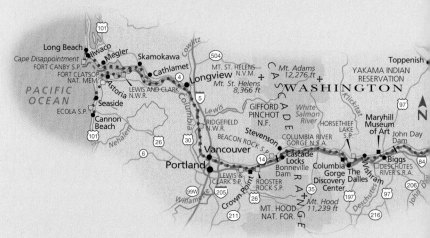

October 7, 1805 – March 23, 1806

Beginning in western Idaho and ending on the Pacific coast, this chapter describes the expedition's trip down the Clearwater, Snake, and Columbia Rivers to winter quarters at Fort Clatsop, near present-day Astoria, Oregon. Aside from a few brief departures, today's roads hug the Lewis and Clark route all the way from the river canyons of western Idaho to the misty rain forests of the Columbia River estuary. While much of the neck-craning scenery remains more or less as it was in 1805, the Snake and Columbia have been dammed. As a result, many of the Indian villages and the rapids, falls, and cascades that Lewis and Clark encountered have been submerged. Still, the landscape is achingly beautiful, and the route dotted with evocative Lewis and Clark sites, parks, and museums— including a painstaking reproduction of Fort Clatsop, part of one of the country's finest museums devoted to the Corps of Discovery.

Detail from "Falls of the Colville," Paul Kane, circa 1846

> "Our diet extremely bad...all the Party have greatly the advantage of me, in as much as they all relish the flesh of the dogs"
>
> WILLIAM CLARK, OCT. 10, 1805

OCTOBER 7–9, 1805

Clearwater River

The Clearwater River, still a magnificent sheet of fast-moving, crystalline water, quickly bore the Corps of Discovery west through dozens of rapids—some trivial, but others dangerous enough to slam the canoes headlong into the rocks and crack them open. Then, as now, thickets of berry bushes lined the banks and the same dark canyon walls loomed above the boatmen as they plied their paddles and shouted out the positions of the oncoming rocks. With the men traveled two Nez Perce chiefs, Tetoharsky and Twisted Hair, who would act as interpreters at the dozens of Sahaptian-speaking villages downriver.

The expedition camped near **Lenore,** an ancient village site that has been occupied by the Nez Perce and their ancestors for more than 10,000 years, and sank a canoe the following day in a rapids above present-day **Spalding.** The other canoes ferried the nonswimmers and sodden cargo to shore, then towed the cracked canoe to the bank. There the expedition camped for two days, drying gear and repairing the sprung dugout.

OCTOBER 10, 1805

Nez Perce National Historical Park

◆ US 95, W OF SPALDING ◆ 208-843-2261

The first-rate museum in the visitor center here overlooks the Clearwater and faces a steep range of treeless volcanic hills. Exhibits describe the story of the Nez Perce and their ancestors from roughly 9000 B.C. to the present, and the museum features an excellent film and breathtaking examples of artifacts, traditional Nez Perce tools, clothing, weapons, and other objects.

Of particular interest is a large dugout canoe, built in 1837 using the same burn-and-chip method the Nez Perce taught the expedition's carpenters at Canoe Camp (see pp. 136-37). Here, too, are many of the fishing tools Lewis and Clark would have seen as they paddled past camp after camp of Nez Perce harvesting salmon: fish spears, barbs, nets, paddles, gigs. You'll also find a tattered strip of silk ribbon and an original Jefferson Peace medal that Lewis and Clark carried on their voyage.

Nearby lie examples of the sorts of trade items the Corps brought with them, and which the Nez Perce fancied: metal ax heads, knives, brass kettles, guns. There's also a copy of an earth sweat lodge very like the one Clark came across the day after gliding past this point.

OCTOBER 10–11, 1805

Lewiston Area

As the Corps approached the confluence of the Clearwater and Snake Rivers, the canoes floated from beneath the last sparse stands of ponderosa pine and entered a region where firewood was scarce and where bare, velvety canyons and swollen shortgrass hills lined the river. This transition to a relatively treeless realm is still apparent as you approach Lewiston.

For a good view of this important confluence, follow US 12 west through town and park at the **Lewiston Levee Parkways Center** on D Street. There, a footbridge crosses the highway and leads to a small concrete shelter on the point of land between the backed up waters of the Snake and Clearwater. The expedition arrived at the confluence late in the day and camped across the Clearwater, beneath the bare rumpled hills that extend along the north bank. The hills looked about the same in 1805, but everything else has changed. The bottomlands are gone, the rivers higher, broader, murkier.

"The Countrey about the forks is an open Plain on either Side," Clark wrote of the confluence area. "The water of the South fork [Snake] is a greenish blue, the north [Clearwater] as clear as cristial…worthey of remark that not one Stick of timber on the river near the forks and but a fiew trees for a great distance up the River we descended[.] I think Lewis's River [Snake] is about 250 yards wide,

> *"The wife of Shabono our interpetr we find reconsiles all the Indians, as to our friendly intentions a woman with a party of men is a token of peace"*
>
> WILLIAM CLARK,
> OCT. 13, 1805

the *Koos koos ke* River [Clearwater] about 150 yards wide and the river below the forks about 300 yards wide."

While camped here, the men dined on salmon, dried roots, and dog meat, all of which they bought from the Indians. These staples would sustain them almost all the way to the Pacific coast, though bartering for them nearly depleted their precious stash of trade goods.

From the confluence, head for **Hells Gate State Park** *(2 miles S of Lewiston on Snake River Ave. 208-799-5015)*, an expansive oasis of shaded lawn and beach along the east bank of the Snake. The park's **visitor center,** perched atop a high hill, offers a fine vista of the Snake and, in the distance, its confluence with the Clearwater. New Lewis and Clark exhibits, opening in 2003, will focus on expedition events from the Bitterroots to the confluence of the Snake and Clearwater. The emphasis here is on the natural history of the mountains Lewis and Clark crossed, the rivers they explored, and the scientific observations they made about the flora, fauna, and geology they encountered. Exhibits also summarize the expedition's relations with the Nez Perce.

In both Lewiston and Clarkston, fine trails lead for miles along the banks of the Snake, offering visitors a chance to stretch their legs or ride bikes.

Beyond Lewiston on US 12, drop by **Chief Timothy State Park** *(8 miles W of Clarkston. 509-758-9580. March-Nov., call for schedule rest of year. Camping)*, which takes in a semiarid island in the middle of the Snake River. Located near the site of an ancient Nez Perce settlement at the mouth of Alpowa Creek, the park offers a small interpretive center *(May–Labor Day)* with revamped exhibits that focus on the early Nez Perce, natural history, and Lewis and Clark's travels through Washington State.

Here, you can watch a video that summarizes expedition events in the immediate area and conveys a sense of what this stretch of the river looked like in 1805. A broad window offers a fine vista of the river corridor.

Outside, a rewarding interpretive trail *(1 mile)* loops around the perimeter of the island. It leaves the bustle of the campground far behind, climbs through gentle short-grass hills dotted with wildflowers, and leads to several peaceful vistas of the river and its rumpled canyon walls.

The expedition stopped at the village the morning of the 11th, bought salmon and dogs, and hired three Indian river guides (probably Palouse) to pilot them through the rapids that lay between this point and present **Pasco.**

From here, the river diverges from modern highways, making it difficult to trace the expedition's westbound route. Happily, though, US 12 follows a leg of the Corps's return trip of 1806, when the men used horses to cross the high plains between present-day **Wallula** and Chief Timothy State Park.

From the park, US 12 climbs alongside a winding stream course to the vast flat top of the Columbia Plateau, which was once a prairie, but now an enormously rich wheat-growing country. Soon the road leads through a narrow trough in the plain, with rows of grass hills on either side.

Near **Pataha,** stop at the historical marker, which identifies a clearly visible remnant of the Indian trail Lewis and Clark followed east in 1806 toward the Snake River. They camped nearby after marching 28 miles through bitterly cold and violent winds, rain, hail, and snow. Supper? Dried meat, Lewis wrote, and "the ballance of our Dogs."

OCTOBER 13, 1805
Lyons Ferry State Park

◆ 30 MILES NE OF DAYTON ON WASH. 261 ◆ 509-646-3252
◆ MID-MARCH–MID-OCT. ◆ CAMPING

This remote but rewarding state park provides a glimpse of the steep canyon country Lewis and Clark paddled through for about a week after leaving the Lewiston area. Here, the Palouse River flows into the Snake through a spectacular desert canyon of abrupt rock-faced walls, where great knobs of terraced lava rise in layers and stand hundreds of feet above the water.

The expedition's canoes rounded the point across from today's park after running a long series of narrow, rocky, dangerous rapids that extended 4 miles upriver and prompted Clark to note that "We Should make more portages if the Season was not So far advanced and time precious with us."

Precious as time was, the captains landed here in a steady rain and poked around among the piled up timbers of a large Palouse village, abandoned for the season by its residents. They also noted the presence of a large Indian burial site. Clark called the confluence a "great fishing place" with many cache pits dug to store salmon. He later named what we call the Palouse River "drewyers River," after expedition member George Drouillard.

Today, the park offers shady campsites, a good beach, and a pleasant walk far out into the confluence area on a narrow levee.

Heading west on US 12 toward Pasco, consider a stop at **Lewis and Clark Trail State Park** *(509-337-6457. See p. 172),* which the expedition passed through during their return trip on May 2, 1806.

OCTOBER 16–18, 1805

Sacajawea State Park

◆ US 12 N ACROSS THE SNAKE RIVER TO PASCO, FOLLOW SIGNS ◆ 509-545-2361 ◆ LATE MARCH–OCT.

Site of Lewis and Clark's meeting with the friendly Wanapam and Yakama, this large shaded park lies on the point of land between the Snake and Columbia Rivers. Breezy, landscaped, and pleasantly removed from the bustle of the Tri-Cities area (Richland, Pasco, and Kennewick), the park also maintains a rewarding interpretive center that focuses on the expedition. Start, though, with a short walk down to the very point of land where the Snake, to your left, meets the Columbia. The expansive view from this spot still squares with the description Clark wrote in 1805.

"In every direction from the junction of those rivers," he wrote, "The Countrey is one Continued plain low and rises from the water gradually, except a range of high Countrey…on the opposit Side about 2 miles distant from the Collumbia." The high country he noted are the Horse Heaven Hills, which extend southwest toward the Cascade Mountains.

The park's plans for the bicentennial years include an interpretive trail that will lead east from this point along the Snake River and then loop back through the park, passing outdoor exhibits related to the expedition, native life, and natural history.

Exhibits inside the **Sacajawea Interpretive Center** *(Fri.-Tues.; donation)* are scheduled for expansion and will concentrate in greater detail on Sacagawea's experiences with the Corps of Discovery. Pertinent expedition events, for instance, will be presented from her point of view, and there will be more information about her infant, Jean Baptiste. Other exhibits and a new video will offer an overview of the expedition.

As the Corps approached this confluence, the men spent their days scouting and paddling white water, gliding past many Indian fishing villages, and scrounging scarce firewood to cook their salmon and dog meat stews. They made good time, but faced some significant delays. Below the present **Lower Monumental Dam,** for example, one of the canoes grounded on a rock, filled with water, and flipped—bedding, clothing, skins, the party's entire stock of dried roots, and the captains' tepee floated away. Most of the gear was retrieved, but they lost several tomahawks, shot pouches, and other irreplaceable items.

Shortly after they reached the confluence, the Corps was joined by about 200 Wanapam, who marched into

camp from their village a quarter mile up the Columbia, singing, dancing, and beating on drums. The captains smoked with the chiefs, handed out Jefferson Peace medals and other gifts, and tried to explain through signs "our friendly disposition to all nations."

Accompanied by 18 canoes of curious Wanapam and Yakama the following afternoon, Clark and a couple of men paddled up the Columbia to the mouth of the Yakama, near present **Richland.** The rivers teemed with salmon (probably coho or sockeye), and the banks were lined with mat lodges and scaffolds laden with drying fish.

Along the way, Clark visited a Wanapam family in their mat lodge and was treated to a meal of salmon boiled in a waterproof basket. There, he noted for the first time the distinctive shape of the Indians' foreheads, which had been flattened in infancy.

The expedition departed on the 18th with 40 dogs in the canoes, but no salmon. "Those which was offerd to us," Clark said, "we had every reason to believe was taken up on the Shore dead."

Elsewhere in the Tri-Cities area, stroll or bike along the **Sacagawea Heritage Trail** *(For map contact Tri-Cities Visitor Bureau, 800-254-5824 or 509-735-8486)*, which runs along both banks of the Columbia east of the I-182 crossing. For a jet boat tour, contact Columbia River Journeys *(888-486-9119 or 509-734-9941)*.

From Pasco, follow US 12 southeast to US 730, which follows the Columbia's abrupt turn to the west and leads into a towering desert chasm lined with nearly vertical cliffs. This is **Wallula Gap,** a spectacular canyon that continues for several miles, with turnouts and footpaths leading to black sand beaches shaded by small, scrubby trees.

The Corps paddled into the gap on the evening of October 18, floated past the village of the Wallawalla's principal chief, Yellept, and camped above the present Oregon border.

After they landed, the captains asked Twisted Hair and Tetoharsky to go to Yellept's village and invite him to spend the night. He arrived late, with 20 others, and gave Lewis and Clark a large basket of mashed berries. The next morning the captains held a brief but friendly council, handed out medals and other small gifts, and shoved off.

OCTOBER 19, 1805
McNary Dam

Worth a stop to get the U.S. Army Corps of Engineers' take on why salmon populations have plummeted since Lewis and Clark's time, the interesting **Pacific Salmon Information Center** *(1 mile E of Umatilla on US 730. 541-922-4388)* also offers the chance to get eyeball to eyeball with migrating salmon as they swim up a fish ladder.

Above the dam, stop at the overlook to take in the plateau landscape. Clark walked along the rim of this bluff on October 19 with several others while Lewis and the rest of the expedition wrestled the canoes through a treacherous 2-mile-long rapid.

Gazing across the river, Clark saw a village of Umatilla Indians near present **Plymouth.** Eager to greet them, he scrambled down the bluff and crossed over in one of the first canoes through the rapids. The village lanes were empty, the houses tightly shut. Clark pushed his way into one of the houses and found it full of men, women, and children "in the greatest agutation, Some crying and ringing there hands, others hanging their heads." He and the others did their best to seem friendly, and the Umatilla relaxed a bit after the Nez Perce guides joined them. But it wasn't until Sacagawea arrived, Clark noted, that the villagers "appeared to assume new life."

OCTOBER 19–20, 1805
Umatilla N.W.R.

◆ W OF PLYMOUTH OFF WASH. 14 ◆ 509-545-8588

As the Corps boomed through this area making 30 to 40 miles a day, the captains noted the presence of white pelicans, ducks, double-crested cormorants, sage grouse, and sandhill cranes. You can get a look at most of those birds—as well as many others that probably caught Lewis's eye—at this national wildlife refuge, which stretches along the backed up waters of the Columbia for a dozen miles or so. Along the Washington side, look for unmarked turnouts with paths leading beneath the cliffs.

The western edge of the refuge adjoins **Crow Butte State Park** *(509-875-2644)*, where a 30-minute stroll from the campground to the top of the butte opens up a splendid vista of the river corridor and the spacious lands of the Columbia Plateau.

OCTOBER 20–21, 1805

Crow Butte to John Day Dam

From Crow Butte, Wash. 14 continues to cross the vast desert plain, hugging the river course, traversing short-grass hills, and overlooking the lowlands to the south. Soon, though, barren land rises on both sides of the river and high terraced ledges of basalt protrude from the grass and sagebrush to form a capacious, reddish brown trough—miles across, hundreds of feet high, with the shining waters of the Columbia rippling down the center like a silver ribbon. A turnout at the top of the grade beyond the **John Day Dam** provides a spectacular vista of the gorge and Mount Hood.

The expedition camped near the dam on October 21. Wood was so scarce they had to buy it from neighboring Indians and use it only for cooking, though the nights were cold. They ate their usual menu of dog meat and fish, but were able to toast one another with an unexpected beverage. "Collins presented us with Some verry good *beer*," Clark wrote, made from "wet molded & Sowered" camas root bread.

As usual, the river that day had been full of rapids and its banks crowded with Indians drying salmon, pounding the fish into pulp, and packing it away in underground storage pits. But now some of the people were wearing scarlet and blue cloth robes, one a sailor's jacket: signs that the party was approaching the coast.

Maryhill Museum of Art

◆ 5 MILES NW OF BIGGS OFF WASH. 14 ◆ 509-773-3733
◆ MID-MARCH–MID-NOV. ◆ ADM. FEE

Perched on a high grassy bluff, this intriguing mansion-cum-art museum includes a marvelous collection of baskets and other items made by the Wishram and Wasco peoples, who lived in this area in Lewis and Clark's day. The site also offers a stunning view of the gorge above what was once the Great Falls, or Celilo Falls, of the Columbia.

From the front lawn, a locator helps identify the mouth of the Deschutes River, which Lewis and Clark reconnoitered, and Miller Island. The Great Falls, now inundated, roared just downstream of the island.

Inside, you'll find a large display of objects Lewis and Clark saw in use among various peoples of the Columbia Plateau and Northwest coast. There are burden baskets, digging sticks, cradleboards, exquisite sheep horn bowls, game pieces, and woven hats like those the captains bought at the mouth of the Columbia from the Clatsop.

OCTOBER 22, 1805

Deschutes River State Recreation Area

◆ 4 MILES W OF BIGGS ON OREG. 206
◆ 541-739-2322 ◆ CAMPING

This narrow oasis of a park lies along the riparian bottoms of the Deschutes River, which still flows freely into the Columbia from a deep side canyon of bare grass hills. Lewis and Clark walked through the park on October 22, striking the Deschutes, Clark wrote, "at the foot of a verry Considerable rapid" a quarter mile up from its mouth.

You can walk beside the same rapids on a verdant riverside trail, or view them from above on paths traversing the dry hillsides. If you'd been here in 1805, you could have looked out over the Columbia and seen "Indians in canoes killing fish with gigs" and nets, and women wading in the swampy bottomlands, pulling up wapatoo roots with their feet.

OCTOBER 22–23, 1805

Wishram Overlook

◆ HISTORICAL MARKER ON WASH. 14 N OF WISHRAM

The Great Falls of the Columbia, or Celilo Falls, which forced Lewis and Clark out of the water here on October 23, thundered off this small town until 1957, when The Dalles Dam submerged and silenced it. Still, from this overlook you can trace the expedition's rough course.

Columbia River
near The Dalles,
Oregon

The expedition paddled toward this point from the mouth of the Deschutes (visible upriver), skirted the lower end of Miller Island (to your left), and landed somewhere beneath your feet at a large Wishram village. There, the inhabitants and their horses helped portage the baggage to a camp 1,200 yards downriver. The following morning, they took the canoes across to the south bank, portaged them 457 yards around a 37-foot falls, then paddled down a narrow channel to an 8-foot falls, over which they lined the canoes with stout, elk-skin ropes.

While camped beside the falls, Clark described how local Indians dried, pounded, and tightly packed tons of salmon into elongated bear grass and bullrush baskets lined with salmon skins. "Thus preserved," Clark wrote, "those fish may be kept Sound and Sweet Several years." Each bundle weighed about 90 pounds, and hundreds of them were stacked in neat piles on the rocky ledges above and below the falls.

What Clark saw could be called a warehouse for a vast and ancient trade network that centered on the Wishram and Wasco villages. Had he arrived a month or so earlier, he would have seen a bustling market with thousands of Indians haggling for items unobtainable in their own regions.

From the Pacific coast came wapatoo root and European trade goods, such as guns, blankets, beads, knives, kettles, and cloth. From the western foothills of the Rockies came horses, buffalo meat, and beautifully decorated leather clothing. The locals supplied tons of preserved salmon in portable bundles and acted as middlemen between the upriver Sahaptian-speaking peoples and the many Chinookan who lived below.

The going rate for fish was high, the captains poor. Still, they managed to buy eight fat dogs for the men's supper. Lewis also replaced one of their lumbering dugouts with a lightweight Chinookan canoe, wide in the middle, tapering to each end, with "curious figures" carved into the bow.

OCTOBER 24, 1805

Horsethief Lake State Park

◆ N OF THE DALLES ON WASH. 14 ◆ 509-767-1159
◆ APRIL-OCT. ◆ CAMPING

Nestled in a cliff-lined cove that shows clearly on Clark's map of the area, this riverside park lies between what were once two spectacularly dangerous rapids known as the Short and Long Narrows. Like Celilo Falls, both sets of rapids lie anonymously beneath the surface of today's reservoir, but in Lewis and Clark's day they posed a major challenge to all who traveled the river. More than navigation hazards, the rapids were also extremely important Native American fishing and trading sites—which explains why a large village of Wishram had been living here for many generations before Lewis and Clark paddled into view.

The expedition camped near the village after facing the Short Narrows, just a few miles upriver. Before attempting the rapids, Clark had scouted them from a high rock with Pvt. Pierre Cruzatte, the expedition's best boatman. What they saw was a quarter-mile stretch of shocking white water where the full force of the Columbia rushed through a rock-walled channel 45 yards wide. The Indians considered it impassable, but Clark and Cruzatte thought the expedition's paddlers could handle it.

"Accordingly," Clark wrote, "I deturmined to pass through this place notwithstanding the horrid appearance of this agitated gut Swelling, boiling & whorling in every direction (which from the top of the rock did not appear as bad as when I was in it;[)] however we passed Safe to the astonishment of all the Ind[ian]s."

The next day, the Corps repeated its bravura performance in the forbidding white water of the Long Narrows, and paddled downriver to The Dalles.

For a panoramic view of this section of the river, you can park above the cove on Wash. 14 and walk the **Horsethief Butte Trail** along the base of a fortresslike bluff east of the park. The park also contains ancient pictographs (*Accessible only on guided hikes Fri.-Sat.*).

By 2003, the park will open exhibits depicting what the site looked like when Lewis and Clark landed in 1805. They will describe plank houses reminiscent of the 20 Wishram dwellings the Corps encountered here, convey a sense of the Wishram's lives, and outline the far-flung trading network that centered on this and several other villages in the vicinity. Here, too, plans call for interpretive trails, exhibits on the expedition's relations with neighboring Indians, and depictions of the Short and Long Narrows.

Touring the Gorge

Docked at Cascade Locks Marine Park, the modern stern-wheeler *Columbia Gorge* (*Cascade Locks. 503-223-3928. Fare*) offers two-hour narrated voyages through the Columbia River Gorge from mid-June through September.

Tired of the traffic? Head for the **Historic Columbia River Highway** (*Bonneville Dam exit off I-84*), which winds for about 20 miles among cliffs, waterfalls, and misty rain forests. It offers spectacular vistas of the gorge at an unhurried pace.

OCTOBER 25–28, 1805

The Dalles

After running the Long Narrows, the expedition landed at the site of this city and camped atop a flat promontory of blocky rock, which they dubbed "Fort Rock Camp." They spent the next three days drying out gear, repairing canoes, and hunting in the wooded foothills of Mount Hood.

The site (*I-84 City Center exit, follow signs*) still offers a commanding view of the river, which Clark described as "a butifull jentle Stream of about half a mile wide." Harbor seals bobbed in the current, and whooping cranes flapped overhead. Indians paddled over for a visit, feasted with the men on fresh venison, and happily watched York dance to Cruzatte's fiddle.

The expedition shoved off again the morning of the 28th and continued downriver, stopping at various Chinook villages, compiling vocabularies, admiring the cut of the local canoes, and noting the increasing frequency of European trade goods—brass kettles, cutlasses, a musket, a man in a sailor's jacket and pigtail.

They logged just 4 miles before heavy winds forced them to land their clumsy dugouts on the south bank. There, they waited in vain for better weather, then pitched camp for the night. Not far from the site of their camp, you'll find the **Columbia Gorge Discovery Center and Wasco County Historical Museum** (*Discovery Dr., off*

I-84, 3 miles W of The Dalles, follow signs. 541-296-8600. Adm. fee). Built on a grassy shelf of basalt overlooking the river, this facility offers a rundown on the geology, vegetation, wildlife, and people of the Columbia River Gorge. Exhibits include excerpts from Clark's journal covering the voyage from Celilo Falls through the Cascade Range, reproductions of his maps of the Short and Long Narrows, and copies of the box compasses, telescopes, and spearlike espontoons he and Lewis carried.

Soon, the center will open a painstaking exhibit devoted to trade items, or "Indian presents," that Lewis and Clark packed specifically for barter and gift-giving among tribes they encountered. The exhibit will convey the magnitude and variety of the items involved and explain their important role in the success of the expedition. Both sides of the ledger will be represented: European manufactured goods for Native American foods, tools, and clothing.

Because the area ranked as a major trade center, the exhibit will also take in items Lewis and Clark saw but did not buy, such as works of tribal art from throughout the Pacific Northwest. It is the first phase of a major installation that will depict the full extent of Lewis and Clark's cargo—both what they brought with them, and what they carried back.

OCTOBER 29–30, 1805

The Dalles to Stevenson

This portion of the journey—Wash. 14 from The Dalles to Stevenson—retraces the Corps's plunge into the lush, western forests of the Columbia River Gorge, where the sodden climate of the Pacific coast stalls out against the Cascade Range. Within a half hour's drive, you leave the semiarid shortgrass hills behind and enter a region of waterfalls, moss-laden rocks, ferny glens, and thickly timbered mountain slopes.

For Lewis and Clark, it was also a plunge into an entirely different culture. The various Chinookan peoples who lived along the Columbia from Celilo Falls to the coast spoke an entirely different language from those above, built large plank houses decorated with elaborate wood carvings, paddled elegant canoes, practiced infant head-flattening, and tended to drive a hard bargain for their fish, roots, sea otter skins, and conical woven hats.

Their dickering skills annoyed the captains, whose stock of trade goods was fast diminishing. But it was the petty thievery—a knife here, a tomahawk there—that enraged the entire expedition. It didn't help that the Corps had almost daily contact with the Chinookan at

Mount Hood at sunrise

Yakama fisherman with Chinook salmon, Columbia River

their villages, on the water, or at the expedition's camps. The party was beginning to feel poor, preyed upon, and gouged at every turn.

Just west of Stevenson, consider a stop at the **Columbia Gorge Interpretive Center** *(990 S.W. Rock Creek Dr., off Wash. 14. 509-427-8211 or 800-991-2338. Adm. fee).* This terrific museum has just one tiny exhibit on Lewis and Clark, but offers a rich interpretation of the Cascade, Watlala, Wishram, and Wasco peoples whose villages dotted the banks of the Columbia when the Corps of Discovery paddled through.

Here, you'll find a wealth of artifacts dating back thousands of years—stone tools, fishing gear, baskets, carved wooden images, loads of jewelry—as well as many early photographs of gorge Indians dressed up for their portraits, going about their daily tasks, and paddling their amazing canoes. There are diagrams of the sort of pit houses and plank longhouses Clark visited and described in his journal, exhibits on burial practices and vision questing, and even a rendition of how the mythical coyote created the Columbia River with a root-digging stick.

A short distance beyond the interpretive center, pull in at the **Bridge of the Gods Overlook,** where you will see how a massive landslide several hundred years ago narrowed the Columbia here and created a 10-mile series of difficult rapids known as the Cascades.

Lewis and Clark arrived at the head of the rough water on a dark, dreary day of cold rain and camped on an island near this overlook and just below a Chinookan village. The steep, densely forested mountains look roughly the way they did in 1805, but, even though the current remains swift here, the white-water barrier faced by the expedition has been submerged by Bonneville Dam.

OCTOBER 30–NOVEMBER 1, 1805
Cascade Locks

At the foot of the Bridge of the Gods, follow the signs to **Cascade Locks Marine Park** (see sidebar p. 151), where you can walk over the historic locks to a small island offering a good view of the river. Clark spent a solid day scouting the rapids. He hiked 20 miles round-trip along the north bank, following a well-worn portage trail past vacant villages (the inhabitants off hunting) and burial vaults where the bones lay 4 feet deep. At the end of his walk he stopped at a place he named **Beacon Rock.** There he happily noted that the river appeared to be influenced by ocean tides.

On November 1, the expedition portaged their baggage and wrestled the dugouts over poles to the vicinity of **North Bonneville.** The following day, they cleared the last of the rapids, running some, lining the boats through others, and sending baggage and nonswimmers around the worst. While the Corps toiled, parties of Chinookan bypassed the men, portaging their cedar canoes on their shoulders or bobbing through the white water.

OCTOBER 31 & NOVEMBER 2, 1805
Beacon Rock State Park

◆ 10 MILES W OF STEVENSON ON WASH. 14
◆ 509-427-8265 ◆ CAMPING

Shaped a bit like a bell jar, this massive, 848-foot tower of dark rock marked the end of the Cascades rapids for Lewis and Clark and the beginning of their voyage through tidewater to the Pacific coast. While scouting the Cascades, Clark had walked beneath Beacon Rock and had seen that the Columbia River widened below and appeared to have no white water for as far as he could see. The absence of rapids would be a welcome change, but the tides and currents of the Columbia River estuary ahead would present the captains with a different and much more frustrating set of challenges.

Today, a 20-minute walk up fairly steep switchbacks takes you to the top of Beacon Rock and a marvelous vista of river, gorge, and bottomlands. The park offers a more limited view from its **Upper Picnic Area.** Beneath the rock, the park takes in a wide swath of bottomland and riverfront where you can walk to the Columbia, relax on a beach, and enjoy roughly the same view of Beacon Rock that the expedition saw (*Access from Beacon Rock Moorage Rd., W of the rock; park just beyond railroad crossing*). This area will soon offer Lewis and Clark exhibits and a developed trail.

Beacon Rock, in the distance, overlooking the Columbia River Gorge

After negotiating the Cascades, the expedition glided easily past Beacon Rock, logging 29 miles for the day as the men paddled among harbor seals, trumpeter and tundra swans, geese, brant, various ducks, gulls, and plover.

They camped near **Rooster Rock State Park** (*NE of Corbett off I-84. 503-695-2261*) and woke to fog so thick a man could not be seen at 50 paces. While they waited for the mists to lift, they probably did not know they were about to paddle back onto the map for the first time since leaving the Mandan villages in early April. That steep, wooded point across the river from today's park was laid down by one of Capt. George Vancouver's lieutenants in 1792.

NOVEMBER 3–5, 1805
Portland to Skamokawa

The Corps of Discovery hurried down this stretch of the Columbia, racking up roughly 30 miles a day from the mouth of the Willamette to the abrupt widening of the Columbia River estuary, west of present Skamokawa. Hurrying through is still the recommended approach. The manifold attractions of Portland and Vancouver have little to do with the expedition, and roads rarely approach any meaningful portion of the Columbia until you clear Longview.

As the Corps passed through the **Portland-Vancouver** area on November 4, the party breakfasted at a large Skilloot village. The villagers had at least 52 canoes hauled up on the bank and owned a wealth of European goods, including muskets, pistols, swords, and powder flasks. Several canoes of well-armed Skilloot followed the expedition downriver, joined up for the noon meal, and stole Clark's ceremonial pipe tomahawk and one of the men's cloaks. The party retrieved the cloak, but not Clark's pipe. The incident contributed further to the Corps's festering resentment of all Indians on the lower Columbia.

North of Vancouver, you might drop by the **Ridgefield National Wildlife Refuge** *(3 miles W of I-5 on Wash. 501. 360-887-4106)* to walk its **Oaks to Wetlands** nature trail *(1 mile N of Ridgefield)*, which leads through riverside habitats that members of the Corps became intimately familiar with as they hunted the forests and bottomlands.

The expedition camped in the vicinity of the refuge amid the raucous nattering of thousands of geese, swans, ducks, and sandhill cranes. "I could not Sleep for the noise," Clark wrote. "They were emensely numerous and their noise horrid."

The following morning, the expedition passed through the current refuge and came upon a village where 900 Cathlapotle were living in fine cedar plank houses. It was one of the largest villages on the Columbia, and it occupied, Clark said, a quarter mile of riverfront.

As the men paddled on toward present-day **Cathlamet,** the hunters began to see signs of elk, which would become their principal source of food and clothing during the winter of 1805-06.

NOVEMBER 6–7, 1805

Skamokawa

Set aside some time to walk the beautiful beach at **Skamokawa Vista Park** *(Off Wash. 4. 360-795-8605)*, which offers a splendid view of the estuary—wide but full of islands, with a promisingly open western horizon and dark, forested highlands rising on either side. Here you'll find a kiosk devoted to expedition events in the immediate

The Chinookan Peoples of the Lower Columbia

In Lewis and Clark's time, 12 different tribes spoke the Chinookan language and lived in villages along the Columbia River from The Dalles to the Pacific coast. They included the Clatsop, the Chinook proper, and many others. Master canoe builders, they thrived in the river and coastal environments. Salmon, roots, and berries were their staples, but they also hunted elk, deer, and waterfowl. They practiced head-flattening and slavery was common.

Ravaged by 19th century smallpox epidemics, the Chinook still live along the Columbia.

> *"The Indians
> left us and
> Crossed the
> river which
> is about
> 5 miles wide
> through
> the highest
> Sees I ever
> Saw a Small
> vestle ride…
> Certain it is
> they are the
> best canoe
> navigators
> I ever Saw"*
>
> WILLIAM CLARK,
> POINT ELLICE,
> WASH.
> NOV. 11, 1805

area and information about Native Americans the Corps encountered nearby. Soon, the park will add a 2.5-mile nature trail that hugs the shoreline and leads through dense forests west of the campground. Signs will focus on matters other than Lewis and Clark, but the steep terrain, giant trees, and tangled understory convey a sense of why the expedition's hunters often found the forests of the estuary too thick to hunt.

The Corps landed in a thick fog at a Wahkiakum village near present-day Skamokawa on November 7 in order to barter for fish and roots.

"Here," Clark wrote, "we purchased a Dog Some fish, wappato roots and I purchased 2 beaver Skins for the purpose of making me a roab, as the robe I have is rotten and good for nothing."

By now the men knew they were getting close to the end of their voyage. They had identified Mount St. Helens, were in view of the Coast Ranges, and the rise and fall of the tide was more obvious. Still, morale was low. Their clothes were rotting, their bedding full of lice, the food dull, the forests difficult to hunt in, and the weather miserable. Everyone, Clark said, was "wet and disagreeable." Then, later the same day near present **Altoona**, spirits suddenly soared and Clark scribbled the magnificent line: *"Ocian in view! O! the joy."*

The party halted soon afterward and camped within sight of **Pillar Rock,** a slender column still visible a half mile offshore from Altoona but now topped with navigational aids.

"Great joy in camp," Clark wrote, "we are in *View* of the *Ocian,* this great Pacific Octean which we been So long anxious to See. and the roreing or noise made by the waves brakeing on the rockey Shores (as I Suppose) may be heard distictly."

Actually, the men were still looking at the Columbia River estuary. The ocean lay 20 miles to the west, no great distance, but violent storms and high waves were about to end their exhilarating sprint through tidewater, stranding them in a series of desperate camps along the north shore. Nine days would pass before any member of the expedition waded in the true surf of the Pacific.

NOVEMBER 8–9, 1805
Grays Bay

From Skamokawa, Wash. 4 climbs into the forested hills and bypasses Grays Bay, home to the Wahkiakum for at least 2,500 years and site of Lewis and Clark's first stormbound camp on the estuary. They laid up along the bay's west shore after the swells had threatened to swamp the canoes.

Hemmed in by steep, rocky slopes, they were forced to spend two days of wind and rain on a patch of ground so small it flooded completely at high tide. Driftwood logs 200 feet long and 7 feet in diameter rolled into camp on the waves, threatening to crush their canoes to pieces. Everyone was soaked. Everyone was cold. Everyone was elated.

"Not withstanding the disagreeable time of the party for Several days past," Clark wrote, "they are all Chearfull and full of anxiety to See further into the ocian."

On November 10, they got their chance when the wind and waves moderated. But they made just 8 miles before waves pinned them down again—this time to Point Ellice, a broad highland across the estuary from present **Astoria.**

Chinookan Canoes

Lewis and Clark saw five kinds of Native American canoes as they came down the Columbia. The small ones were used in quiet backwaters by one or two people, while the larger were for riding the rough Columbia River estuary and coastal seas.

"Some of them particularly on the sea coast are waxed painted and orimented with curious images at bough and Stern," Lewis wrote.

The Chinookan carved their canoes from cedar or fir, hollowing the tree to a thickness of about an inch at the gunwales. They tapered most models as they carved, then filled them with hot water to make the wood pliable and spread the walls with thwarts to accentuate the curves.

NOVEMBER 10–15, 1805

Megler Rest Area

◆ JUST E OF ASTORIA BRIDGE ON WASH. 401

Located near the tip of Point Ellice and right on the estuary, this narrow highway rest stop lies in the vicinity of Lewis and Clark's second stormbound camp, where they sheltered for six days in what Clark described as a "dismal nitich" or cove surrounded by cliffs and high hills.

Today's level roadbed and mowed lawn do little to convey the cramped and appalling conditions the Corps faced here. Since there was no ground safe from high water, they formed their camp on a mass of drift logs that floated every high tide. They sank their canoes under piles of rocks to keep the waves from smashing them against the cliffs. Monstrous trees surged toward them on waves. It rained continuously. Their shelters were worthless. There was no food but roots and dried fish. Small stones rattled down on them from the bluffs. Perhaps most frustrating of all, Indians paddled in and out of camp with no apparent difficulty.

After a couple of days, they found a slightly better spot a half mile west, and, on the 13th, three men managed to take the expedition's lightweight Chinookan canoe around Point Ellice. There they found a much better place—a large, abandoned village on a long sand beach. Lewis followed them on the 14th and took a small party on to the coast. If he could find a trading post or hail a vessel, he could present his letter of credit from Jefferson and replenish the expedition's meager stock of trade goods. Once in funds, they could buy whatever they needed from the Indians. Meanwhile, Clark and the bulk of the party waited for a break in the weather. They got it late on the 15th, threw the baggage in the canoes, and hurried around the point.

NOVEMBER 15–24, 1805

Lewis and Clark Campsite S.P.

◆ 2 MILES S OF CHINOOK OFF US 101

Little more than a turnout, this noisy roadside picnic area marks the approximate location of Lewis and Clark's last major encampment on the north shore of the Columbia River estuary. Here they spent nine relatively comfortable days before doubling back and crossing south to build Fort Clatsop in the foothills visible across the estuary and to the southwest of present Astoria. Here, too, the captains led separate parties overland to Cape Disappointment, the finger of land bending around from your right.

Conditions here were good, considering. The men built comfortable huts with lumber scrounged from the vacant village. They shot deer, sandhill cranes, snow geese, and ducks. Parties of Chinook and Clatsop frequented the camp, offering roots, fish, baskets, hats, and furs.

Still, relations with the Indians remained tense. Lewis had to force some Chinook to give up two precious rifles they had stolen from the expedition's small scouting party. Clark retrieved other gear at gunpoint, and told all the Chinook who came into camp that anyone who stole a rifle would be shot.

After Lewis concluded his coastal reconnaissance (no trading post, no ship), Clark, York, and ten other men set off on their own three-day jaunt around Cape Disappointment. They carved their names in trees, found curious bits of marine animals washed up on the beach, shot a California condor, and, in general, savored their transcontinental triumph.

When they returned to camp, the whole party weighed the options for where best to spend the winter. They could stay where they were, return upriver, or investigate the south shore where the elk were said to be abundant. The captains wanted to stay close to the coast, where the weather was warmer and where they could make salt and hail the odd ship.

But rather than simply announce their decision, Lewis and Clark polled their comrades. Everyone got a vote,

including Sacagawea and York. Nearly everyone voted to examine the south shore.

NOVEMBER 24–26, 1805

Fort Canby S.P. and Vicinity

◆ 1 MILE W OF ILWACO OFF US 101 LOOP

◆ 360-642-3078 ◆ CAMPING

Straddling Cape Disappointment and facing the wild, unrestricted surf of the Pacific, this gorgeous park lies right along Lewis and Clark's overland routes and brings their oceanside experiences vividly to life. Here, you can pluck crab shells from the same beaches, watch waves explode against the same black rock headlands, and swat bugs in the same dense and boggy coastal forests where the expedition finally attained its western goal. Aside from the area's natural beauty, you'll find two useful interpretive centers—one within the park and one in the neighboring town of Ilwaco.

Start, though, by walking up to the **Cape Disappointment Lighthouse** *(0.25 mile from Coast Guard station),* which offers the best north shore vista of the estuary and the river's treacherous bar. From this vantage point, you can trace the paths of Lewis and Clark's overland parties around Baker Bay to the cape. Little is known of Lewis's route except that he got this far. Clark, though, kept a journal, so we know that after reaching this point his party continued north to McKenzie Head (the baldish headland just up the coast), and beyond for another 9 miles.

Back at the parking area, take a moment to look at the tiny island of rock tight against the shore. That's probably the site Clark mentions in his journal as an anchorage for trading vessels. Near it, both parties carved their names on trees (now gone). If the spot seems an unlikely mooring, remember that many trading vessels of the time drew just 12 feet and that the bay has silted up considerably since 1805.

Next, drive up to the park's **Lewis and Clark Interpretive Center,** built on an old gun emplacement overlooking the sea. Slated for major renovation and expansion during the bicentennial years, the center's exhibits offer an overview of Lewis and Clark's entire voyage from the mouth of the Missouri to the Pacific. A new wing, scheduled to open in 2003, will focus more intently on the expedition's experiences near the mouth of the Columbia.

The new exhibits are expected to express the expedition's elation over finally reaching the Pacific and also to convey a clear sense of the desperate conditions the men faced at the close of their westbound journey—the ferocious weather, lousy food, and the disintegration of their clothing and shelters. Here, too, plans call for a depiction of a Chinookan village, reproductions of Clark's surveying equipment, maps tracking the overland parties' excursions along the coast, and much, much more.

Elsewhere in the park, you can hike up **McKenzie Head** *(0.5-mile trail begins on campground road),* where Clark got his first good view of the coast to the north and where a small marble obelisk at the trailhead marks the approximate location of one of Clark's campsites. Or, take a walk out to the **North Head Lighthouse** *(1 mile N of park entrance on US 101 loop),* for its spectacular view of the open ocean and of the beach that runs north for miles. Clark and his party walked that beach to the vicinity of present **Long Beach** before calling it quits and turning back for Point Ellice.

The park's trail system makes it possible for ambitious hikers to link most of these landmarks while roughly following Clark's overland route. Starting from the Cape Disappointment Lighthouse, the trails lead 0.75 mile to the Lewis and Clark Interpretive Center; then 0.6 mile to the base of McKenzie Head; 1.6 miles to North Head; and 1 mile from North Head to Beard's Hollow.

Long Beach lies a few miles to the north. There, you'll find a lovely paved trail called **Clark's Last Mile** *(W on*

Bolstad Blvd., park at the beach), which leads north a short distance to a Lewis and Clark monument and then winds among the rolling dunes of the town's oceanfront. Soon, the trail will be extended to the south, perhaps reaching as far as Beard's Hollow.

Before heading across the estuary to Astoria, consider stopping at the **Ilwaco Heritage Museum** *(115 S.E. Lake St., Ilwaco. 360-642-3446. Closed Sun. Oct.-May. adm. fee)*. It offers an exhibit summarizing Lewis and Clark's experiences along the estuary through journal excerpts, photos of important landmarks, and reproductions of expedition equipment. The museum also presents an assortment of Chinookan artifacts, including basketry, horn spoons, and wooden knives. Here, too: charts and an enormous relief map of the estuary, canoe models, photos, and a case of beachcombed whale bones.

NOVEMBER 27–DECEMBER 7, 1805

Astoria

This pleasant, steep-sided harbor town offers a cartographic view of the estuary and its surroundings—especially from the top of **Astoria Column** *(Coxcomb Hill on 16th St., follow signs. 503-325-2963)*, a 125-foot spire standing on the town's highest hill. Beginning in 2003, the column grounds will include a new visitor center with several modest exhibits on Lewis and Clark. From the balcony at the top of the column, you can follow Lewis and Clark's movements along both the north and south shores of the estuary.

Point Ellice is clearly visible, along with the curve of Baker Bay to Cape Disappointment. Along the south shore you can see Tongue Point, that tiny peninsula just east of town, where the Corps was stranded for a third time. To the southwest you get a clear view of Youngs Bay and the mouth of the Lewis and Clark River, which the Corps ascended to build Fort Clatsop.

But linger on Tongue Point. There, Clark and most of the men spent ten wretched days in conditions even worse than what they had known on the north shore. In addition to rain, hail, cramped quarters, and wave-tossed tree trunks, there was wind so violent that it knocked over trees 200 feet tall and 10 feet in diameter.

When the wind didn't blow, thick wood smoke lingered in the air and stung the men's eyes. All the tents had rotted through. So had the captains' tepee. Their clothes were in tatters, the food as bad as ever, and now some of the men came down with severe diarrhea, an illness Clark attributed to their unrelenting diet of dried pounded fish mixed with salt water. Clark himself got so sick that when a

" We are all wet, bedding and Stores, haveing nothing to keep our Selves or Stores dry, our Lodge nearly worn out, and the pieces of Sales and tents So full of holes and rotten… wind to high to go either back or forward and we have nothing to eate but a little Pounded fish… This is our present Situation! truly disagreeable"

WILLIAM CLARK, STORMBOUND ON TONGUE POINT, OREG. NOV. 28, 1805 hunter finally shot an elk, he dared not eat its meat.

"O! how disagreeable my Situation," he wrote, "a plenty of meat and incaple of eateing any."

Fortunately, Lewis and several men managed to paddle their Indian canoe into Youngs Bay. After several days of scouting, they found an acceptable wintering site 3 miles up Lewis and Clark River. On December 7, the entire expedition moved there and began construction of Fort Clatsop.

DECEMBER 7, 1805–MARCH 23, 1806

Fort Clatsop National Memorial

◆ 5 MILES SW OF ASTORIA OFF US 101 ◆ 503-861-2471
◆ ADM. FEE

Built within a moccasin toss of Fort Clatsop's original site, this convincing reconstruction of the Corps's winter quarters stands in a muffled, moss-laden forest of towering sitka spruce. Staffed by well-versed Lewis and Clark buffs in period garb, spiced up with whiffs of wood smoke and tanned elk skin, the fort forms the centerpiece of an exceptional memorial to the expedition, which also includes one of the finest Lewis and Clark museums anywhere.

Like the original fort, the reproduction is 50 feet square, gated front and back, with two shed-roofed buildings that face one another across a narrow parade ground. All of the rooms have been furnished—the captains' with particular care—and you're welcome to handle much of what you see. Stretch out on Clark's bed. Heft a jawbone from Lewis's desk. Try on a buckskin jacket or a threadbare cocked hat. Ask a question, and the interpreter will offer a detailed reply.

Behind the fort, you can walk to the same spring the expedition tapped for fresh water. Or, stroll down to the canoe landing, where you'll find reproductions of the expedition's clumsy dugouts. Wherever you walk, you'll come across plaques identifying trees and other plants first described for science by Lewis or Clark.

Inside the visitor center, incisive exhibits cover all major aspects of the voyage—historical context, preparations, weapons, Indian diplomacy, mapping, and natural history observations. Here, you'll find examples of the simple tools the expedition's carpenters used to fell the trees, shape the logs, and split the planks that built Fort Clatsop. Nearby, a genuine Harpers Ferry 1803 flintlock rifle shares space with other weapons the men carried, such as an American long rifle, and a 1795 Army musket. There is also a fascinating exhibit on the Chinook and Clatsop, arranged around an elegant coastal canoe outfitted with paddles, herring rake, harpoon, double-bladed knife, and other

" We are infested with swarms of flees [lice] already in our new habitations; the presumption is therefore strong that we shall not devest ourselves of this intolerably troublesome vermin during our residence here."

MERIWETHER LEWIS,
FORT CLATSOP,
JAN. 2, 1806

fishing and hunting gear. Accompanying panels explain how the canoe was carved and the gear used.

Throughout this rich assortment of reproduced and genuine artifacts, one finds a variety of fascinating documents, including a copy of Clark's 1805 map of the West. Drawn at Fort Mandan, it shows the Missouri River stretching within a few hundred miles of the Pacific Coast, thus revealing the captains' high hopes for an easy water route. Other documents include an expedition roster, Lewis's estimates of expenses, diagrams of the keelboat, and long lists of equipment, sup-

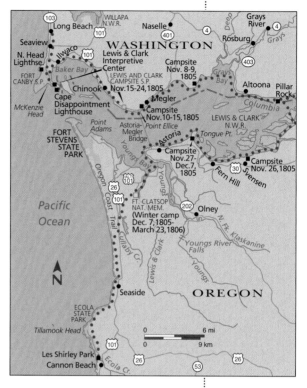

plies, medicines and Indian presents. A collection of short films demonstrates various tasks that the expedition's men performed while at Fort Clatsop, such as tanning hides, making moccasins and candles, and building fires with flint and steel.

The expedition landed at this wooded site grateful to find a safe haven at last from the stormy shores of the Columbia River Estuary.

The location was, as Clark said, a "most eligable Situation" close to the ocean but well above high tide, with fresh water, and trees for lumber. Working in nearly continuous rain with occasional hail, snow, and lightning, the men felled trees, split timbers, roofed their huts, and were "Snugly fixed," Clark said, in time for a grim Christmas repast of tainted elk, spoiled pounded fish, and a few roots.

The expedition's winter here was dull, wet, lean, sick, and lonely. Rain fell most of the time. Fires were hard to keep going. The diet was monotonous—elk, elk, and more elk, supplemented by fish, roots, and the occasional dog bought from the Clatsop. Meat spoiled quickly. The men

> *"Some of the large canoes are upwards of 50 feet long and will carry from 8 to 10 thousand lbs. or from 20 to thirty persons and some of them particularly on the sea coast are waxed painted and ornimented with curious images at bough and Stern; those images sometimes rise to the hight of five feet"*
>
> MERIWETHER LEWIS, FEB. 1, 1806

came down with colds, flu, strained muscles, and venereal disease. There was no liquor, little tobacco. And relations with the neighboring tribes were tepid, at best. The Clatsop, who eventually gained a grudging respect, visited almost daily and were admired for their mastery of the coastal environment. But even with them, there was none of the whole-hearted, cross-cultural merriment the expedition had enjoyed with the Mandan the previous year.

Work helped pass the time. The men hunted in an ever widening radius of the fort and hauled the meat and hides back through boggy forests. They jerked or smoked the meat, scraped the hides, and tanned them with elk brains. They sewed moccasins, chopped firewood, mounted guard, and made occasional forays to Salt Camp, in present **Seaside,** where a few of the men boiled seawater to make salt.

But if most of the winter passed in drudgery and discomfort, the spirits of the men were leavened by the sure knowledge that they had accomplished a great deed and that they would return home as heroes.

The captains kept busy overseeing the men's work, trading and visiting with various Indians, and doctoring the men. Between interruptions they wrote, sketched, charted, and prepared specimens to take back to Jefferson.

Clark worked on his map of the country from Fort Mandan to the mouth of the Columbia, substituting hard geographic facts for the enormous expanse of white space and conjecture that filled previous maps of the American West. He and Lewis pored over it, savoring the knowledge that they had fulfilled Jefferson's request to find the most practical and navigable route to the Pacific. Less gratifying was the fact that the map would obliterate the President's hope for an easy route to the coast.

Lewis, who had written almost nothing since crossing the Bitterroot Range, wrote at a ferocious pace all winter, filling page after page with descriptions and sketches of dozens of plants and a hundred animals. Of these, 10 plants, 11 mammals, 2 fish, and 11 birds were new to science. He also wrote about various Native American peoples—how they prepared food, flattened the heads of their infants, and made houses, canoes, fishing tackle, and clothing.

Lewis expected to stay at Fort Clatsop until April 1, but by early March it was getting difficult to feed the men. Elk were now scarce and the captains so poor that they could not afford to buy much food from the Clatsop. Besides, everyone was eager to clear out. The captains decided to shove off early.

Before they left, Lewis set out to buy two canoes from the Indians. Prices were high, and Lewis was desperate for better boats. He managed to pay for one with his own uniform coat, but felt he could not afford the second. So he ordered the men to steal it. Thus equipped, the Corps of Discovery departed Fort Clatsop on March 23, after posting in the captains' quarters a list of the men's names and a sketch of Clark's map of their route from St. Louis to the Pacific.

SEASIDE

Snuggled beneath the steep dark cliffs of Tillamook Head, this small resort town lies along a beautiful beach where, at a small bivouac called **Salt Camp**, a handful of expedition members spent nearly the first two months of 1806 boiling seawater in five large kettles to make three to four bushels of salt. An approximation of their works stands in a residential area at the south end of town (*Lewis and Clark Way, follow signs*).

Herbarium sheet, Fort Clatsop National Memorial

During the winter, Clark passed through this coastal area with 14 others, including Sacagawea, to see a beached whale near present **Cannon Beach.** To get there, they had to scramble over Tillamook Head, which Clark called "the Steepest worst & highest mountain I ever assended." Today, a 6-mile portion of the **Oregon Coast Trail** approximates their route, starting at the end of Tillamook Head Road and leading through deep forest to Ecola State Park.

LES SHIRLEY PARK

This picnic area, located in the town of Cannon Beach's north end, off Fifth Street, offers access to a breathtaking beach at the mouth of Ecola Creek. Here Clark and his party of 14 found the beached whale the Clatsop had told them about. Unfortunately, the whale had been picked clean by the Tillamook, who lived nearby. Clark traded for a few gallons of oil and about 300 pounds of blubber, complaining that the Tillamook were "averitious, & independent in trade."

The following day, the party lugged the greasy bundles back over Tillamook Head, passing through present **Ecola State Park** (*N of Cannon Beach off US 101, follow signs. 503-436-2844. Adm. fee*), a stunning coastal preserve of sand and surf-beaten pinnacles, where sea lions bask on the rocks and elk slip through the damp forests. Trails here connect with Clark's route over Tillamook Head.

Homeward Bound

March 23 – September 23, 1806

For most of their six-month journey home, Lewis and Clark retraced the route they had followed to the Pacific. They paddled up the Columbia and crossed the worst of the Rockies on horseback. However, in present-day Montana the captains divided the men into as many as five separate parties in order to explore uncharted land along the Marias and Yellowstone Rivers.

After reuniting near Williston, North Dakota, they coasted down the Missouri to St. Louis—where they were received as heroes who had been given up for dead. Because the Corps's return trip backtracks over much of the outbound route, this chapter concentrates on their divergent explorations of Montana.

Detail from "Buffalo and Elk on the Upper Missouri," Karl Bodmer, 1833

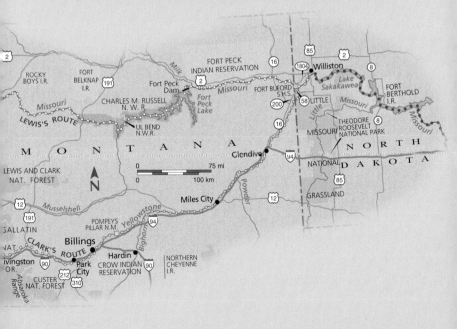

Fort Clatsop reproduction, near Astoria, Oregon

Fort Clatsop to Wallula Gap

The expedition departed from Fort Clatsop March 23, after waiting out a morning of high winds and heavy rain. As the boat crews dipped their paddles and dug in for home, Lewis and Clark looked back over the preceding months and took some satisfaction in how the Corps had fared through all the drizzle, confinement, tainted meat, and poverty of Fort Clatsop.

"At this place," Clark wrote, the expedition had "lived as well as we had any right to expect, and we can Say that we were never one day without 3 meals of Some kind a day either pore Elk meat or roots."

Going upriver was tough. The Columbia's muscular current often slowed the Corps to half its downstream pace. Rapids they had paddled through the previous autumn now required them to tow the canoes or portage. The men had no comforting kegs of flour or salt pork in the canoes, no whiskey, no tobacco, no tents, no surplus elk, and very little merchandise to buy anything. Indeed, the captains wrote that the sum total of their remaining trade goods would fit easily into two large handkerchiefs.

After just a week of upstream travel, the party began hearing disturbing reports from Indians of widespread hunger farther up the Columbia. "This information," Clark wrote, "gives us much uneasiness with respect to our future means of Subsistence."

Accordingly, the captains halted for several days near present-day **Washougal** to shoot and jerk enough meat to carry with them to the Nez Perce country. While the men hunted and prepared the meat, Clark explored the Willamette River, which the captains had not seen in 1805 as the Corps made its quick descent of the Columbia. Lewis passed the time poking around in the woods looking for new plants and animals.

Added to the challenges of navigation and food gathering was the maddening, nearly constant harassment the Corps endured from various bands of Indians all the way to The Dalles and beyond. As during the previous autumn, the Indians not only traded on terms the captains considered rapacious, but some stole whatever they could lay their hands on.

Tomahawks disappeared. Knives vanished. A hunk of lead went missing here, an ax there, then a robe, a packsaddle, even—temporarily—Lewis's dog Seaman. The thefts and the grappling attempts at theft enraged the men and drove them to the brink of serious violence. Lewis at one point was ready to burn down a village, and the men, he said, seemed "well disposed to kill a few of them." Fortunately, during the tensest moments Lewis was able keep tempers, including his own, under control.

As they approached The Dalles, the captains bought horses, which they used to portage the Long and Short Narrows. Once beyond those awesome rapids, though, Lewis decided to ditch the canoes and burn them along with all the paddles and setting poles in order to deny the Indians the windfall. Thereafter, the expedition marched overland along the north side of the Columbia, slowly adding to their horse herd as they went.

South of present Pasco, the Corps's relations with the locals took an abrupt turn for the better. On April 27, near the mouth of Wallula Gap, they met up again with Chief Yellept and the Wallawalla, who feted the Corps and invited the Yakama to come join in an evening of festivities. Cruzatte whipped out his fiddle, and the men danced their jigs and reels. The Indians egged them on, then began their own powerful dance. Some 550 men, women, and children sang and moved in unison, with members of the Corps joining in. It was quite a change from the dreary days at Fort Clatsop.

Now stocked with 23 horses, the expedition crossed the river and followed a Nez Perce guide up onto the high plains south of the Snake River. They traveled through the present-day towns of **Waitsburg, Dayton,** and **Pomeroy** before descending again to the Snake several miles west of present **Clarkston.**

"the wind is pretty high but it seems to be the common opinion that we can pass point William. we accordingly distributed the baggage and directed the canoes to be launched and loaded for our departure. — at 1 P.M. we bid a final adieu to Fort Clatsop."

MERIWETHER LEWIS, DEPARTING FORT CLATSOP, MARCH 23, 1806

"we are obliged to have recourse to every subterfuge in order to prepare...to meet that wretched portion of our journy, the Rocky Mountain, where hungar and cold in their most rigorous forms assail the waried traveller; not any of us have yet forgotten our sufferings in those mountains in September last, and I think it probable we never shall."

MERIWETHER
LEWIS,
AT KAMIAH, IDAHO
JUNE 2, 1806

MAY 2, 1806

Lewis and Clark Trail S.P.

◆ 5 MILES W OF DAYTON, OFF US 12. ◆ CAMPING
◆ 509-337-6457

As the Corps crossed the plains, they followed the Touchet River through this lovely wooded park, where otters, beaver, and deer can still be seen along the trails. During the day, three Wallawalla accompanying the expedition showed Lewis how to cut cow parsnip, a plant that still grows abundantly within the park. "I tasted of this plant," Lewis wrote, "found it agreeable and eat heartily of it without feeling any inconvenience."

Outdoor exhibits focus on the expedition's eastbound journey, describe the Corps's day-to-day life with horses, and detail the area's natural history.

MAY 14–JULY 3, 1806

Kamiah to Traveler's Rest

From Clarkston, the expedition followed the north bank of the Clearwater into the heart of Nez Perce territory. Here, the men began to meet and camp with some of the Nez Perce who had been of such great help the previous autumn after the Corps's ordeal on the Lolo Trail. The Indians told Lewis and Clark that heavy snow in the high country would prevent any eastbound trip over the Lolo for at least a month.

This came as disappointing news to men so eager to return home, but the Corps made the best of their time at a camp on the east bank of the Clearwater, about a mile and a half northwest of present-day Kamiah.

During the expedition's wait, the captains recovered 21 of the horses and about half the saddles they had left with the Nez Perce the previous autumn. They also found that Clark's skills as a physician were so highly regarded among the Nez Perce that they would trade food, sorely needed by the Corps, for treatment. Clark successfully treated ailments ranging from sore eyes and ulcers, to rheumatism and paralysis. While Clark doctored, Lewis botanized, traded for more horses, and visited with the Nez Perce. The enlisted men passed the time hunting, horse racing, and playing various games with the Nez Perce.

In mid-June, the captains moved camp up to the blossoming camas meadows near present Weippe and prepared, against all Nez Perce advice, to force the Lolo Trail. They now had 65 horses, enough to carry both men and baggage. But they had no guides. They struggled in the snow for two days before turning around and sending

Drouillard back to the Nez Perce with an army rifle as a reward for guide services.

On June 25, with excellent guides, the expedition set off again. This time, they glided right over the Bitterroot barrier, taking just six days to reach Traveler's Rest, in Lolo, south of present Missoula. The previous autumn, the journey had taken 12 days.

Lewis and Clark lingered at Traveler's Rest for a few days to rest the men and horses, acquire some meat, and put the finishing touches on their plan to split the expedition and explore new territories.

Lewis would head northeast, taking a Nez Perce shortcut to the Great Falls of the Missouri. There he would pick up the Marias River and follow it northwest, hoping that this Missouri River tributary extended far into British Canada. This unknown ending point marked the boundary of U.S. territory. He also hoped to meet the Blackfeet and arrange a truce between them and the Nez Perce, so American goods could pass easily over the mountains.

Clark, meanwhile, would head south along the Bitterroot River and backtrack the expedition's 1805 route as far as Three Forks. There, he would break off to float the Yellowstone River and rejoin Lewis at the confluence of the Missouri and Yellowstone. As the captains pursued their separate routes, they would detach other groups to portage the Great Falls and to take the Corps's horse herd overland to the Mandan villages.

It was an elaborate plan, full of promise, but also fraught with risks that jeopardized the expedition's primary objective—to find the quickest, most practical route from the Missouri to the Pacific and get back safely with all the maps, notes, specimens, and journals. At 8 a.m. July 3, Lewis and Clark shook hands and parted company.

JULY 3–27, 1806
Lewis's Return Trip

From Traveler's Rest, Lewis's party of nine men rode north along the Bitterroot River to its confluence with the Clark Fork and struggled across the raging current on makeshift rafts. They had so much baggage that they had to make several crossings. On the last trip, Lewis's raft whisked a mile and a half downriver.

"On our approach to the shore the raft sunk," Lewis wrote, "and I was drawn off the raft by a bush and swam." Meanwhile, the Nez Perce had easily ferried their belongings in small, inflatable deerskin rafts, which they towed across behind their horses.

The party camped that night in bottomlands so thick

> *"It is now the season at which the buffaloe begin to coppelate and the bulls keep a tremedious roaring we could hear them for many miles and there are such numbers of them that there is one continual roar."*
>
> MERIWETHER LEWIS, ON THE BISON RUT NEAR THE GREAT FALLS, JULY 11, 1806

with mosquitoes they had to build large smudge fires to protect the horses. "These insects tortured them in such manner," Lewis wrote, "that I realy thought they would become frantic."

The following morning, some of the men turned out early to hunt for their Nez Perce guides, who were about to part company. "I was unwilling to leave," Lewis wrote, "without giving them a good supply of provision after their having been so obliging as to conduct us through those tremendious mountains."

After parting "with these friendly people," Lewis led his party east along the Clark Fork's north bank through what is now **Missoula.**

Though city traffic and suburban sprawl have swallowed up most reminders of Lewis's passage, you can still get a feel for some of the terrain he trotted across by visiting **Maclay Flat** (*2 miles SW of town, off US 93 on Blue Mountain Rd.*). Here, a short walk leads through ponderosa pine forest to a section of the Bitterroot River and a fine view of the surrounding mountains. Warblers, kingfishers, red-tailed hawks, and many other birds still enliven the scenery, just as they did when Lewis rode through.

Beyond Missoula, head east on Mont. 200, which roughly follows Lewis's route up the Blackfoot River to the Continental Divide. Along the way, it passes through a magnificent river canyon and glides through expansive high country meadows and valleys surrounded by forests and mountains.

Lewis and his men made excellent time along this stretch, logging 25 to 30 miles a day as they followed a clear Nez Perce path to the buffalo country. Their passage from Traveler's Rest to the Great Falls would take just nine days, cutting off roughly 400 miles and seven weeks from the route they had taken the previous summer when, without horses, they had been compelled to boat far to the southwest before crossing the divide.

About 9 miles east of **Bonner,** the highway pulls away from the river and its canyon of steep ponderosa pine and larch forests. If you want to continue along the canyon—and don't mind jarring potholes or a snoot full of dust—follow the signs for the **Blackfoot River Recreation Corridor.** There, a dirt and gravel road hugs the river for about 18 miles before rejoining Mont. 200. It's a terrific, though sometimes bumpy, drive that offers many opportunities to walk or bike a portion of Lewis's route along the north bank.

After clearing the Blackfoot's canyon, Lewis emerged onto what he described as a high extensive plain surrounded by low, timbered hills and high, broken mountains.

Soon, the surface of the valley broke into "a vast number of little hillucks and sinkholes" that Lewis called "prairie of the knobs." The land, on both sides of present-day **Ovando,** looks much the same today as in 1806.

On July 5, Lewis's party camped near today's **Monture Fishing Access** *(6 miles W of Ovando),* an appealing stop where a bend of Monture Creek slips around a small meadow of waist-high grass and undercuts a hillside topped with ponderosa pine. On July 6, they camped just west of present **Lincoln.** The following day, they reached the Continental Divide at what is now called **Lewis and Clark Pass.** Here, Lewis and his men stepped back into U.S. territory for the first time in nearly 11 months. From the top of the pass, he could see Square Butte, a prominent landmark to the northeast, which showed him the way to the Great Falls.

To follow in their footsteps, pick up a map and visitor regulations at the **Helena National Forest Lincoln Ranger District** *(1.5 miles E of Lincoln on Mont. 200. 406-362-4265)* and drive to the end of Alice Creek Road *(10 miles E of Lincoln).* There, an exceptionally rewarding trail branches off to the right and climbs a mile or so to the pass—an open saddle of grass, wildflowers, and dwarf evergreen trees. The site, which is virtually unchanged since Lewis's time, opens up an incredible vista of the Great Plains spilling down from the Rocky Mountains like a vast sea of grass. Nearby, you'll find travois ruts left in the ground by generations of Indians crossing the mountains.

From the pass, Lewis angled down to the north in order to pick up the Sun River and follow it to the Great Falls. You can cross the divide on Mont. 200 at **Rogers Pass** *(5 miles SE of Lewis and Clark Pass)* and descend through gorgeous mountain country to the rumpled, wind-raked surface of the plains. At the foot of the mountains, take a left on US 287, which runs north and picks up Lewis's trail near **Augusta.** There turn east onto Mont. 21, which follows the Sun River and Lewis's footsteps past flat river terraces, cottonwood groves, and the occasional butte or high hill.

As Lewis and his men descended the river, they stored a surplus of skins and meat for the three nonhunters who would be left at the Great Falls to portage the expedition's cached goods. Just west of present **Simms,** they killed "a

Expedition Medicine

During the course of the 28-month expedition, Lewis and Clark dealt with a wide variety of illnesses and injuries. Considering their blissful ignorance of bacteria and the physical dangers inherent on such a journey, it is truly remarkable that they lost just one member of the party—Sgt. Charles Floyd, probably to appendicitis (see pp.40-41).

Expedition ailments and injuries included: colds and sore throats, snakebite, snowblindness, abscesses, boils, dysentery, high fever, malaria, rheumatism, poisoning, diarrhea, malnutrition, scurvy, gonorrheal infection, strained back, skin disease, sea sickness, syphilis, muscle strain, influenza, cuts, wolf bite, sunstroke, dislocated shoulder, and gunshot wound.

To treat the men, the captains bled, purged, lanced, greased, poulticed, and prescribed various medicines such as powerful laxatives, laudanum, zinc sulphate, lead acetate, and mercury.

very fat buffaloe bull"—their first in nearly a year. Closer to the Missouri, the hunting improved. Large herds of elk and incredible numbers of bison crowded the land along the river bottoms. Lewis estimated he could see 10,000 bison within a 2-mile radius.

Home on the Plains

While in the Browning vicinity, you may want to check out the **Museum of the Plains Indian** (Jct. of US 2 and 89W. 406-338-2230. Closed weekends Oct.-May; adm. fee June-Sept.). Well stocked with beautifully decorated clothing, weapons, tools, and assorted ceremonial gear, this fine museum offers an overview of the Plains Indian lifeways, including that of the Blackfeet and other tribes Lewis and Clark encountered during the course of the expedition.

GREAT FALLS UPPER PORTAGE CAMP

Lewis reached the west bank of the Missouri on July 11 and woke the next morning to find that 7 of his 17 horses had been stolen during the night (he blamed the Salish). The men swam the remaining horses across the river, floated their baggage over in bullboats, and settled into the same camp Lewis had established in 1805 at the upper end of the portage route.

Lewis and the men dug up their cached goods (many of which, including Lewis's plant specimens, were ruined), prepared a surplus of mashed roots and dried meat, and made shelters and clothing from animal skins.

Here, too, the men got reacquainted with their old nemesis, the grizzly. Among other incidents, Pvt. Hugh McNeal was thrown by his terrified horse right in front of a bear, which rose to its hind legs. McNeal clubbed it with his musket, knocking it to the ground and breaking the gun. While the griz pawed at its head, McNeal scrambled up a tree. He stayed there for several hours until the angry bear finally wandered off.

On the 16th, all was ready for Lewis's trip up the Marias. He and three others crossed the Missouri and headed down its north bank to the Great Falls. On the 17th, they struck north for the Marias.

Those left behind were joined by a detachment of Clark's men, who arrived in the canoes the expedition had cached the previous autumn southwest of present Dillon. Together, the two groups portaged the canoes and baggage, picked up a cached pirogue, and set off for a rendezvous with Lewis near the mouth of the Marias.

THE MARIAS RECONNAISSANCE

Lewis's 11-day journey through the heart of Blackfeet territory extended across the High Plains from the Great Falls to the vicinity of present Browning, where Lewis could see that the Marias did not extend into British Canada, as he had hoped. The trip accomplished little, put Lewis and his men in grave danger, and resulted in a violent encounter with two young Blackfeet warriors.

Cottonwoods on semiarid floor of Two Medicine River, near Cut Bank

Today, it's very difficult to follow Lewis's route. Roads merely cross his path, and the locations of his most important camps are either in dispute or lie on private land. Still, a trip northwest on I-15 and US 2 to Browning approximates his trek. Lewis and his men rode due north from the Great Falls, crossing the Teton River and trotting across the plains, which Lewis likened to "a well-shaved bowling-green, in which immence and numerous herds of buffaloe were seen feeding attended by their scarcely less numerous sheepherds the wolves."

Soon, they were on the Marias, where Lewis noted a single bison herd extending without a break for 12 miles. There were also vast numbers of elk, deer, and pronghorn. Firewood was so scarce that the men sometimes cooked their meat over fires made from buffalo dung.

The Marias led them past present **Shelby** to **Cut Bank Creek,** which in turn led them almost to present **Browning** before Lewis threw in the towel on July 22. Clearly, the Marias trended west, not north. He decided his party would rest their horses, which had sore hooves, for a couple of days, and fix the site's longitude before turning back for the Missouri. He named the site **Camp Disappointment.**

CAMP DISAPPOINTMENT MEMORIAL

Though this graffiti-marred monument (*off US 2*) stands several miles south of Camp Disappointment's actual site, its location atop a gravelly knoll conveys a strong sense of the setting and offers a panoramic view of the northern

"The Black- foot indians rove through this quarter of the country and as they are a vicious lawless and reather an abandoned set of wretches I wish to avoid an interview with them if possible"

MERIWETHER LEWIS, JULY 17, 1806

plains and the abrupt face of the Rockies.

Lewis and the men spent four uncomfortable days near here. Game was scarce. For three days they had nothing to eat but root mush flavored with tainted bison grease and a handful of pigeons. Signs of the Blackfeet were everywhere. The weather turned cold, cloudy, rainy. Finally, Lewis despaired of fixing the site's longitude, broke camp the morning of the 26th, and headed southeast toward the Two Medicine River and his violent encounter with a small party of Blackfeet.

The actual site of Camp Disappointment lies on private land posted with NO TRESPASSING signs. You can approach it, though, by driving 10 miles east of Browning off US 2. Then turn north on County Road 444, which crosses Cut Bank Creek a couple of miles east of the site.

TWO MEDICINE FIGHT SITE

Here again, the actual site of Lewis's skirmish with the Blackfeet is difficult to reach—not only because of terrain, roads, and private lands, but because the precise location of the site is in dispute. But you can get very close, as long as you don't mind nosing around on back roads (ask first before entering private land).

Perhaps the easiest approach is to double back on US 2 to Cut Bank, take Valier Road south about 6 miles, go west on Gov. Hugo Aronson Road about 10 miles, and turn south on Lenoir Road (2nd major left). This leads you to the edge of a deep, meandering rut carved into the high plains by the Two Medicine River. Across the way and to the left, high badlands bluffs crowd the south bank.

Lewis and his men came in from the west, keeping to the south bank of the river while George Drouillard hunted ahead. As the hills closed in on the south bank, Lewis rode up to the plains and soon spotted 30 horses and several Blackfeet a mile ahead of him. The Indians seemed to be watching Drouillard. "This was a very unpleasant sight," Lewis wrote. With escape being impossible, Lewis decided to make the best of things. Both parties advanced cautiously toward one another, shook hands, and agreed to ride down to the river and camp together—somewhere along the base of the steep, badlands bluffs.

There were eight Indians, from the Piegan division of the Blackfeet Confederation. Lewis smoked with them late into the night. Through Drouillard's sign language, he outlined his plan for an American trading network that would deliver manufactured goods, including guns, to the region's various tribes. Lewis meant well, but to the Blackfeet his proposal was appalling news. It threatened to break their existing monopoly on firearms by supplying rifles to their enemies.

At first light, the Blackfeet tried to steal the party's rifles and horses. All of the men recovered their guns, but in doing so Pvt. Reuben Fields stabbed one of the Blackfeet through the heart. Then, as Lewis sprinted after some of the horses, an Indian turned toward him with a musket. "I shot him through the belly, he fell to his knees and on his wright elbow," Lewis wrote, "from which position he partly raised himself up and fired at me…being bearheaded I felt the wind of his bullet very distinctly." Lacking his shot pouch to reload, Lewis ran back to camp, gathered his men and seven horses, burned the Indians' remaining gear, and fled southeast across the plains.

The men rode all day and long into the night, covering 100 miles by 2 a.m., when they finally stopped briefly to sleep. They reached the Missouri the following morning, caught up with the boat crews near the mouth of the Marias, and headed downriver to rendezvous with Clark.

JULY 3–AUGUST 3, 1806
Clark's Return Trip

Though Clark backtracked over the expedition's 1805 route most of the way from Traveler's Rest to Three Forks, he started the return trip with a shortcut that he and Lewis had learned about the previous year from the Flathead, or Salish. The shortcut started at Ross's Hole, near the upper end of the Bitterroot River Valley, and climbed over what is now called **Gibbons Pass** to the Big Hole Valley. From there, the party would make its way to **Camp Fortunate** (see pp. 111-14), where the expedition had cached its canoes and other gear the previous autumn.

Today's highways and several excellent back roads make it easy to follow Clark's route all the way to Camp Fortunate.

From Traveler's Rest, it took Clark just two days to reach Ross's Hole, near present **Sula,** where he camped on July 5 near today's **Sula Ranger Station** *(US 93).* With him were 21 men as well as Sacagawea and her toddler, Pomp, and 50 horses.

The shortcut Clark took was a well-beaten path that angled up into the long row of forested hills east of the modern highway. Today's **Bitterroot-Big Hole Road— Forest Road 106** *(1st left beyond ranger station, follow signs)* follows roughly the same course and is well worth the detour from the ordinary route into the Big Hole Valley *(S on US 93, then E on Mont. 43).* The back road climbs across steep slopes of ponderosa pine to **Gibbons Pass,** a featureless hump amid deep lodgepole pine, then descends to Mont. 43 through the same broad and gentle meadows that Clark described as "handsom glades" full of sky blue camas flowers and busy ground squirrels.

Whichever route you take, you'll soon emerge from the trees onto the expansive floor of the Big Hole Valley. Here, Clark said, the "Indian trail Scattered in Such a manner that we Could not pursue it." Fortunately, Sacagawea had been in the valley many times. She told Clark how to get to Camp Fortunate. The party veered southeast of the present highway and was soon overtaken by a ferocious storm of wind and rain.

Big Hole National Battlefield

Though it has little direct connection with Lewis and Clark, this battlefield *(10 miles W of Wisdom on Mont. 43. 406-689-3155. Adm. fee Mem. Day–Labor Day)* is still worth a visit. It commemorates a bloody battle in 1877 between the Nez Perce and the U.S. Army. Visitors learn how relations between white Americans and the previously peaceful Nez Perce (a tribe that had greatly helped the expedition) came to such a woeful state. Trails through beautiful bottomlands and forest hills give you a chance to stretch your legs on the kind of land that Clark once roamed.

As Clark's party crossed the Big Hole Valley on July 7, they stopped at present-day **Jackson** to boil meat in the hot springs that now supply warm water to the swimming pool of a motel. The hot springs, Clark said, "has every appearance of boiling, too hot for a man to endure his hand in it 3 seconds." He directed that two different size pieces of meat be placed in the water. "The one about the Size of my 3 fingers Cooked dun in 25 minits the other much thicker was 32 minutes before it became Sufficiently dun."

Beyond Jackson, County Road 278 makes a gradual, rising curve to the east, more or less following Clark's route over **Big Hole Pass** *(Unmarked)* and down to the willowy meanders of Grasshopper Creek, where you'll find a turnoff for **Bannack State Park** *(406-834-3413. Adm. fee. Camping)*. That road follows Clark's route past Bannack, an 1860s gold-mining town, and over the rolling sagebrush and grass hills to the vicinity of present **Grant**. There, you can pick up County Road 324 and trace the expedition's 1805 route to Camp Fortunate, which is what Clark did.

The party spent two nights at their old encampment. They raised their submerged canoes, repaired them, and dug up their cached goods, which included a precious stash of tobacco. The men were so anxious to get at the tobacco, Clark wrote, "that they Scercely gave themselves time to take their Saddles off their horses before they were off to the deposit." They departed Camp Fortunate on the morning of July 10, some in the canoes, some on horses.

MISSOURI HEADWATERS STATE PARK

It took Clark's party just three and one-half days to descend the Beaverhead and Jefferson Rivers to today's beautiful state park *(Cty. Rd. 286. 406-994-4042. Adm. fee. Camping)*. The previous August, fighting against the current and in low water, they had covered the same ground in 17 days.

Clark tarried at the confluence of the Madison and Jefferson Rivers just long enough to let the horses graze and sort out gear between the 11-man canoe party, which would continue down the Missouri to the Great Falls, and the horse party, which he would lead east over the **Bridger Range** to the Yellowstone.

By 5 p.m., the canoes had shoved off, and Clark's group was headed east along the Gallatin River toward present-day Bozeman. As they rode, he pointed out a promising opening to the east in the Bridger Range, **Flathead Pass.** But Sacagawea "who has been of great Service to me as a pilot through this country recommends a gap in the mountain more South which I shall cross." That gap is **Bozeman Pass,** now crossed by I-90.

William Clark's inscription on Pompeys Pillar, east of Billings

THREE FORKS TO PARK CITY

As Clark skirted the northern edge of the valley and approached present **Bozeman,** the party picked its way among lush, sometimes swampy, creek and river bottoms where countless beaver dams had backed up and divided the waters into a confusing web of channels and ponds. Deer, elk, and pronghorn were everywhere, and there were even signs of bison. Just east of Bozeman, the men rode up Kelly Canyon, crossed Bozeman Pass, and descended along the route of today's I-90 to the Yellowstone River, near present-day **Livingston.**

The phenomenal scenery they passed through for the next few days can still leave you slack-jawed with admiration, especially if you travel early or late in the day when the light is warm and the sun low enough to cast a shadow from every rock and blade of grass. The Yellowstone flows north between the dark, hulking mass of the Gallatin and Absaroka Ranges, then bends eastward, cutting an enticing, rimrocked gash across the plains.

Clark's party remained on horseback almost all the way

Confluence of the Yellowstone and Missouri Rivers

to present **Billings,** looking for trees big enough to build canoes, charting the course of the river, feasting on bison, and shooting the occasional grizzly. Some of the horses got so lame the men made bison-hide moccasins for them.

Trees were so rare that Clark considered building bullboats (see sidebar p. 62) from bison hides and willow branches, but rejected the idea. Bullboats were unwieldy, he thought, the river's current too swift, and the presence of dangerous falls or rapids unknown. "No other alternative for me," Clark wrote, "but to proceed on down untill I can find a tree Sufficently large &c. to make a Canoe."

Just south of **Park City,** Clark finally found cottonwoods big enough to make two narrow canoes—each 28 feet long, but only about a foot and a half wide. To steady them, he had the canoes lashed together, perhaps a bit like a catamaran, with a small platform between them. But before the boat could be launched, Clark lost several horses to the Crow Indians. There was no skirmish. The party just woke up one morning and saw that many were missing. They were never recovered.

On the 24th, Clark headed downriver in the boat accompanied by six men, Sacagawea, and little Pomp. They

flew down the Yellowstone, logging 69 miles that day, 58 the next, then averaging about 60 miles each day all the way to the Missouri, which they reached on August 3.Meanwhile, Sgt. Nathaniel Pryor and three others tried to take the remaining horse herd across the plains to the Mandan villages. They didn't get far. The second night out, near present **Hardin,** the Crow stole every single horse. Pryor and his men trudged back to the Yellowstone, where, at Pompeys Pillar, they built two bullboats and chased Clark downriver.

POMPEYS PILLAR NATIONAL MONUMENT

As Clark raced eastward, he stopped to climb and carve his name into this squat, flat-topped peg of perpendicular sandstone that juts 127 feet above the flat bottomlands of the Yellowstone River. Named for Sacagawea's toddler, Pompeys Pillar (*28 miles E of Billings off I-94. 406-875-2233. Adm. fee*) still bears Clark's dated inscription, along with the many Native American pictographs and petroglyphs he noted in his journal.

The view from the top remains much the same as when Clark stood there late in the day admiring the Pryor and Bighorn Mountains, the plains, and the meandering course of the Yellowstone, where "high romantic Clifts approach & jut over the water for Some distance both above and below." Clark camped just a few miles downriver, shortly after shooting two bighorn sheep and pulling a fossilized dinosaur rib from the crumbling face of a bluff.

A short interpretive trail from the base of the pillar leads to the Yellowstone River. Stations along the way discuss the river's importance as a transportation corridor and describe how Clark's party constructed its boat. A full-scale reproduction of the boat lies along the riverbank.

Inside the **visitor center** (*Mem. Day–Sept.*), you'll find an example of a bison-hide bullboat very much like the admirable vessels Pryor's party paddled on the Yellowstone. During summer, the center offers interpretive walks and a campfire program every Friday at 7 p.m.

TO THE MISSOURI

I-94 parallels Clark's sweep down the Yellowstone all the

"The party all considerable much rejoiced that we have the Expedition completed and now we look for boarding in Town and wait for our Settlement and them we entend to return to our native homes to See our parents once more as we have been so long from them."

SGT. JOHN ORDWAY,
ST. LOUIS, MO.
SEPT. 23, 1806

way to **Glendive,** where Mont. 16 picks up the river route and carries on nearly to the Yellowstone's confluence with the Missouri. Beyond Glendive you'll find opportunities to pull over to fish, stroll the bottomlands, or have a picnic.

Clark's party made quick and largely pleasant work of the Yellowstone. Forty-five miles was a slow day. The weather was usually good, there was always plenty of food, and the men finally had enough skins to make clothes and shelters. Large herds of elk were seen on every point. Grizzly bears dozed on the sandbars and sometimes charged into the river after the boat.

Northeast of present-day Glendive, Clark had to pull over for a full hour to let a huge herd of bison swim across the river. Though the Yellowstone was a full mile wide, Clark wrote, the bison herd stretched from bank to bank "as thick as they could Swim."

On August 3, Clark reached the Missouri at today's **Fort Buford State Historic Site,** North Dakota (see p. 80). The mosquitoes were so bad and the hunting so poor that he dropped downriver for several days. As the party descended, Pryor caught up with them and reported that the bullboats had performed splendidly.

"He [Pryor] informed me that they passed through the worst parts of the rapids & Shoals in the river without takeing a drop of water," Clark wrote, "and waves raised from the hardest winds dose not effect them."

AUGUST 12–SEPTEMBER 23, 1806

The Last Leg

On August 12, south of present **Williston,** North Dakota, Lewis and his group finally rejoined Clark and the others. He lay face down in the white pirogue with shot-through buttocks. But he reassured Clark that the wound would heal in a few weeks and that his unwitting assailant—Pvt. Pierre Cruzatte, blind in one eye and nearsighted in the other—had mistaken him for an elk.

"I instantly supposed that Cruzatte had shot me," Lewis wrote of the accident, "as I was dressed in brown leather and he cannot see very well." Cruzatte, for his part, denied all knowledge. Lewis believed the wounding was unintentional, but he found evidence of his assailant's identity in his own pants. "The ball had lodged in my breeches which I knew to be the ball of the short rifles such as that he had," Lewis wrote, "and there being no person out with me but him and no Indians that we could discover I have no doubt in my own mind of his having shot me."

The wound itself could have been far more serious, as the ball narrowly missed Lewis's hipbone. But perhaps its treatment—regular rinsings with Missouri River water—placed him in even greater peril from infection. Still, Lewis's luck held and the wound healed as the combined party headed east.

Together again, the Corps of Discovery charged down the Missouri River. By August 14, they were at the Mandan villages. There, they convinced Chief Sheheke to accompany them east to meet Jefferson. They also allowed John Colter to leave the party so he could return to the mountains as a trapper. "His services could be dispensed with," Clark wrote, "and as we were disposed to be of Service to any one of our party who had performed their duty as well as Colter had done, we agreed to allow him the prvilage."

The captains also paid off Charbonneau and bid adieu to Sacagawea and Pomp. Clark offered to take Pomp—"a butifull promising Child who is 19 months old"—and educate him as if he were his own son. Charbonneau and Sacagawea thought Pomp too young, but agreed to send him to Clark when he was older. They would do so when the boy was about 6, and he would stay with Clark until he was about 17.

On the road, near Bozeman, Montana

By late August, the Corps passed through the Arikara villages. Farther along, they met the Teton Sioux and paddled by without serious incident, though Clark berated them and threatened to kill any who came near the party's camp. Then it was on to the Yankton Sioux, who smoked a friendly pipe. Near present-day **Sioux City,** Iowa, they visited the grave of Sgt. Charles Floyd.

As they pressed on toward home, they met trading parties headed upriver who filled them in on two years worth of news and gave them food, tobacco, and the first whiskey they'd drunk in more than a year.

On September 20, the men received an enthusiastic welcome at La Charette, Missouri. The next day, they were in St. Charles. On the 23rd, they crossed the Mississippi, stopped briefly at their old Wood River encampment, and paddled across to St. Louis.

"The people of the Town gathered on the bank and could hardly belive that it was us," wrote Sgt. John Ordway, "for they had heard and had believed that we were all dead and were forgotten." ◆

National Signature Events

NATIONAL COUNCIL OF THE LEWIS AND CLARK BICENTENNIAL
0615 Palatine Hill Road,
Portland, OR 97219
503-768-7996 or 888-999-1803
www.lewisandclark200.org

During the expedition's bicentennial years, 14 sites across the country will host national Lewis and Clark commemorative events. Each event will offer a wide variety of formal ceremonies, celebrations, and educational activities focusing on expedition events pertinent to the area. Dates and locations follow.

January 18, 2003, "Bicentennial Kick-off" at Monticello and Charlottesville, Va. The date marks the 200th anniversary of President Jefferson's confidential message to Congress requesting funds for the expedition. 434-984-9802.

October 24–26, 2003, "Falls of the Ohio" near Louisville, Ky. and Clarksville, Ind. Events commemorate the rendezvous here between Lewis and Clark in October 1803. The captains and their men continued down the Ohio on the keelboat October 26, 1803. 502-292-0059.

Spring, 2004, "Three Flags Ceremony/ Expedition Departure" at St. Louis, Mo, St. Charles, Mo., and at Hartford and Wood River, Ill. The "Three Flags Ceremony" will commemorate the March 10, 1804 transfer of the Louisiana Purchase territory to the United States. The "Expedition Departure" event will mark the 200th anniversary of the start of the expedition's voyage up the Missouri River on May 14, 1804. 618-467-2288, 314-516-6853, or 636-946-6899.

July 3–4, 2004, "A Journey Fourth" at Atchison and Fort Leavenworth, Kansas, and Kansas City, Mo. The event commemorates the first American Independence Day celebrated west of the Mississippi. 816-691-3851.

July 30–August 3, 2004, "Tribal Council" at Fort Atkinson, Nebr. The dates mark the anniversary of Lewis and Clark's first diplomatic council with native peoples of the West, which occurred north of Omaha. 402-471-3368.

Summer 2004, Pending event involves the local tribes (who Lewis and Clark knew as the Sioux) and the state of South Dakota. 605-773-3301.

Late fall, 2004, "Circle of Cultures, Time of Renewal and Exchange" at Bismarck, N. Dak. The commemoration recalls the convivial autumn and winter of 1804–05 that Lewis and Clark spent among the Arikara, Mandan, and Hidatsa peoples. 701-462-8535 or 701-328-2532.

July 3–4, 2005, "Discovering the Big Sky" at Great Falls and Fort Benton, Mont. Events focus on reconciliation between the Blackfeet and Euro-American cultures, and on the expedition's successful portage of the Great Falls. 406-455-8451.

Fall, 2005, "Destination 2005: The Pacific" at Fort Clatsop National Memorial and neighboring communities. Events commemorate the expedition's arrival at the Pacific coast and its dreary winter of 1805-06. 503-861-2471.

Spring 2006, Pending event involves the Nez Perce Tribe and the state of Idaho. 208-843-2253 ext. 2305.

July 25, 2006, "Clark on the Yellowstone" at Pompeys Pillar National Monument near Billings, Mont. The event focuses on Clark's exploration of the Yellowstone, and the date marks the anniversary of his inscription on this sandstone tower, which he named after Sacagawea's infant son. 406-256-8628.

August 17–20, 2006, "Home to Sakakawea" at Four Bears Peninsula, near New Town, N. Dak. Events commemorate the expedition's return to the Mandan villages, examine Sakakawea's contributions, and contrast President Jefferson's hopes for the venture with those of tribal leaders who met Lewis and Clark. 701-627-2870.

Early Fall, 2006, Pending "Commemorating the Expedition's Return" at St. Louis, Mo. 573-751-4115 ext. 3250.

Late Fall, 2006, Pending "Final Event" at Philadelphia, Penn. 215-440-3405 or 215-299-1013.

Other Lewis & Clark Sites

MONTICELLO
2 miles SE of Charlottesville, Va.
Route 53
Charlottesville, VA 22902
434-984-9822
www.monticello.org
President Jefferson's elegant and ingenious home reflects the character and intellect of the man who Clark so accurately described as the "Author of our Enterprise." In fact, Jefferson's intense interest in exploring the trans-Mississippi West predated the Lewis and Clark Expedition by at least a decade. Beginning January 18, 2003, the home will open a new exhibit, "Framing the West at Monticello: Thomas Jefferson and the Lewis and Clark Expedition." The exhibit will re-create Jefferson's "Indian Hall," which he adorned with natural history specimens and Native American works of art that Lewis and Clark collected on their voyage. The exhibit will continue through December 2003.

HARPERS FERRY NATIONAL HISTORIC PARK
Off US 340
Harpers Ferry, WV 25425
304-535-6298
www.nps.gov/hafe
Lewis spent more than a month at Harpers Ferry in the spring of 1803, procuring rifles, powder flasks, tomahawks, bullet molds, and other items. He also attended to the fabrication of an iron-frame boat that he hoped to assemble after portaging the Great Falls of the Missouri.

FALLS OF THE OHIO STATE PARK
Clarksville, Ind.
Jeffersonville exit off I 65
Jeffersonville, IN 47131
812-280-9970
www.fallsoftheohio.org
It was here on the Indiana-Kentucky border that Lewis, bringing the keelboat down the Ohio River from Pittsburgh, rendezvoused with Clark in mid-October, 1803, thus forming their famous partnership. The captains spent two weeks at Gen. George Rogers Clark's nearby home, recruited and enlisted more men for the voyage, and set off on October 26.

TALLGRASS PRAIRIE NATIONAL PRESERVE
North of Strong City on Kans. 177
Route 1, Strong City, KS, 66869
620-273-8494
www.nps.gov/tapr/home.htm
This 10,894-acre preserve embraces a precious remnant of the tallgrass prairie that once covered over 400,000 square miles of North America. Here visitors glimpse the sort of prairies Lewis and Clark saw as they followed the Missouri north.

TAMASTSLIKT CULTURAL INSTITUTE
7 miles E of Pendleton, on Ore. 331
72789 Highway 331
Pendleton, OR 97801
541-966-9748
www.umatilla.nsn.us/tamust.html
This superb interpretive center traces the history and lifeways of three Sahaptian-speaking peoples encountered by Lewis and Clark as they followed the Columbia River: the Umatilla, Wallawalla, and Cayuse. Exhibits cover pre-Columbian times to the present, and the center orients visitors to various Lewis and Clark sites in the region.

YAKAMA NATION CULTURAL CENTER
US 97
Toppenish, WA 98948
509-865-2800
Lewis and Clark met the Yakama shortly after arriving at the confluence of the Snake and Columbia Rivers in mid-October, 1805. They also spent a few days with the Yakama the following spring, as the expedition made its way home. This outstanding cultural center illuminates the indigenous lives of the Yakama people from prehistoric time forward.

MERIWETHER LEWIS NATIONAL MONUMENT
Off Tenn. 20, 7 miles E of Hohenwald
2680 Natchez Trace Parkway
Tupelo, MS 38804
800-305-7417
www.nps.gov/natr
Location of Lewis's death and burial, the monument grounds take in the site of Grinder's Inn, where Lewis is believed to have killed himself October 11, 1809. A tall, broken shaft of marble marks his grave, and a rustic log building recalls the character of Grinder's Inn.

General Information

For overall information including trail maps, contact the **Lewis and Clark National Historic Trail**
1709 Jackson St.
Omaha, NE 68102
402-514-9311
www.nps.gov/lecl/

State and local information may be obtained from the **Lewis and Clark Trail Heritage Foundation, Inc.**
P.O. Box 3434
Great Falls, MT 59403
*406-454-1234
or 888-701-3434*
www.lewisandclark.org

For information on the Lewis and Clark Expedition's bicentennial celebration or for how to get in touch with the pertinent tribal governments and state bicentennial commissions, contact the **National Council of the Lewis and Clark Bicentennial**
0615 Palatine Hill Rd.
Portland, OR 97219
*503-768-7996 or
888-999-1803*
www.lewisandclark200.org

Camping

For camping in national forests, call **U.S. Forest Service Reservations**
800-280-2267

State by State:

MISSOURI

Missouri Division of Tourism *573-751-4133
or 800-877-1234*
www.missouritourism.org
Missouri Dept. of Natural Resources *Parks 573-251-2479 or 800-334-6946*
www.dnr.state.mo.us/dsp/homedsp.htm

State Historical Society of Missouri *573-882-7083*
St. Louis Convention & Visitors Bureau *314-421-1023 or 800-916-0040*
Jefferson City Convention & Visitors Bureau *573-632-2820 or 800-769-4183*

IOWA

Iowa Division of Tourism *512-242-4705 or 800-345-4692*
www.traveliowa.com
Department of Natural Resources *Parks 515-281-5145* www.state.ia.us/parks
State Historical Society of Iowa *515-281-6200*
Council Bluffs Area Chamber of Commerce *712-325-1000 or 800-228-6878*
Sioux City Convention Center *712-279-4800 or 800-593-2228*

NEBRASKA

Nebraska Division of Tourism *402-471-3796 or 800-228-4307*
www.visitnebraska.org
Game & Parks Commission *402-471-0641*
www.ngpc.state.ne.us/
Nebraska State Historical Society *402-471-3270*
Omaha Convention & Visitors Bureau *402-444-4660 or 866-937-6624*

SOUTH DAKOTA

South Dakota Dept. of Tourism *605-773-3301 or 800-732-5682*
www.travelsd.com
Division of Parks and Recreation *605-773-3391 or 800-807-4723*
www.state.sd.usgfp
South Dakota State Historical Society *605-773-3458*

Chamberlain Chamber of Commerce *605-734-4416*
Pierre Chamber of Commerce *605-224-7361 or 800-962-2034*

NORTH DAKOTA

North Dakota Tourism Department *701-328-2525 or 800-435-5663*
www.ndtourism.com
Parks and Recreation Department *701-328-5357 for state parks and campground information,
800-807-4723 for campground reservations*
Bismarck-Mandan Convention & Visitors Bureau *701-222-4308 or 800-767-3555*

MONTANA

Travel Montana *406-444-2654 or 800-847-4868*
www.visitmt.com
Department of Fish, Wildlife and Parks *406-444-2535*
http://fwp.state.mt.us
Montana Historical Society *406-444-2681*
Butte Convention & Visitors Bureau *406-723-3177 or 800-735-6814*
Dillon Chamber of Commerce *406-683-5511*
Great Falls Chamber of Commerce *406-761-4434 or 800-735-8535*
Missoula Chamber of Commerce *406-543-6623 or 800-526-3465*
Three Forks Chamber of Commerce *406-285-4556*

IDAHO

Idaho Division of Tourism *800-847-4843*
www.visitid.org

**Idaho Department of
Parks and Recreation**
208-334-4199
www.idahoparks.org

**Clearwater National
Forest** *208-476-4541*

**Salmon-Challis National
Forest** *208-756-5100*

**Lewistown Chamber of
Commerce** *208-743-3531
or 800-473-3543*

**Idaho Outfitters and
Guides Assocation**
208-342-1919

WASHINGTON

**Washington State
Tourism** *360-586-2088*
www.tourism.wa.gov

Washington State Parks
360-902-8844
www.parks.wa.gov/

**Washington State
Historical Society** *253-272-
3500 or 888-238-4373*

**Clarkston Chamber of
Commerce** *509-758-7712*

**Tri-Cities Visitor &
Convention Bureau** *509
735-8486 or 800-254-5824*

**Bed & Breakfast
Reservation Service**
206-439-7677

OREGON

Oregon Tourism
800-547-7842
www.traveloregon.com

Oregon State Parks
www.oregonstateparks.org

**Oregon Guides & Packers
Association** *800-747-9552*
www.ogpa.org
*Information on white-water
rafting and hiking*

Oregon Historical Society
503-222-1741

**The Dalles Chamber of
Commerce** *541-296-2231*

**Portland Visitor's
Information Center**
*503-275-8355
or 800-345-3214*

About the Author

Thomas Schmidt has written extensively about the nature and history of the Rocky Mountain region. His work includes books on Glacier, Rocky Mountain, and Grand Teton National Parks, and on Wyoming history. He is the author of *The Rockies* in National Geographic's Driving Guides to America series, a contributor to several other National Geographic guidebooks, and co-author of *The Northern Rockies* in the Smithsonian Guides to Natural America series. Schmidt lives in Bozeman, Montana with his wife, Terese, and their two children, Pat and Colleen.

A Note on Quotations

The journal quotations used in this guide were taken from *The Journals of the Lewis and Clark Expedition* (Vols. 1-11), Gary E. Moulton, ed.; University of Nebraska Press, 1983-1997. Original spelling and punctuation have been retained.

Illustrations Credits

Arrow Creek, Mont. 87
Arrow Rock S.H.S., Mo. 23
Astoria, Oreg. 159, 163–164
Atchison, Kans. 29

Baker, Idaho 120
Bannack S.P., Mont. 180
Beacon Rock S.P., Wash. 155–156
Beartooth Wildlife Management Area, Mont. 100
Beaverhead Rock, Mont. 109–110
Big Hole Pass, Mont. 180
Billings, Mont. 181–182
Bismarck, N. Dak. 63–64
Bitterroot Big Hole Road, Mont. 179
Bitterroot River, Mont. 126, 173
Black Sandy S.P., Mont. 102
Blackfoot River Recreation Corridor, Mont. 174
Bonner, Mont. 174
Bozeman, Mont. 181
Brockton, Mont. 82
Browning, Mont. 176–177
Brownville, Nebr. 31–32

Cahokia Mounds S.H.S., Collinsville, Ill. 16
Camp Disappointment, Mont. 177–178
Camp Fortunate Overlook, Mont. 112
Camp Wood, Ill. 12–16
Canoe Camp, Idaho 136–137
Cape Disappointment, Wash. 161–162
Cardwell, Mont. 107
Cascade Locks Marine Park, Oreg. 155
Cathlamet, Wash. 157
Chamberlain, S. Dak. 51–53
Charles M. Russell N.W.R., Mont. 83–84
Chief Timothy S.P., Wash. 142–143
Clark Canyon Reservoir, Mont. 111–112
Clark's Lookout, Mont. 110
Clearwater River, Idaho 140
Columbia Gorge Interpretive Center, nr. Stevenson, Wash. 154–155
Conner, Mont. 126
Council Bluffs, Iowa 33
Cow Creek, Mont. 87
Cross Ranch Nature Preserve, N. Dak. 71
Cross Ranch S.P., N. Dak. 71
Crow Butte S.P., Wash. 147
Crow Flies High H.S., N. Dak. 78
Culbertson, Mont. 81
Cut Bank Creek, Mont. 176, 178

Dakota City, Nebr. 40
The Dalles, Oreg. 151, 153, 171
De Soto N.W.R., Iowa-Nebr. 37–38
Dearborn Fishing Access, Mont. 98–99
Departure Point (campground), Mont. 99
Deschutes River S.R.A., Oreg. 148
DeVoto Memorial Grove, Idaho 131–132
Double Ditch Indian Village S.H.S., N. Dak. 64
Drouillard boat ramp, Jefferson River, Mont. 105
Dry Camp, Idaho 135

Ecola S.P., Oreg. 167
Elk Point, S. Dak. 44

Falls of the Ohio S.P., Ind. 187
Farm Island S.R.A., S. Dak. 54–55
First Shoshone Village Site, Sandy Creek, Idaho 118–119
Fort Abraham Lincoln S.P., N. Dak. 62–63
Fort Atkinson S.H.P., Nebr. 35–37
Fort Benton, Mont. 88–89
Fort Buford S.H.S., N. Dak. 80, 184
Fort Canby S.P., Wash. 161–162
Fort Clatsop National Memorial, Oreg. 164–167, 170
Fort Leavenworth, Kans. 27–28
Fort Mandan S.H.S., N. Dak. 66–71
Fort Osage, Mo. 26
Fort Peck, Mont. 83
Fort Pierre, S. Dak. 54, 55–58
Fort Pierre National Grassland, S. Dak. 58
Fort Randall Dam, S. Dak. 50
Fort Rock (promontory), Mont. 104–105
Fort Union Trading Post N.H.S., N. Dak. 80–81

Gates of the Mountain, Mont. 99–100
Gavins Point Dam, Nebr.-S. Dak. 47–49
Giant Springs Heritage S.P., Mont. 91
Gibbons Pass, Mont. 179
Gibbonsville, Idaho 124
Glade Creek Camp, Idaho 130, 131
Glendive, Mont. 183–184
Grant, Mont. 115, 180
Grasshopper Creek Fishing Access, Mont. 111
Grave Creek, Mont. 129
Grays Bay, Wash. 158–159
Great Falls, Mont. 90–93, 175, 176
Greensward Camp, Idaho 135

Hardin, Mont. 183
Harpers Ferry N.H.P., W. Va. 187
Hauser Lake, Mont. 101
Helena, Mont. 102–103
Hell Creek S.P., Mont. 84
Hells Gate S.P., Idaho 142
High Road Fishing Access, nr. Twin Bridges, Mont. 109
Holter Dam, Mont. 99
Holter Lake Recreation Area, Mont. 99–101
Horsethief Lake S.P., Wash. 150–151
Howard Creek Picnic Area, Mont. 129
Huff Indian Village S.H.S., N. Dak. 61–62
Hull Creek, Idaho 123–124

Ilwaco Heritage Museum, Ilwaco, Wash. 163
Indian Cave S.P., Nebr. 31
Indian Post Office, Idaho 134
Indian Trees Campground, Mont. 125
Ionia Volcano, Nebr. 45–46

Jackson, Mont. 180
Jefferson City, Mo. 20–21
John Day Dam, Oreg.-Wash. 147

Kamiah, Idaho 172
Kansas City, Kans.-Mo. 27
Katy Trail S.P., Mo. 18, 21
Knife River Indian Villages N.H.S., N. Dak. 72–73

La Hood, Mont. 107
LaFramboise Island Nature Area, S. Dak. 58
Lee Creek Campground, Mont. 130
Lee Metcalf N.W.R., Mont. 126
Lemhi Hole Fishing Access, nr. Salmon, Idaho 120–121
Lemhi Pass, Idaho-Mont. 114–117
Lenore (ancient site), Idaho 140
Les Shirley Park, Oreg. 167
Lewis and Clark Campsite S.P., Wash. 160–161
Lewis and Clark Caverns S.P., Mont. 106–107
Lewis and Clark Grove, Idaho 135
Lewis and Clark Interpretive Center, Washburn, N. Dak. 64–65
Lewis and Clark Lake, Nebr.-S. Dak. 48–49
Lewis and Clark National Historic Trail Interpretive Center, Great Falls, Mont. 90–91
Lewis and Clark Pass, Mont. 175
Lewis and Clark S.H.S., Ill. 12

Lewis and Clark S.P., Iowa 38–39
Lewis and Clark S.P., Mo. 29
Lewis and Clark S.P., N. Dak. 79
Lewis and Clark Trail S.P.,
    Wash. 172
Lewis Rock, Mont. 104
Lewiston, Idaho 141–142
Little Missouri S.P., N. Dak. 76
Little Sioux, Iowa 38
Livingston, Mont. 181
Lolo, Mont. 127–128
Lolo motorway, Idaho 133–136
Lolo Pass, Idaho-Mont. 128,
    130–131
Lolo Trail, Idaho-Mont. 127,
    128–130, 172–173
Loma, Mont. 87, 88
Long Beach, Wash. 162–163
Lost Trail Pass, Mont. 123–125
Lower Portage Camp., Mont. 92
Lyons Ferry S.P., Wash. 143

Maclay Flat, Mont. 174
Mandan, N. Dak. 63
Marias River, Mont. 87–88,
    176–177
Maryhill Museum of Art,
    nr. Biggs, Wash. 147–148
Malta Bend, Mo. 24
McNary Dam, Oreg.-Wash. 146
Megler Rest Area, Wash. 159–160
Meriwether Lewis National
    Monument, Miss. 187
Missoula, Mont. 174
Missouri Headwaters S.P., Mont.
    103–106, 180–181
Missouri National Recreational
    River, Nebr. 44
Missouri River Recreation Road,
    Mont. 98–101
Mobridge, S. Dak. 59–61
Monticello, Va. 187
Monture Fishing Access, nr.
    Ovando, Mont. 175
Morony Dam, Mont. 92

Nebraska City, Nebr. 32, 33
New Town, N. Dak. 78–79
Newcastle, Nebr. 45–46
Nez Perce N.H.P., Idaho 140
Niobrara S.P., Nebr. 49
North Fork, Idaho 123
North Head Lighthouse,
    Wash. 162

Oacoma, S. Dak. 51
Oahe Dam, S. Dak. 57
Omaha, Nebr. 34–35
On-A-Slant Village, N. Dak. 62–63
Oswego, Mont. 82
Ovando, Mont. 175

Packer Meadows, Idaho 130, 131
Park City, Mont. 182
Pasco, Wash. 142, 171
Pataha, Wash. 143
Pelican Point Fishing Access,
    Mont. 98
Pheasant Camp, Idaho 135
Pierre, S. Dak. 53–54, 55–58
Pines Recreation Area, Mont.
    83–84
Plymouth, Wash. 146
Pompeys Pillar N.H.L., Mont. 183
Ponca S.P., Nebr. 44–45
Poplar River, Mont. 82
Portland, Oreg. 156–157
Powell, Idaho 129, 133
Powell Ranger Station, Idaho 132

Rainbow Falls, Mont. 91
Rattlesnake Cliffs, Mont. 110–111
Reunion Bay, N. Dak. 78
Richland, Wash. 145
Ridgefield N.W.R., Wash. 157
Rocheport, Mo. 21, 23
Rooster Rock S.P., Oreg. 156
Ryan Dam, Mont. 91–92

Sacagawea Monument,
    nr. Tendoy, Idaho 117
Sacagawea Spring, Mont. 92
Sacajawea Interpretive Cultural
    and Education Center,
    Idaho 120
Sacajawea S.P., Wash. 144–145
Saddle Mountain, Mont. 125
Sakakawea, Lake, N. Dak. 76–78
Salmon, Idaho 120–121
Sandy Creek, Idaho 118
Seaside, Oreg. 166, 167
Second Shoshone Village Site,
    Kenney Creek, Idaho 119–120
Sibley, Mo. 26
Silver Star Fishing Access,
    Jefferson River, Mont. 108
Sinque Hole Camp, Idaho 134
Sioux City, Iowa 40–41, 185
Skamokawa, Wash. 156–158
Smoking Place, Idaho 135
Snake Creek S.R.A., S. Dak. 50–51
Snowbank Camp, Idaho 133
Spirit Mound, S. Dak. 46–47
Spring Gulch Campground,
    Mont. 126
Squaw Creek N.W.R., Mo. 30
St. Charles, Mo. 18–19, 185
St. Joseph, Mo. 29–30
St. Louis, Mo. 16–17
Stanton, N. Dak. 66, 71–72, 76
Stevenson, Wash. 153–155
Sula, Mont. 125–126, 179
Sun River, Mont. 175

Tallgrass Prairie National
    Preserve, Kans. 187
Tamastslikt Cultural Institute,
    Oreg. 187
Tendoy, Idaho 117–118
Three Tribes Museum, N. Dak.
    78–79
Three Forks, Mont. 103, 105
Tonwontonga (site), Nebr. 39
Tower Rock Campground,
    Idaho 121
Townsend, Mont. 103
Trail Creek, Mont. 116
Traveler's Rest, Mont. 127, 173,
    179
Twin Bridges, Mont. 107–109
Twin Creek Campground,
    Idaho 124

Ulm, Mont. 96–98
Ulm Pishkun S.P., Mont. 96–98
Umatilla N.W.R., Wash. 146–147
Upper Missouri National Wild
    and Scenic River, Mont.
    84–85, 87
Upper Portage Camp, Mont. 93,
    176

Van Meter S.P., Mo. 23–25
Vancouver, Wash. 156–157
Vermillion, S. Dak. 45, 47

Wagonhammer Springs Picnic
    Area, Idaho 121
Wallula Gap, Wash. 146, 171
Washburn, N. Dak. 64–66
Waverly, Mo. 25–26
Weippe, Idaho 129, 135, 136
Weippe Prairie, Idaho 136
Weldon Spring Conservation
    Area, Mo. 19–20
Wendover Campground, Idaho
    132–133
West Bend S.R.A., S. Dak. 53
West Whitlock S.R.A., S. Dak. 59
Western Historic Trails Center,
    Iowa 33–34
Weston Bend S.P., Mo. 28
White Cliffs Area, Mont. 87
White Earth Campground,
    Mont. 102
Whitehall, Mont. 107
Williston, N. Dak. 79, 184
Winston, Mont. 102
Wishram Overlook, Wash.
    148–150
Wolf Point, Mont. 82

Yakama Nation Cultural Center,
    Wash. 187
Yellowstone River, U.S. 79–81
York's Islands Fishing Access,
    Mont. 103

National Geographic Guide to The Lewis & Clark Trail
By Thomas Schmidt
Foreword by Stephen E. Ambrose
Published by the National Geographic Society

John M. Fahey, Jr., *President and Chief Executive Officer*

Gilbert M. Grosvenor, *Chairman of the Board*

Nina D. Hoffman, *Executive Vice President; President, Books and School Publishing*

William R. Gray, *Vice President and Director, Book Division*

Elizabeth Newhouse, *Director of Travel Publishing*

Caroline Hickey, *Project Manager*

David Griffin, *Art Director and Design Director*

Barbara A. Noe, Margaret Bowen, *Text Editors*

Vickie Lewis, *Illustrations Editor*

Sean M. Groom, Mary E. Jennings, *Researchers*

Kristin M. Edmonds, *Copy Editor*

Carl Mehler, *Director of Maps*

Joe Ochlak, *Manager*

Thomas L. Gray, Sean M. Groom, Keith R. Moore,Sven M. Dolling, Mapping Specialists, Ltd., *Map Research and Production*

Meredith Wilcox, *Illustrations Assistant*

Richard S. Wain, *Production Project Manager*

Elisabeth MacRae-Bobynskyj, *Indexer*

Additional Staff for 2002 edition

Lyle Rosbotham, *Designer*

Marilyn Gibbons, *Illustrations Editor*

Lise Sajewski, Jane Sunderland, and Connie Binder, *Contributors*

Printed in U.S.A.

Library of Congress Cataloging-in-Publication Data

Schmidt, Thomas, 1959-
  The Lewis & Clark Trail / by Thomas Schmidt ; foreword by Stephen E. Ambrose.
  p. cm.
  Cover title: National Geographic guide to the Lewis & Clark Trail.
  Includes index.
  ISBN 0-7922-6471-1 (alk. paper)
  1. Lewis and Clark National Historic Trail--Guidebooks. 2. Lewis and Clark Expedition (1804-1806) I. National Geographic Society (U.S.) II. Title. III. Title: Lewis and Clark Trail. IV. Title: National Geographic guide to the Lewis & Clark Trail.

   F592.7.S1265 2001
   917.804'34--dc21   2001007003

Composition for this book by the National Geographic Society Book Division. Printed and bound by R.R. Donnelley & Sons, Willard, Ohio. Color separations by Quad Graphics, Martinsburg, West Virginia. Cover printed by Miken Inc., Cheektowaga, New York.

One of the world's largest nonprofit scientific and educational organizations, the National Geographic Society was founded in 1888 "for the increase and diffusion of geographic knowledge." Fulfilling this mission, the Society educates and inspires millions every day through its magazines, books, television programs, videos, maps and atlases, research grants, the National Geographic Bee, teacher workshops, and innovative classroom materials. The Society is supported through membership dues, charitable gifts, and income from the sale of its educational products. This support is vital to National Geographic's mission to increase global understanding and promote conservation of our planet through exploration, research, and education.

For more information, please call 1-800-NGS LINE (647-5463) or write to the following address:

National Geographic Society
1145 17th Street N.W.
Washington, D.C. 20036-4688 U.S.A.

Visit the Society's Web site at www.nationalgeographic.com.